Brian Fleming Research & Learning Library
Ministry of Education
Ministry of Training, Colleges & Universities
900 Bay St. 13th Floor, Mowat Block
Toronto, ON M7A 1L2

D1803327

BILINGUAL TODAY, UNITED TOMORROW

Bilingual Today, United Tomorrow

Official Languages in Education and Canadian Federalism

MATTHEW HAYDAY

McGill-Queen's University Press
Montreal & Kingston · London · Ithaca

© McGill-Queen's University Press 2005
ISBN 0-7735-2960-8

Legal deposit fourth quarter 2005
Bibliothèque nationale du Québec

Printed in Canada on acid-free paper that is 100% ancient forest free (100% post-consumer recycled), processed chlorine free.

This book has been published with the help of a grant from the Canadian Federation for the Humanities and Social Sciences, through the Aid to Scholarly Publications Programme, using funds provided by the Social Sciences and Humanities Research Council of Canada.

McGill-Queen's University Press acknowledges the support of the Canada Council for the Arts for our publishing program. We also acknowledge the financial support of the Government of Canada through the Book Publishing Industry Development Program (BPIDP) for our publishing activities.

Library and Archives Canada Cataloguing in Publication

Hayday, Matthew, 1977–
  Bilingual today, united tomorrow: official languages in education and Canadian federalism / Matthew Hayday.

  Includes bibliographical references and index.
  ISBN 0-7735-2960-8

  1. Language policy – Canada – History. 2. Language and education – Government policy – Canada. 3. Official Languages in Education Program (Canada) 4. Education, Bilingual – Canada. I. Title.

FC145.L3H39 2005   306.44'971   C2005-902258-2

This book was typeset by Interscript in 10/12 Sabon.

Contents

Tables   vii

Acknowledgments   ix

Acronyms   xi

Introduction: A Linguistic Divide, a Crisis of Canadian Unity   3

1   A Century of Language Conflict in Canada   16

2   From Royal Commission to Government Policy, 1963–1970   35

3   Growing Pains and Intergovernmental Squabbles, 1970–1976   63

4   Lévesque's Gambit Fails: A New English Canadian Consensus, 1976–1979   100

5   The Constitutional Débâcle and the Rise of Language Rights, 1979–1983   128

6   A New Equilibrium: Official-Languages Discourse and Canadian National Identity   168

Appendix: Federal Funding of the Official Languages in Education Program   187

Notes   193

Bibliography   229

Index   249

Tables

1.1 Rates of Anglicization and Exogamy in French Canada, 1971/1976   31
1.2 Percentage of Canadians Claiming to Be Bilingual, 1961 and 1971   33
3.1 Student Participation in Minority-Language Education and Second-Language Instruction, 1970–1973   66
3.2 Provincial Spending on Special Projects, 1972–73 to 1975–76   97
4.1 Federal Contributions for Bilingualism in Education, 1970–1983   109
5.1 Average Cost of Education per Student per Year, 1977–78   145
5.2 Enrolment in Immersion and Minority-Language Education Programs, 1984–85   164
A1 Federal Contributions under the Elementary- and Secondary-Level Minority-Official-Language Education Formula   188
A2 Federal Contributions under the Elementary- and Secondary-Level Second-Official-Language Instruction Formula   189
A3 Federal Contributions under the Special Projects Program   190
A4 Federal Contributions under All Official Languages in Education Programs, 1970/71–1982/83   191
A5 Federal Contributions under All Official Languages in Education Programs, 1983/84–2001/2   192

Acknowledgments

This book could not have been completed without the support and encouragement of numerous individuals and organizations. I am particularly indebted to my thesis director, Michael Behiels, for his thoughtful comments, keen insights, and prompt revisions. I have also had the good fortune to receive extensive financial support for this work from the Social Sciences and Humanities Research Council of Canada, the SSHRCC Federalism and Federations Program, Ontario Graduate Scholarships, the University of Ottawa Department of History's Gaston Héon and Julian Gwyn scholarships, and the Fonds pour l'émergence des projets de recherche from the Centre de recherche en civilisation canadienne-française.

My research entailed visits to the archives and departmental libraries of six provinces and the federal government and to the archives of many community associations, where I received much-needed help from many dedicated archivists and librarians. I would also like to thank the dozens of individuals who gave me their time and insights in our interviews and who pointed me to new avenues for my research.

During the writing process many people provided invaluable support to me, whether by proofreading sections of my work, letting me bounce ideas off them, or just listening to my long diatribes. In particular, I would like to thank Marcel Martel, Jeff Keshen, Nicole Neatby, Cornelius Jaenen, Chad Gaffield, Donald Davis, Yves Frenette, Sacha Richard, Cynthia Toman, Jean-Pierre Morin, Krista Robertson, Rachel Sheer, and Brenda Zimmerman. I would also like to thank my parents, Jan and Bryan, and my sisters, Catherine and Sarah, who all patiently endured my prolonged explanations of my work and provided emotional support. My path through the Canadian scholarly publication process has been deftly guided by Kyla Madden, Joan Harcourt, and Joan McGilvray at McGill-Queen's University Press and by two anonymous, but very thoughtful, reviewers of my manuscript. Most importantly, I want to thank my husband, Matthew Kayahara, without whose love and support I might never have finished this book.

Acronyms

ACA	Archives du centre acadien, Université Ste-Anne
ACELF	Association canadienne d'éducation de langue française
ACFA	Association canadienne-française de l'Alberta
ACFEO	Association canadienne-française d'éducation d'Ontario
ACFO	Association canadienne-française de l'Ontario
AEBA	Association des éducateurs bilingues de l'Alberta
AECFM	Association des éducateurs canadiens-français du Manitoba
AEFNB	Association des enseignants francophones du Nouveau-Brunswick
AEFO	Association des enseignants francophones de l'Ontario
ASFO	Association des surintendants francophones de l'Ontario
ANQ	Archives nationales du Québec (Quebec City)
AO	Archives of Ontario
APEC	Alliance for the Preservation of English in Canada
AQ	Alliance Quebec
BEF	Bureau de l'éducation française (Manitoba)
BEP	Bilingualism in Education Program, or Federal-Provincial Programme of Cooperation for the Promotion of Bilingualism in Education
BNA Act	British North America Act, 1867
CEA	Centre d'études acadiennes, Université de Moncton
CHSPTF	Canadian Home and School and Parent-Teacher Federation
CMEC	Council of Ministers of Education, Canada
CNPF	Commission nationale des parents francophones
COL	Commissioner of Official Languages

CP	Centre du patrimoine (Saint-Boniface)
CPF	Canadian Parents for French
CQM	Council of Quebec Minorities
CRCCF	Centre de recherche en civilisation canadienne-française
CTF	Canadian Teachers Federation
CUSB	Collège universitaire de Saint-Boniface
CVF	Conseil de la vie française
ESL	English as a second language
FANE	Fédération acadienne de la Nouvelle-Écosse
FCFAC	Fédération des communautés francophones et acadiennes du Canada
FCFO	Fédération canadienne-française de l'Ouest
FFHQ	Fédération des francophones hors-Québec
FFNE	Fédération francophone de la Nouvelle-Écosse
FLIU	French-language instructional units
FLQ	Front de Libération du Québec
FML	French minority language
FPANE	Fédération des parents acadiens de la Nouvelle-Écosse
FPCP	Fédération provinciale des comités de parents
FSL	French as a second language
FTE	Full-time equivalent
MAIG	Ministère des Affaires intergouvernementales
MIS	Mouvement pour l'intégration scolaire
MLE	Minority language education
NAC	National Archives of Canada
NBTA	New Brunswick Teachers' Association
NSARM	Nova Scotia Archives and Records Management
OISE	Ontario Institute for Studies in Education
OJC	Ordre de Jacques Cartier
OLEP	Official Languages in Education Program
OLMG	Official Language Minority Groups Program
PAA	Provincial Archives of Alberta
PAM	Provincial Archives of Manitoba
PANB	Provincial Archives of New Brunswick
PCH	Patrimoine canadienne/Canadian Heritage
PQ	Parti Québécois
PSBGM	Protestant School Board of Greater Montreal
QFHSA	Quebec Federation of Home and School Associations
RCBB	Royal Commission on Bilingualism and Biculturalism
SANB	Société des Acadiens du Nouveau-Brunswick
SFM	Société franco-manitobaine

SLI	Second language instruction
SNA	Société nationale des Acadiens
SSJB	Société St-Jean Baptiste
WNA	weighted national average

BILINGUAL TODAY, UNITED TOMORROW

INTRODUCTION

A Linguistic Divide, a Crisis of Canadian Unity

BILINGUAL TODAY, FRENCH TOMORROW?

In the spring of 2003 Stéphane Dion, the minister for intergovernmental affairs in Jean Chrétien's Liberal government, launched an action plan for official languages in Canada. Entitled *The Next Act: New Momentum for Canada's Linguistic Duality*, the plan recommitted the federal government to supporting official-languages programs from coast to coast, while increasing the funding attributed to this end. Dion's announcement coincided with the fortieth anniversary of the establishment of the Royal Commission on Bilingualism and Biculturalism (B & B Commission), whose repercussions are felt to this day and whose recommendations provided the foundation for a host of Canadian official-languages programs. Most notably, it provided the impetus for the Official Languages Act, 1969, which declared English and French to be the official languages of Canada, as well as the justification for federal financial support for minority- and second-language education programs, which began in the 1970s.

The decision to continue on the language-policy route established by the Trudeau government in the late 1960s is not uncontroversial. When that government's policies were originally launched, they were rejected by a substantial portion of the Canadian population. While much of the opposition stemmed from reasoned arguments, some opponents responded from fear. In particular, Lt Commander Jock V. Andrew published *Bilingual Today, French Tomorrow: Trudeau's Master Plan and How it Can Be Stopped*, a virulent polemic alleging that a francophone conspiracy to take over Canada was at the root of the new language policies. Both the success of his 1977 book and the proliferation of anti-French organisations such as the Orange Lodge, Loyalist Associations, and the Alliance for the Preservation of English in Canada (APEC) testify to the hostility with which these programs were received in some quarters.

Since the 1970s the Canadian government's official-languages policy has also been widely criticized by Canadian political scientists, including Kenneth McRoberts, Guy Laforest, and Léon Dion. Their critique begins with the B & B Commission, which, they argue, ended in failure. In particular, they point to the Commission's inability to suggest possible political and constitutional solutions to Canada's linguistic divide and national unity crisis of the 1960s.[1] Their critique then turns to the policies adopted by the government of Prime Minister Pierre Elliott Trudeau in response to the commission's reports. Trudeau's government, they argue, betrayed André Laurendeau's vision of Canada by adopting policies that were based on a fundamental misreading of Canada.[2] In essence, Laurendeau, co-chair of the B & B Commission, argued that Canadian bilingualism had to be rooted in two unilingualisms: an English unilingualism rooted in English-speaking Canada and a French unilingualism rooted in a strong Quebec.[3] He believed further that French Canada itself could prosper only if it was rooted in a strong Quebec and thus that a special status was needed for Quebec to protect the strength of its French character. According to McRoberts and his supporters, if the Trudeau government had followed Laurendeau's approach of decentralizing power to the provinces and granting special protections and powers to the province of Quebec, Canada's national unity crisis could have been resolved.

The route proposed by Laurendeau and taken up by McRoberts et al. of establishing a language policy based on territoriality was indeed considered; it had been followed with some success in countries such as Switzerland and Belgium. However, the framers of Canada's language policies faced a substantially different distribution of its language populations. True, francophones predominated in Quebec and anglophones elsewhere in the country. Yet there were also minority official-language populations in every province. Indeed, over 35 percent of New Brunswick's population was French-speaking. Even in provinces where the minority official-language population was not as large, there were still regions in each where the concentrations were significant, ranging from the affluent English-speaking community of Montreal's suburban West Island to the largely rural Franco-Albertan communities in the northern half of Alberta. If the Canadian government wished to preserve and support the communities of official-language minorities across the country, a different route would need to be followed.

Indeed, by the early 1960s the continued existence of a number of these communities, particularly those of the francophone minorities, was in jeopardy. They had survived to this point without the government services in their own language that the anglophone majorities (and the anglophone minority in Quebec) were able to take for granted. Owing in no small part to the support of the Catholic Church and voluntary organizations, French Canadian and Acadian communities had been able to maintain some demographic, social, and cultural vitality. However, as Marcel Martel and Gaétan Gervais point out, this system of supports began to unravel in the 1960s, when the Catholic Church's influence and financial resources began to decline, traditional nationalist organizations such as the Conseil de la vie française and the Ordre de Jacques Cartier began to fade, and the Quebec state became increasingly inward-looking.[4]

Shifts in Quebec politics had repercussions far beyond their impact on French Canadian and Acadian minority communities. Starting in the late 1940s and continuing throughout the 1950s, a cohort of middle-class, university-educated Quebecers began to demand changes that would permit the French language to flourish as the working language of Quebec and French Canadians to fully participate in the decision-making processes of the province. Following the death of Premier Maurice Duplessis, these neonationalists had a major influence on the policies of the Liberal government of Jean Lesage, elected in 1960. The Lesage government launched a series of wide-ranging reforms, collectively referred to as the Quiet Revolution, which modernized the Quebec state and significantly increased the role played by francophone Quebecers in the management of the provincial economy. Many leaders of the Quiet Revolution believed that the Quebec government would need additional powers to implement the types of changes that were needed for French Canadians to achieve their cultural and social objectives. Bolstered by their success at the provincial level, they sought changes to the structure of the federal government to give French-Canadians an active presence in this body as well. While moderate neonationalists sought a new status for their province within the Canadian federation, others increasingly sought to create the apparatus of a sovereign state. Understandably, these desires created a crisis of national unity.

The language policies adopted by the Trudeau government were thus driven by two primary considerations. First, the government wanted to craft policies that would respond to a pan-Canadian linguistic duality, offering government services and educational programs to English and

French speakers across the country, where viable communities existed. Second, it sought to respond to the challenges posed by Quebec's Quiet Revolution in a manner that would make the federal government relevant to French Canadians, while staving off the possibility that Quebec might separate from the rest of Canada. To accomplish these objectives, Ottawa adopted a policy based on the language rights of individual Canadians, set about creating official bilingualism in government institutions, and promoted a vision of a French Canada that stretched across the country, rather than one that was rooted solely in Quebec. The Trudeau government would also fight vigorously against attempts by the Quebec government to acquire additional powers and promote French unilingualism in the province.

Trudeau's critics claim that this approach failed to respond to the needs of Québécois nationalists, strengthened the hand of Québécois separatists, and doomed Canada to a prolonged crisis of national unity. On the whole, they consider Trudeau's response to the B & B Commission to be an unmitigated failure that jeopardized the future of the country. Indeed, given the political socialization of the Canadian adult population, it is not surprising that in the short term Ottawa's policies met with firm resistance and did little to radically alter the dynamics of English-French conflict in Canada or to strengthen the government of Quebec. Moreover, the promotion of official languages could do little in the short run to address the demographic trends that were decimating French Canadian and Acadian minority communities outside Quebec.

A REEVALUATION OF THE TRUDEAU-ERA LANGUAGE POLICIES

The criticisms of the Trudeau-era language policies that have been raised over the past thirty-odd years have a certain validity if one accepts their ideological premises. But to accept these criticisms is to accede implicitly to the disappearance of francophone minority communities in all provinces other than Ontario and New Brunswick, to accept that the English-speaking populations of Quebec must compromise their language rights in the interests of the French-speaking Québécois majority, and to accept a dramatically weakened federal government and decentralized Canadian federation. To deem these policies an abject failure is also to ignore the longer-term impacts of the language programs, particularly the educational initiatives undertaken in the past three decades.

The impacts of the programs established under the auspices of the Secretary of State and continued under Canadian Heritage to support French immersion, second language instruction, and minority-language education have all been more or less overlooked by academics to date. This is a critical oversight. The language policies of the Trudeau era, particularly the education programs, held the potential to inculcate in the next generation of Canadians different conceptions of bilingualism and the place of the English and French languages and their related communities in Canadian society. Moreover, through the use of the spending power, the cultivation of interest groups, and constitutional reform, the Trudeau government was able to lay the groundwork for a lasting language regime that bound the provinces into a commitment to official languages in education. The long-term impacts of these policies and their readoption by recent governments suggests that a reassessment of them and their impacts on Canadian identity politics is needed.[5]

Central to this reassessment are the policies regarding education, which developed from the recommendations of the B & B Commission produced in the first two volumes of its report in 1967 and 1968. Drawing on these recommendations, the federal government and the provinces entered into a program to promote Canada's official languages in education. Education had long been seen as central to the survival of French Canadian cultural identity; this was the primary reason why the province of Quebec had fought to keep it under the jurisdiction of the provinces in the British North America Act, 1867. The commission dedicated the second of its four books to the subject and made several key recommendations for promoting bilingualism in education, notably including federal assistance to the provinces to provide minority-language education and the promotion of second-language teaching in schools.

In 1970, in accordance with these recommendations, Secretary of State Gérard Pelletier announced that the Canadian government would provide financial assistance to the provinces to fund minority-language education for their official-language minorities (English in Quebec, French in the other nine provinces) and second-official-language instruction for the children of the majority-language communities. This was commonly known as the Bilingualism in Education Program (BEP) until its name was officially changed in 1979 to the Official Languages in Education Program (OLEP). It continues to exist under the latter name, and several billions of dollars have been spent to promote its objectives. The original objectives were to "ensure, insofar as it is feasible, Canadians have the opportunity to educate their children in the official language of their choice and that children have the opportunity to learn, as a second language, the other official language of their country."[6] To accomplish these objectives, the Canadian government agreed to pay a percentage of the per-student costs for students enrolled in minority-language education programs and second-language instruction classes. In addition, the federal government established programs of grants and bursaries for such related aspects as teacher training, student exchanges, and language training centres.

Over the next decade and a half, the provinces implemented the OLEP. How they did so, however, differed markedly from one province to the next. While some provinces actively developed their second-language and minority-language programs, others took very little interest in them, while still others allowed them to continue to erode. Some provinces favoured one aspect of the program over the other. Others tried to completely rework their education systems in the light of a new bilingual model. By 1984, as the provinces began a new series of multi-year agreements under the OLEP, although the state of minority-language education and second-language instruction had improved greatly since the 1960s, it was far from uniform across the country.

CRAFTING CANADIAN LANGUAGE POLICY – MAJOR CONSIDERATIONS

This book analyzes the development of language programs in education and language policy in Canada for the first fifteen years of federal government involvement in language planning. It explains how a diverse patchwork of programs could still exist after almost fifteen years of a standard federal formula for funding official languages in education. A comparative perspective on the evolution of these programs and a representative sample of the Canadian language experience is provided by focusing on the development of official-languages programs in education in six Canadian provinces: Alberta, Manitoba, Ontario, Quebec, New Brunswick, and Nova Scotia. This sample includes two Western provinces, two Maritime provinces, and two Central Canadian provinces. It includes a province with a francophone majority (Quebec), provinces with the largest francophone minorities (New Brunswick, around 33 percent, and Ontario and Manitoba, around 6 percent each), and provinces with much smaller concentrations of francophones (Alberta and Nova Scotia, around 3 percent each). It also includes provinces that were very active in the development of French immersion and second-language programs. Most importantly, it includes provinces that represent the spectrum of governmental opinions on the OLEP negotiations, and it includes all the key players in this process. While the OLEP did involve the other four provinces (and two territories), their governments were largely peripheral to the developmental process and followed the lead of the six representative provinces.

In order to understand the decisions that were made by federal and provincial politicians and civil servants, it is necessary to understand the dynamics of Canadian federalism and how these decisions both affected and were in turn affected by the development of Canadian language policy in education. Education is under provincial jurisdiction in the Canadian constitution, and thus to develop a language policy targeted at this sector, the Canadian government had to obtain provincial cooperation. Its success in this respect varied substantially. The federal and provincial governments each had their own set of objectives for language policies, objectives that were sometimes compatible, sometimes not. The provinces differed widely in terms of their preexisting language-education programs. Moreover, education was a key battleground in the conflicts between the provinces and Ottawa during constitutional talks in this period.

Two concepts are particularly important in the analysis that follows: the interstate/intrastate dynamic of Canadian federalism and the role of the embedded state. Under interstate federalism, the collective interests of citizens in the regions are primarily represented by the governments of the constituent units of the federation; in the Canadian context, this role is played by the provincial governments. Intergovernmental conflict is pervasive in this system, and conflict is resolved through intergovernmental negotiations and bargaining. Moreover, the national government has very limited ability to impose policy in areas of provincial jurisdiction.[7] In intrastate federalism, the same regional interests and conflicts are represented and resolved in the national decision-making structures; in Canada, this role is played by Parliament and the Supreme Court.

In the years immediately following the Second World War, Canadian federalism was described as cooperative federalism, which favours the operation of intrastate federalism. Under cooperative (or administrative) federalism, the federal and provincial governments engaged in many collaborative ventures. Negotiations between the two levels were largely carried out by bureaucrats with the authority to negotiate agreements on the behalf of their governments. Issues of jurisdiction were often blurred, to the benefit of pragmatism, compromise, and flexibility. In Canada, this type of federalism led to the creation of a number of conditional-grant or shared-cost programs.[8]

In the late 1960s, a transition began towards executive federalism, which favours the operation of interstate federalism. Executive federalism is characterized by a concentration of authority in the upper levels of government, highly publicized federal-provincial conferences, and the strict attention that is paid to jurisdictional issues. This type of federalism began to emerge in Canada as a result of the Quiet Revolution, as it became evident that Quebec's grievances could not be addressed through the cooperative federalism that had predominated in the postwar era.[9] This shift polarized the governments and made it difficult for the federal government to implement programs that involved provincial jurisdiction. Moreover, while Canada's national government theoretically includes strong regional representation, particularly through the Senate, by the 1970s the upper house came to be increasingly seen as a body of patronage appointees, rather than of regional representatives. Moreover, strict party discipline in the elected House of Commons undermined the ability of members of Parliament to effectively act as champions of regional interests, as did the decline of strong regional ministers.[10] Consequently, these institutions lost credibility as forums in which regional conflicts could be sorted out and compromises reached, further weakening intrastate federalism in the 1970s. The OLEP was developed at the height of the transition between these two phases (collaborative/intrastate and executive/interstate) in Canadian federalism.

In order for the Trudeau government to proceed with its national-unity strategy of promoting bilingualism and protecting official-language minority communities, it would need to exercise a fair deal of control over the development of the OLEP, but the reemergence of interstate federalism, coupled with Quebec nationalism, threatened its ability to do so. Although a conjunction of forces conducive to provincial acceptance of an intrastate program existed at the outset of the OLEP, the rise of interstate federalism in the early 1970s threatened Ottawa's ability to continue to direct the evolution of the program. In order to reassert control over the OLEP, the federal government needed to bolster the operation of intrastate federalism. It had to confirm its role as an effective broker of regional interests and convince Canadians that a strong central government, rather than a decentralized federation, would provide the route to national unity. Understanding the extent to which the Trudeau government was able to implement this plan is central to an analysis of this period, as is understanding how the provinces balked the federal government. For Canadian federalism is never exclusively of an interstate or an intrastate variety: both varieties are always present, but the dominance of either one in a given period will determine which level of government has the upper hand in setting policy.

This analysis of the impact of Canadian federalism on the development of language policy accepts the basic tenets of the neo-institutionalist theory of policy formation. This theory posits that governments, bureaucracies, and states have their own vested interests in the policy-making process, interests that are independent of the options put forth by interest groups, and it posits that they exert a directing influence on policy formation.[11] According to this model, there will thus be jockeying on the part of the provincial and federal states to protect their agendas and interests. In the Canadian context, beyond simply asserting their own interests, governments also fund interest groups to advance and bolster their agendas and to apply pressure on other governments.[12]

This phenomenon is part of what has been termed the "embedded state."[13] In Canadian federalism, voters elect at least two levels of government, each of which has its own set of jurisdictions under the Constitution. In theory, these governments, and thus their actions, draw their legitimacy from the fact that they are the elected representatives of the citizenry. Thus, in intergovernmental negotiations, both the national and provincial governments can rightfully claim to be representing the will of their respective electorates. However, since the provinces are subsets of the nation, the two electorates overlap: the same people have elected both levels of government, and they make demands on both levels. It is from this starting point that the embedded state comes into operation.

New governmental programs and policies do not simply come into existence in a vacuum. They enter a landscape littered with policies and ongoing programs from the past that are embedded in the present terrain of state-society relations and that must be contended with when new policies are being crafted. Thus, the actions of the "states" of the past constitute an ongoing "embedded state" in the present.

In the modern era, the number of state-society relationships in Canada has multiplied dramatically, owing to the fragmentation of the population along a host of different cleavages: by race, by gender, by class, by ideology, and so on. Moreover, an individual's identity may incorporate aspects of multiple cleavages. Government authority is also fragmented between its various levels. Thus, on any given issue citizens might sympathize with the position of either the national or their provincial government, depending on which aspects of their identity they consider to be important. They can then use their influence to advance that position by voting or lobbying or through daily work as civil servants. In a federal system such as Canada's, state actors seek to maximize the number of cleavage groups that are allied to their level of government. This is an ongoing process, and thus embedded group-state relations form an important consideration in policy-making.

Governments must deal with the embedded state from the past, but they will also try to reconfigure and restructure state-society relationships into new relationships that will then become embedded legacies for the future, if they are successful. This dynamic is crucially important to understanding the evolution of Canada's official-languages policies. In particular, the federal government provided funding to lobby groups, who then applied pressure on provincial governments to advance the federal vision of official languages (and their own agendas as well). Moreover, a cohort of civil servants at both the provincial and federal levels who were committed to programs such as the OLEP, were at times able to use their positions to overcome the reluctance of their respective governments to commit themselves to these policies and programs. The creation of these official-languages policies would also solidify the allegiances of new groups to the federal government. Furthermore, the programs were in and of themselves new elements for the embedded state of the future. The conflict over which model of federalism would predominate in the Trudeau era – interstate or intrastate – is closely related to the ways in which the federal and provincial governments used the embedded state to further their own interests.

The response of Canadians to the new language programs was affected by a host of demographic trends. By the late 1960s, sociolinguists such as Richard Joy were predicting the disappearance of French as a viable language outside a narrow "bilingual belt" between Sault Ste Marie, Ontario, and Moncton, New Brunswick.[14] They identified several factors at play in the Canadian context that influenced this trend, including exogamy (marriage outside the linguistic community), urbanization, industrialization, and intergenerational transfer. These trends would all play a role in shaping the decisions made by Canadians, both English- and French-speaking, as to whether or not to support the new language programs, either politically or by enrolling their children in them. Members of majority-language populations could either choose to support the continued existence of the minority-language group or encourage its disappearance, to support national bilingualism or support French as the language of Quebec alone. Members of the minority could opt to fight for linguistic survival or accept assimilation.

HISTORIOGRAPHY

While the language policies of the Trudeau era have received some limited attention from the political science community, most of it critical and primarily focussed on the Official Languages Act and civil service training programs,[15] the policies comprise largely virgin territory for historians. In recent years, Marcel Martel, Michael Behiels, and other historians have begun to explore the development of French-Canadian minority communities and their relations with their provincial and federal governments in the postwar years, chronicling this important transitional period.[16] Like most of the existing literature on French Canada and like their colleagues in sociology, education, and linguistics, these historians focus primarily on relations between the francophone minority communities and their respective provincial and federal governments, as well as on internal concerns of these communities.[17] This book builds on the foundations provided by these authors and examines some of the same issues, but with an eye to understanding the processes that framed the development of these policies and the diverse combination of players, including both anglophone and francophone lobby groups,[18] federal and provincial governments, civil servants and teachers, who influenced the direction of the language policies created in this period.

Much of the literature on language issues in Canada tends to focus on either anglophones or francophones and on either minority-language education or second-language education. It is my view that these elements need to be studied as interdependent elements in the development of Canadian language policy. Yet, other than the work of Garth Stevenson, Marc Levine, and Ronald Rudin,[19] there is a dearth of literature on the anglophone minority in Quebec. Almost nothing has been written about the politics of French immersion and French second-language education in postwar Canada: the elements of the Trudeau-era language policies that were directly experienced by the most Canadians.[20] These strands will be woven into my examination of this period.

PRIMARY SOURCES

In an ideal world, a comparative study such as this would be based on more-or-less identical primary source materials. However, were this an ideal world, there would be none of the conflicts that provide such fruitful material for historical research. Even in the four short decades that have elapsed since the B & B Commission began its research, mountains of potentially useful documentation have been destroyed, key individuals have passed on, and memories have faded. I have done my best with the material that remains to reconstruct this tale. My research is based primarily on the archival holdings of the federal government, the six provinces that are studied in depth, and numerous lobby groups. This material is uneven, whether because of access provisions or documentary conservation policies. While I was blessed with fantastic material at the Provincial Archives in Manitoba, I met with a dearth of documentation in Nova Scotia. In other cases, a rigorous archivist might have maintained detailed, well-organized records from a five-year period, but the same record group would be almost empty for another.

While these gaps are regrettable, it has been possible to reconstruct the historical record based on other sources. Published documents from this period, including demographic and educational studies, annual reports of government ministries, and newspapers, have helped provide overviews and key details. In addition, several civil servants, lobbyists, and senators who were intimately involved in the development of the OLEP and provincial language programs were kind enough to let me interview them to gain their perspectives on these events. While there are some limitations to oral history, including incomplete memories (as virtually all my research subjects hastened to caution me), these interviews nevertheless provide an important overall context for the research and stories that would never appear in an official government report. Moreover, they supplement the details omitted in the textual sources and often point the way to other avenues of research and different interpretations of the printed documents.

There has been little written of a descriptive nature about the development of language policy in relation to education since the B & B Commission submitted its report in 1968. While my primary purpose was to analyze the reasons underlying the path taken by governments in this regard, I first had to determine what that path was. Consequently, a fair deal of this book is dedicated to chronicling the development of provincial official-language policies, particularly as they affected the sectors of minority-language education, second-language instruction, and French immersion for the period from 1968 to 1984. I hope that this narrative will serve as a useful reference for other scholars interested in the history of Canadian language policy, Canadian federalism and intergovernmental relations, and the history of education.

Chapter 1 provides the background to this story, looking at official languages in education in the provinces from Confederation to the 1960s. In chapter 2, I examine the process that led to the formation of a federal-provincial agreement on official languages in education, starting with the formation of the B & B Commission in 1963 and continuing through the constitutional renewal process of the late 1960s until this agreement was reached in 1970. Chapter 3 looks at the early years of the OLEP and federal involvement in language policy, a period in which many new initiatives were launched in the English-speaking provinces to make education systems more bilingual. Conversely, these developments were matched by a retrenchment towards unilingualism in Quebec and increased assertiveness on the part of its Liberal government, which sought to expand its jurisdiction and decentralise the Canadian federation. This process came to a head with the election of the Parti Québécois in November 1976, where chapter 4 begins. This election inaugurated a fierce battle between Trudeau and Quebec premier René Lévesque over the nature and future of Canada, its federal system, and the role of its language groups. The chapter looks at Lévesque's gambit to win the other provinces over to his vision of the future of Canada and the impact it had on how the other premiers viewed Trudeau's vision. This was make-or-break time for the OLEP, as the provinces, the federal government, minority-language-community groups, and new national pressure groups entered the fray over the future development of Canada's language policies. The outcome would be crucial to establishing whether Canadian federalism would become completely decentralized, remain stable, or be marked by increased federal dominance. By 1979, when the OLEP agreements lapsed, the players were at a stalemate. Chapter 5 shows how this stalemate was resolved, a process that took four tumultuous years and included two federal elections, a referendum in Quebec, the patriation of the Constitution and a new framework for language rights in Canada under the Canadian Charter of Rights and Freedoms. Finally, chapter 6 looks at developments in Canadian language policy since Trudeau's time and concludes with an assessment of the OLEP and the language policies of this era and of the impacts they had on Canadian federalism, national unity, identity politics, and language learning in Canada. Through this analysis, I propose that a reevaluation of the Trudeau legacy on language policy is needed, both in terms of its impacts at the time and in its repercussions since then.

CHAPTER ONE

A Century of Language Conflict in Canada

The decision of the governments of Lester B. Pearson and Pierre Elliot Trudeau to actively promote two official languages in the 1960s marked a decisive break with how governments had historically addressed language issues in Canada. Indeed, during the pre-Confederation era and the first hundred-odd years of Canada's existence as a country, the best treatment that French-speaking minorities could hope for from their government was benign neglect. Most met with active attempts either to assimilate them or to prevent them from using their mother tongue. The dawn of the Quiet Revolution in Quebec heralded a new era in how both the federal and the provincial governments addressed the issue of bilingualism. As we shall see, the 1960s witnessed the slow opening up of provincial governments to increased tolerance of their linguistic minorities and an opportunity for Ottawa to take decisive action in this respect.

THE PRE-CONFEDERATION ERA

The question of what languages would be spoken in the territory to become Canada dates to the British Conquest of 1760. From this point forward, the legal status of the French language underwent a succession of expansions and contractions. It was initially quite restricted by the Royal Proclamation of 1763, then was gradually accorded increased status through the Quebec Act of 1774 and the Constitutional Act of 1791. Following the rebellions of 1837 and 1838, Lord Durham submitted his *Report on the Affairs of British North America*. He concluded that Lower Canada's problems were rooted in the cleavage between the English and French races. To resolve these problems, he proposed the fusion of Upper and Lower Canada and the introduction of responsible government. English speakers would be the majority population in the revamped colony, and the legislative council and assembly would both operate in English only. Through these measures, the French component of British North America was to be assimilated to the English language and culture.

Durham's proposed assimilation did not come to pass. The French language was rapidly accorded increased status in the legislature and courts, particularly those of Canada East (Quebec). Indeed, for all intents and purposes, the United Province of Canada was officially bilingual by 1849, when Lord Elgin read the Speech from the Throne in both English and French.

This bilingual status for the federal government was carried over into section 133 of the British North America Act, 1867 (BNA Act), which reads:

Either the English or the French language may be used by any Person in the Debates of the Houses of the Parliament of Canada and of the Houses of the Legislature of Quebec; and both those Languages shall be used in the respective Records and Journals of those Houses; and either of those Languages may be used by any Person or in any Pleading or Process in or issuing from any Court of Canada established under this Act, and or from all or from any of the Courts of Quebec. The Acts of the Parliament of Canada and of the Legislature of Quebec shall be printed and published in both those Languages.

Although this section made provisions for the official languages of the legislatures and courts of Quebec and the federal government, it notably did not impose any such requirements for federal government services or for the courts and legislatures of the other provinces.

In addition, at the instigation of Canada East's representatives, who were concerned about the preservation of the French language and Catholic education, section 93 of the BNA Act allocated responsibility for education to the provinces. Moreover, confessional education rights in the Canadas were protected for Catholic schools in Ontario and Protestant schools in Quebec. These guarantees were made on the basis of religion, *not* language. Although most Protestants in Quebec were English-speaking and a large proportion of the Catholics in Ontario were francophones, it was not deemed necessary to enshrine language rights in education in the BNA Act. It was assumed that religious schools would de facto protect language rights. This omission would have far-reaching implications in the post-Confederation era.

ONTARIO

Almost two decades passed in Ontario before the government paid any attention to the language of instruction of the province's schools. To this point, teachers in the francophone counties of Eastern Ontario taught primarily in French. However, owing to the influence of Egerton Ryerson, superintendant of education from 1846 to 1876, Ontario's education system had been moving towards standardization: in textbooks, in teacher training, in courses of study. As part of this broader trend, in 1885 the government issued a regulation requiring that English be taught in all the province's schools and that teachers obtain teaching certificates that proved their competency in English grammar, among other subjects. In 1890, the government restated that English was to be the language of instruction in the province, "except insofar as this is impracticable by reason of the pupil not understanding English."[1] For the most part these regulations were not rigorously enforced, and instruction continued to be provided in French in much of the province, despite the protestations of the anti-French Protestant Orange Order.

Over the following two decades, Ontario's francophone population began to shift its children from the public schools into the separate-school system, creating conflict between the French and Irish Catholics of Eastern Ontario. By 1910, the French Canadian élite was convinced that its "bilingual" schools, many of which in fact functioned in French, were threatened by a movement to transform them into English-language schools. Through the newly formed Association canadienne-française d'éducation d'Ontario (ACFEO), they began to push for recognition of French-language schooling. ACFEO was now on a collision course with opponents of French-language schooling. An investigation by schools inspector F.W. Merchant showed that the "bilingual schools," rather than accelerating the transition from French to English, were in fact functioning largely in French and teaching the English language very poorly.[2]

The Ontario government responded to Merchant's report in 1912 with the controversial and provocative regulation 17. Regulation 17 made English the sole language of instruction for the province after grade 2 and called for strict enforcement of this regulation by school inspectors. French-as-a-second-language instruction was permitted for only one hour per day in the higher grades. These restrictions caused an uproar, the legacy of which is still felt. Overturning regulation 17 and restoring French-language education rights would be ACFEO's raison d'être for the next fifty-six years.[3] During the First World War, the regulation further enflamed existing tensions between English and French Canadians, particularly during the conscription crisis. In 1927, the implementation of regulation 17 was softened to permit the functioning of "bilingual" elementary schools in practice, although the regulation was not completely taken off the books.[4] However, for the next four decades, publicly funded French-language secondary schools did not exist in Ontario, and ACFEO continued its battle.

NEW BRUNSWICK

New Brunswick entered Confederation with a substantial French-speaking Acadian population, which accounted for between 35 and 40 percent of the total population for most of the post-Confederation era. The New Brunswick Acadians dwelt predominantly in rural areas, and their children overwhelmingly attended Catholic schools, which existed side by side with Protestant schools in 1867. Unlike in Ontario, New Brunswick's confessional schools were not protected under the BNA Act.

In 1871 the New Brunswick government passed the Common Schools Act, declaring that all publicly funded schools must be nondenominational and imposing regulations on teacher certification. The act was seen as an attack on the Acadian population, since most Acadian children were enrolled in Catholic schools, which used French as the language of instruction. Four years of conflict ensued, until an agreement was reached in 1875 exempting members of religious orders from the new teachers' certificates and permitting religious teaching after regular school hours. While the Common Schools Act did not explicitly bar French-language instruction, the provincial Department of Education provided school manuals and official services in English only.[5]

By 1920, a dichotomy existed in New Brunswick. English speakers benefited from an education system that was reasonably well funded by local property taxes and well supported by the Department of Education. The Acadians, by contrast, were served by an odd network of "bilingual schools" with a weak funding base. Local property taxes from the poorer, rural areas where Acadians lived were insufficient. Moreover, funding formulas for schools were based on the number of heads of households, rather than the number of children, which worked against the larger Acadian families. In the bilingual schools, French was taught in the early grades, but English was progressively introduced until lessons were essentially English-only after grade 4. Acadian counties tended to have higher rates of illiteracy.[6] Private French-language secondary schools existed but were limited to the élite.

A 1955 inquiry by the Mackenzie Commission into the state of funding in New Brunswick revealed the disparity of funding between the urban (and English) and rural (normally Acadian) districts in the province. This revelation did not, however, lead immediately to any changes. They would have to wait until after the 1960 election of Liberal premier Louis Robichaud.

NOVA SCOTIA

After the 1755 Deportation, Acadians resettled in the more remote parts of the Nova Scotia, with the largest concentrations on Cape Breton Island in Richmond and Inverness counties and in the southwestern counties of Clare and Argyle. Other francophones, drawn by government and military jobs, would eventually settle around the provincial capital of Halifax in the post-Confederation era. By 1971 the Acadian population was split close to evenly between these three regions. They were thus geographically remote from each other, a factor that would have a significant impact on their ability to resist assimilation and form strong community networks.

Acadian schools offering a limited amount of French-language instruction existed in a clandestine and quasi-illegal fashion in Nova Scotia from 1864 until 1902, when the government announced its first official policy on French-language education. The policy permitted the use of French as a language of instruction for grades 1 to 3, after which they were to switch to English as the language of instruction. In 1939 the policy was revised to permit French-language instruction for the primary grades, bilingual instruction for grades 7 to 9, and then English-language instruction for grades 10 to 12. Analysts of Nova Scotia's French-language education system from these decades have noted that this system made sense only if its primary objective was to gradually assimilate the Acadian population. Indeed, if this was the objective, it had been successful through to the mid–twentieth century. By the 1960s, more than half of Nova Scotia's Acadians reported English as their mother tongue.[7] The system also discouraged higher education: fewer than 50 percent of Acadian adults had completed grade 8.[8]

MANITOBA

Carved out of the Northwest Territories in 1870, Manitoba entered Confederation as an officially bilingual province under section 23 of the *Manitoba Act*, with its Catholic schools constitutionally protected. Over the following two decades, large numbers of British Canadians from Ontario settled there and sought to make it a British province. At their urging, the official use of the French language in the Manitoba legislature, the courts, and the civil service was abolished by the Manitoba Official Language Act, 1890.[9] That same year, Manitoba switched to a single, nondenominational education system under the Act Respecting the Department of Education and the Act Respecting Public Schools, eliminating the public funding of Catholic schools.[10] Controversies over this decision raged for the next six years, until Prime Minister Wilfrid Laurier reached a compromise with Manitoba premier Thomas Greenway in 1897. Religious instruction would be permitted after regular school hours, and Roman Catholic teachers would be allowed to continue to teach. Bilingual instruction would also be permitted where ten pupils in a class spoke a minority language, a provision that applied not only to the French Canadian population but also to other immigrant groups such as the Ukrainians and Germans.

The Laurier-Greenway compromise allowed Catholic and French-language education to continue in Manitoba for the next two decades and received official sanction from the Pope. It did not, however, completely resolve the issue. In 1916, during the First World War, the T.C. Norris government, in an effort to anglicize foreigners, eliminated the bilingual schools.[11] French Canadians were caught up in this sweep as the Laurier-Greenway compromise was ended by the Manitoba government's unilateral action.

Franco-Manitoban leaders reacted to the abolition of their schools by creating the Association des éducateurs canadiens-français du Manitoba (AECFM) to lobby for the reinstitution of French-language education rights. Through covert cooperation with the minister of education (who viewed French as a "natural language" for Canada), the AECFM was able to protect French-language education in some homogenous French Canadian pockets of the province.[12] However, the schools relied on the independent resources of Franco-Manitoban community institutions and the Catholic Church and received no official support from the Department of Education.

It would not be until the 1950s that official reinstitution of French-language education would begin to take place in Manitoba. In 1952, the government of Douglas Campbell permitted one hour of French instruction for grades 7 to 12, and this was extended down to grade 4 in 1955. However, Franco-Manitoban education was dealt a setback in 1959, when the McFarlane Commission consolidated the province's school divisions, merging small homogenous Franco-Manitoban divisions into larger divisions containing large numbers of anglophones or other language groups. Franco-Manitobans no longer completely controlled these boards and often found themselves in the minority.[13]

ALBERTA

Under the Northwest Territories Act of 1875, religious minorities were permitted to establish their own separate schools. An 1877 amendment declared the territories to be officially bilingual. This was the high point for the legal status of French in the territory currently known as Alberta. In 1890, the Canadian Parliament transferred authority to the Territories to choose their language status. Two years later, they adopted English as their official language. In 1901, English was made the obligatory language of instruction in schools, although local ratepayers could pay the costs of using other languages, including French, for the first year of instruction.[14]

In 1905 the new provinces of Alberta and Saskatchewan were created out of the Territories. While Wilfrid Laurier, French Canadian members of Parliament, and Roman Catholics hoped that the provinces would adopt the bilingual status the region had enjoyed before 1892, they encountered fierce opposition from Clifford Sifton and other anglophone MPs. Despite Laurier's efforts the pre-1905 language policies were retained in the Autonomy Bills of 1905.

French-language instruction in the province of Alberta was extremely limited for the next several decades. Under regulations adopted in 1925, French could be used as the language of instruction only for grades 1 and 2. Beyond that level, French instruction was limited to one hour per day.[15] The Association canadienne-française de l'Alberta (ACFA) was created in 1926 to work for the improvement of French-language education in the province. Together with the Catholic Church, ACFA and other French Canadian organisations created French-language instructional materials for schools, although no provincial funds were provided for this and French-language courses that fell outside the 1925 regulations were not recognized by the provincial government. Private French-language schools were likewise not accorded any recognition or funds from a hostile Department of Education.[16] Some rural school districts were small enough that French-Canadian parishes were able to elect francophone commissioners to run the schools and hire teachers. However, this type of arrangement worked only in small districts and lacked official sanction. French-language education in Alberta would remain under constant siege until the late 1960s.

QUEBEC

Unlike other provinces, the legislature and courts of Quebec remained officially bilingual for the century following Confederation, and the province's English-language minority was treated very well in comparison with its French-speaking counterparts elsewhere in the country. Two education streams were established in the province along confessional lines: a Protestant stream that catered overwhelmingly to the English-speaking population and a Catholic stream that, although it predominantly served a francophone clientele, also operated English-language schools.

For a brief period, from 1868 to 1875, the Ministry of Public Instruction ran Quebec's education system. The ministry oversaw the Council of Public Instruction, composed of two committees, one Catholic and one Protestant, which supervised the schools of the province. This experiment with government control over education was short-lived, however, as Catholic bishops wrested control of education away from the politicians. The ministry was disbanded in 1875 and replaced by the Department of Public Instruction, which nominally controlled education. The full Council of Public Instruction rarely met in the decades that followed, and Quebec's school system was left to the jurisdiction of the Catholic Committee, which was run by the Catholic bishops of the province, and to the Protestant Committee, which was run by elected representatives of the Protestant minority of the province.

Over the decades that followed, the provincial government provided a nominal amount of funding for education, but local property and corporate taxes paid for most of the school system's costs. This worked heavily in favour of the Protestant school boards, which were able to draw on the substantial financial resources of Montreal's English-speaking business community to pay not only for Montreal's schools but also for those of the Gaspé and the Eastern Townships. The Protestant school boards and the English sector of the Catholic School Commission of Montreal provided education for a large proportion of the allophone communities and Jewish communities of Quebec, who were made to feel unwelcome in the French schools.[17] The management of the English-language schools was left to local authorities, and these schools thrived, offering programs from kindergarten up to the province's three English-language universities.

Quebec also differed from other provinces in the concentration and composition of its minority-language community. The British Canadian community was heavily concentrated on the West Island of Montreal, where it formed the majority. There were also sizeable communities in the Eastern Townships and Western Quebec, thanks to settlement by the Loyalists.[18] Tied closely to the English-speaking majority of North America, Quebec's anglophone community was financially well-off and able to assimilate significant portions of Quebec's immigrant population. Indeed, until the late 1970s, British Canadians in Quebec did not consider themselves to be a minority community at all but rather part of the British Canadian majority of Canada.[19]

In the decades following Confederation, very little was done to promote the status of the French language in Quebec. Before 1960 the only significant piece of language legislation was the 1910 Lavergne law, which required public utilities to provide bilingual signs and communications.[20] A 1937 attempt by the Duplessis government to give supremacy to French-language texts of laws and regulations was repealed one year later under intense pressure from Montreal's British Canadian community.[21] The English-speaking community of the province was very powerful and able to participate fully in all aspects of life in the province, whether social, economic, or political. By the 1950s, however, an increasing proportion of Quebec's educated francophone population had begun to feel that Quebec's anglophone community had succeeded at the expense of its francophone majority, and they sought to improve their status in the province.

PROVINCIAL CHANGES IN THE 1960S

Quebec

The death of Maurice Duplessis, followed shortly by the 1960 election of a Liberal government led by Jean Lesage was the opportunity that educated Quebec francophones had been hoping for. His election heralded the beginning of the Quiet Revolution, a period of intense modernisation and reform in the province designed to bring francophones into full participation in the economy of Quebec.

No new language laws were passed under the Lesage government, but the Parent Commission on Education did indicate that in the effort to improve the status of French in the province, education would be the most important sector, and assimilation of immigrant children should be a priority. In 1965 the government re-created the Ministry of Education, which had been moribund for the previous ninety years, and thus took an important step in reasserting government control over the education system. The anglophone communities were not oblivious to the changes that were afoot. Seeking to improve the French-language capacities of their children, school boards in Montreal and St Lambert pioneered programs in French immersion.

Between 1967 and 1969, under the Union Nationale governments of Daniel Johnson and Jean-Jacques Bertrand, language conflicts came to a head in the Catholic school commission of St-Léonard, a predominantly French-speaking suburb of Montreal that had recently seen rapid settlement by Italian speakers. After the 1967 municipal elections brought a pro-Italian party to power, the Ligue pour l'intégration scolaire was created; it was led by Raymond Lemieux and supported by many French-speaking residents who felt threatened by the increasing predominance of the Italian community. The Ligue orchestrated the take-over of the school commission by its supporters and won a referendum advocating an end to bilingual classes in 1968. (The referendum was boycotted by most of the Italian community.) The school commission then voted to end its policy of providing bilingual classes; the classes were three-quarters English, and ending them would have forced St-Léonard's large Italian community to attend French-language schools.[22] As a result, The St Leonard Parents' Association, composed of Italian parents who wanted the old system protected, clashed with the Ligue pour l'intégration scolaire and the Société St-Jean Baptiste (SSJB).[23] The clashes peaked on 10 September 1969, when the riot act was read to the conflicting groups. The Bertrand government thus found itself trying to balance the interests of francophone neonationalists, who were trying to develop a French-speaking state in Quebec, and parents who wanted the existing system of open access to English-language schools to be protected.[24] In an era when other provinces were moving towards increased bilingualism in their education systems, there were strong pressures for Quebec to use its school system to promote the French language.

New Brunswick

The year 1960 also witnessed the election of another reformist francophone Liberal premier as Louis Robichaud came to power in New Brunswick. The improvement of Acadian education was a major priority of his government, and steps were soon taken to this end. First came a move to translate school manuals into French, followed shortly by the appointment of a francophone deputy minister of education in 1964, the start of a tradition of having two deputy ministers, one from each language group. Steps were also taken to improve second-language teaching throughout the province's schools, with curriculum consultants appointed to supervise the mandatory second-language programs that were adopted in both English and Acadian schools in 1965.

The Robichaud government also fundamentally altered the structure of financing government services. Following the 1963 report of the Byrne Commission on Municipal Taxation, the Liberals introduced their ambitious Equal Opportunities Program. A standard provincial formula for funding schools, paid for by the provincial treasury, replaced the prior system of funding based on local taxation. The number of school divisions in the province was reduced to thirty-three, more or less along linguistic lines, with English-language, French-language, and bilingual districts.[25] A French-language normal school was also established at the Université de Moncton in 1967 to train Acadian teachers, and steps were taken to increase Acadian representation in the Department of Education.

Acadian community activism increased in this period as well. After the bicentennial commemorations of the 1755 Acadian Deportation, held in 1955, community leaders revitalised the Société nationale des Acadiens (SNA), a Maritimes-wide association, to lobby the government on issues important to the community, including education.[26] This association became increasingly activist and radical in its demands throughout the 1960s, particularly as students from the Université de Moncton entered the movement.[27] An era of fundamental change was clearly afoot in New Brunswick, one in which yet another step would be taken in 1969, when the province became officially bilingual.

Ontario

Reforms were also taking place in Ontario under Conservative premier John Robarts, who believed that improving the status of the Franco-Ontarians would demonstrate to Quebec's political class that English Canada was serious about creating conditions for the two dominant language communities to live together. He thus set about gradually responding to the long-standing demand of Franco-Ontarians for publicly funded French-language secondary schools. An initial step was taken in 1963, when the Department of Education authorized the teaching of history, geography, and Latin in the French language. Four years later, on 24 August 1967, Robarts announced his intention to enact legislation providing full funding for public French-language secondary schools. Following a feasibility study by the Bériault Committee, the Ontario government passed Bills 140 and 141 in July 1968, guaranteeing the right of Franco-Ontarians to publicly funded French-language secondary schools if a minimum number of students could be reached. The Robarts government decided to fund French-language public secondary schools, rather than Catholic ones, because Catholic schools, both English- and French-language, received government funding only to grade 10, a situation that would not change until the 1980s.[28] Its fifty-year quest accomplished, ACFEO dissolved to make way for a new organisation, the Association canadienne-française de l'Ontario (ACFO), with a mandate to pursue the improvement of French-language services in a much wider array of sectors.

Robarts also tried to intervene on the constitutional front to resolve tensions between Quebec and English-speaking Canada. In November

1967, a few years after the latest failure of constitutional reform efforts led by the federal government, Robarts brought the provincial governments together for the Confederation of Tomorrow Conference. This conference rekindled interprovincial discussions, setting the stage for new federal-provincial talks while also establishing a precedent for interprovincial talks without the presence of representatives from Ottawa.

Manitoba

Changes to French-language education in the Prairie Provinces were less dramatic than those in Central Canada, but nevertheless represented an increasing openness. In Manitoba in 1967, the Conservative government of Duff Roblin realigned provincial school districts along ethnic lines. In five of the new districts – Seine, Red, St Boniface, White Horse Plains, and Mountain – Franco-Manitobans were in a majority or at least a strong minority.[29] The government also unanimously passed Bill 59, permitting the use of French as a language of instruction for up to 50 percent of the school day, overturning the 1916 restrictions. The AECFM dissolved in 1968 and was succeeded by the Société franco-manitobain (SFM), a provincial organisation with a broader mandate to pursue full-day French-language education programs and a return to the bilingual status that the province had been accorded under the Manitoba Act.

Alberta

Alberta also took some modest steps to improve French-language education. In 1964 French-language education was extended to grade 3, and French-language education (as opposed to French as second language) was permitted for one hour per day in the elementary grades. More importantly, under revisions to the Schools Act passed in 1968, French language instruction was permitted for 50 percent of the day for grades 4 through 12, the first time that any French-language instruction was permitted for grades 9 through 12 since the province had been created. Full-day French-language programs, however, were still a distant vision for leaders of the Franco-Albertan community.

Nova Scotia

Nova Scotia moved slowly to improve its French programs. It was not until the 1950s that the Department of Education even produced French-language grammar texts. But as in the other provinces, steps began to be taken in the 1960s. A committee to advise the department on

Acadian matters was created in 1966, and a consultant was appointed in 1967 with responsibility for Acadian schools and all modern-languages programs. This individual faced a monumental task, as 67 percent of Nova Scotia's FSL teachers were unable to carry on a conversation in French.[30]

The Acadian community was slow to organise as well. It was only in 1968 that the province's first lobby group for French-language issues was created: the Fédération francophone de la Nouvelle-Écosse (renamed the Fédération acadienne de la Nouvelle-Écosse). This group had a major challenge to overcome in the following decades. French-language media in the province were practically nonexistent, aside from *Le Petit Courrier*, a weekly paper whose circulation was restricted to the southwestern counties. Also, the assimilative policies of the Department of Education had taken their toll on the Acadian population, which had been dwindling over the decades. It would take a great deal of effort to institute effective French-language education in Nova Scotia after so many decades of neglect.

NATIONAL OFFICIAL LANGUAGES ISSUES

Very little was done by the federal government between Confederation and the Second World War to promote and recognize the use of two languages, and Ottawa only rarely intervened in provincial matters concerning official languages. Both English and French were permitted for use in the Canadian parliament and its bureaucracy and within federal courts. A traditional practice of appointing a Quebec lieutenant under an English-speaking prime minister had also evolved. However, it was not until 1958 that simultaneous interpretation was introduced in the House of Commons. Likewise, bilingual stamps and bilingual currency were introduced only in the postwar era.

The status of French Canadians within the federal civil service was also generally poor. They were numerically underrepresented, particularly at the level of senior management. (Indeed, this was one of the main reasons why the Ordre de Jacques Cartier had been formed in 1926.)[31] This situation did not sit well in Quebec as neonationalism took hold of the collective imagination in the early 1960s. French-speaking Quebecers increasingly decried their exclusion from positions of power and authority, particularly in the economy of the province, and resolved to change this state of affairs.

It was against this backdrop that Prime Minister Lester Pearson appointed the Royal Commission on Bilingualism and Biculturalism in 1963. Co-chaired by André Laurendeau and Davidson Dunton, the commission was to "inquire into and report upon the existing state of bilingualism and biculturalism in Canada and to recommend what steps should be taken to develop the Canadian Confederation on the basis of an equal partnership between the two founding races, taking into account the contribution made by other ethnic groups to the cultural enrichment of Canada and the measures that should be taken to safeguard that contribution."[32] In particular, the commission was to look into the situation and practice of bilingualism within branches and agencies of the federal administration and to make recommendations to ensure that the federal government would have a bilingual and bicultural character. It was also mandated to consult with provincial governments concerning the opportunities available for Canadians to learn the English and French languages and then recommend what could be done to enable Canadians to become bilingual.

The commission held public hearings and regional meetings throughout 1964 and 1965, received briefs from a wide variety of individuals and associations, and undertook a major series of research studies. Its first report (there would be five in total) was submitted on 8 October 1967; its second, which dealt specifically with education, on 23 May 1968, shortly after the death of co-chair André Laurendeau. The conclusions and recommendations of the commission will be addressed in detail in the next chapter. Suffice it to say here that several of its major recommendations would form the basis for the next few decades of federal language policy and would lead to both the Official Languages Act and the Official Languages in Education Program.

Two other events in 1967, the Centennial year, had major repercussions for official languages, although neither involved the federal government directly. The Confederation for Tomorrow Conference, convened by Premier Robarts, proposed that the federal government provide financial and technical aid for minority-language education programs, particularly in provinces where, for various reasons, the provinces themselves believed they could not afford to provide them.[33] The provinces also created the Council of Ministers of Education, Canada (CMEC), to provide ministers of education with a forum in which to discuss issues of mutual concern and to coordinate cooperation and consultation among the provinces on educational matters.

The CMEC was part of Robarts' strategy to reinforce interstate federalism and curb the Canadian government's use of its spending power. He (and other like-minded premiers) hoped that the provinces could use these agencies of interprovincial cooperation and coordination to address issues of national importance that fell under provincial jurisdiction, thereby preventing the establishment of intrusive, federally controlled, shared-cost programs and the operation of intrastate federalism.[34] The creation of the CMEC dismayed the federal government. Prime Minister Pearson expressed reservations concerning the desire of the council to meet with the federal minister of manpower and immigration, noting that the "creation of interprovincial councils could establish a pattern of 'ganging up' of provincial ministers to pressure the federal government," and his Cabinet agreed to avoid the "development of federal-provincial discussions of a policy nature at provincial initiative through such agencies."[35] Initially, the CMEC had little impact on federal-provincial relations. However, the council would rise to great importance in the mid-1970s as the forum in which the provinces discussed developments in the Official Languages in Education Program. It would be an important component in the provinces' attempt to promote and expand their interstate vision of federalism while holding the federal government at bay.

While these political changes were certain to affect the climate in which a new language policy for Canada would be crafted, a host of other considerations – demographic, social, and economic – also had to be borne in mind. In all provinces except New Brunswick, francophone minority communities were shrinking relative to the total population. The percentage of Alberta's population that declared French as its mother tongue had slipped from 3.9 percent in 1931 to 2.9 percent by 1971, lower than either the German or the Ukrainian populations.[36] The comparable figure in Manitoba had risen from 6.1 percent to a high of 7.1 percent in 1941 but had dropped back to 6.1 percent by 1971, slightly lower than the 6.3 percent in Ontario (a figure that had similarly risen from 6.9 percent in 1931 to 7.4 percent in 1951 and then steadily fallen).[37] New Brunswick's francophone population had actually climbed from 32.6 percent in 1931 to 34 percent in 1971. Across the border in Nova Scotia, however, the figure had dropped from 7.6 percent in 1931 to 5 percent by 1971.[38] In many of these provinces, the census figures for those of French origin was significantly higher, indicating that the process of anglicization was having a significant impact on the size of the francophone populations.

In 1982, University of Ottawa mathematician Charles Castonguay published a report on language transfer in the provinces. He based his figures on the language primarily spoken in the home by individuals aged thirty-five and over who identified French as their mother tongue. He took this figure as a good indicator of the language that the children of these individuals would be raised in.[39] The second column in table 1.1 indicates the percentage of these individuals who had "anglicized," that is, who had adopted English as their language of daily use in the home. Castonguay's methodology has been contested by a num-

Table 1.1
Rates of Anglicization and Exogamy in French Canada, 1971/1976

Province	Rate of Anglicization, Castonguay (1971)	Rate of Anglicization, Alternate (1971)	Rate of Exogamy (1976), 25-34 year age bracket
Nova Scotia	42	30.8	45
New Brunswick	12	7.7	13
Ontario	38	–	37
Manitoba	45	34.6	45
Alberta	64	51.2	60

Source: Castonguay, "The Decline of French," 93; Viaud, "La géographie du peuplement francophone," 85; Johnson and McKee-Allain, "La société et l'identité," 215.

ber of demographers, so alternate figures on anglicization, based on raw data comparing French mother tongue to French language of usage are given in column 3.[40] While these figures paint a less bleak picture, it is nevertheless clear that by the 1970s francophone communities were rapidly being assimilated in all the provinces, except perhaps New Brunswick.

Many demolinguists identify exogamy, the practice of marrying outside one's language group, as a crucial factor in the assimilation process, a practice that in the overwhelming number of cases leads to the use of the majority language in the home.[41] As the figures in table 1.1 demonstrate, exogamy was a significant phenomenon in the provinces listed, where the rates of exogamy closely parallel the anglicization rates. Other measures and methodologies producing slightly different anglicization and exogamy rates have been used by various demographers, but their results do tend to closely parallel the figures in table 1.1. Clearly, anglicization was ravaging the francophone minority communities of Canada by the 1960s and 1970s.

The survival of Canada's francophone minority communities was not helped by the disappearance of their two main pillars of support. The Catholic Church in Quebec, once a moral and financial source of support for French-speaking communities across the country, was in a period of decline by the 1950s. Other organisations that had historically supported these communities, such as the Conseil de la vie française (CVF) and the Ordre de Jacques Cartier (OJC), were faced with internal crises in the early 1960s that ultimately led to the dissolution of the OJC and a declining funding base for the CVF, depriving many small and isolated French-speaking communities of their major sources of revenue and moral support.[42]

The decline of these organisations coincided with the rebirth and reorganization of the Quebec state described earlier. Francophone Quebecers increasingly turned to their provincial government over the Catholic Church as a means for economic and social advancement. Francophone Quebecers became more inward-looking, seeing themselves as *Québécois* rather than *Canadiens-français*. Quebec's Ministère des affaires culturelles did take a brief interest in supporting French-speaking minority communities in the mid-1960s, but it too largely withdrew from this role by 1969.[43] French Canadian communities in the other provinces were aware of their exclusion from Quebec's new orientation. In an attempt to rebuild their institutional supports, they increasingly adopted provincial orientations and turned to their provincial governments for support.[44] As we shall see, community leaders also turned to the federal government for support and urged the B & B Commission to recommend federal support for official language minorities, so as to halt their disappearance and fragmentation.

Canada was dramatically divided along linguistic lines by the 1960s. Demographer Richard Joy determined the percentage of the Canadian population that claimed to be bilingual in 1961 and 1971, producing the results in table 1.2. Joy's studies indicated a very low level of bilingualism nationally, at 13.4 percent by 1971, particularly considering that his statistics are based on self-reported bilingualism, which might have inflated his figures. Moreover, these figures mask the much higher proportion of native French speakers who were bilingual, relative to native English speakers. These figures also indicate the very low levels of bilingualism outside Central Canada and New Brunswick, which would make the promotion of bilingualism on a national level a major challenge indeed.

The baby boom, which had propelled a huge influx of students into the education system and necessitated the hiring of significant numbers of new teachers and administrators, was petering out by the mid-1960s. Elementary and secondary school enrolments thus steadily declined through the 1960s and 1970s, exerting major financial pressures on the school boards that had expanded to meet the needs of the previous generation. These boards were now stuck with more schools and teachers than were either necessary or affordable for the shrinking student population. Several provinces, including Ontario, New Brunswick, and Manitoba in the 1950s and 1960s, began consolidating their school boards, eliminating small boards in favour of larger regional boards, a phenomenon that would soon spread to Nova Scotia. As a result, small school districts that once had contained a majority of francophones, were absorbed into larger school boards where francophones were in a minority.[45]

Table 1.2
Percentage of Canadians Claiming to Be Bilingual, 1961 and 1971

Region	1961	1971
Canada, nationally	12.2	13.4
Quebec	25.5	27.6
New Brunswick	19.0	21.5
Ontario	7.9	9.3
Other provinces	4.6	5.3

Source: Joy, *Canada's Official Languages*, 121.

The impetus for English-speaking Canadians to study French was changing as well. Many Canadian universities that had once required knowledge of a second language as a prerequisite for admission dropped this requirement in the 1960s. Accordingly, a major reason for students to continue with the study of French, the most widely available second-language course, had disappeared by the late 1960s.[46]

Despite these demographic, social, and economic constraints, there were some promising signs that a new course could be charted for official languages in Canada. Major constitutional negotiations took place in the 1960s between the federal and provincial governments, including negotiations over the failed Fulton-Favreau formula and negotiations at the provincially driven Confederation of Tomorrow Conference. These negotiations provided a convenient forum for the discussion of language issues. Moreover, Expo 67 and the Centennial celebrations fostered feelings of national optimism and an openness to language questions that had not previously existed.[47] More importantly, the national economic picture had been generally rosy since the early 1950s, and economic optimism reigned in the late 1960s. Consequently, the federal government was well disposed to spend large sums of money to promote its agenda and areas of concern, including official languages,[48] particularly in the late 1960s when Canada elected a prime minister strongly committed to bilingualism, in the person of Pierre Elliot Trudeau.

CONCLUSION

Although during the first century of Canada's post-Confederation history there had proved to be little support for bilingualism, either in terms of a supportive climate for francophone minority communities or in the promotion of bilingualism among individual Canadians, there was cause for some limited optimism by the 1960s. Provinces that had once been hostile to French-language education were loosening restrictions and opening up the provincial purse. Constitutional and economic trends in the country were pointing towards a greater openness to change and a willingness to spend money to this effect. Even though the provincial governments of Ontario, Quebec, and Alberta were increasingly militant about preventing federal interventions in their jurisdiction and were leaning towards provincially driven solutions to national questions, the overall atmosphere in the country seemed to indicate that federal involvement in the language dossier might not be rejected. Consequently, a critical juncture had been reached in Canadian language education, the future of which would largely be shaped by how the federal and provincial governments responded to the recommendations of the Royal Commission on Bilingualism and Biculturalism.

CHAPTER TWO

From Royal Commission to Government Policy, 1963–1970

By the 1960s, it was clear that continuing to run Canada as if it contained only English speakers was no longer a viable option. With the dawn of the Quiet Revolution, the province of Quebec was now front and centre in constitutional debates, demanding that the rights of its French-speaking majority be acknowledged and that the provincial government be given additional powers to this end. Provincial premiers such as John Robarts and Louis Robichaud were calling for new arrangements to respond to the needs of French-speaking Canadians. Even provinces that had outlawed the teaching of French in their schools were beginning to adopt more permissive positions. The decade was marked by ongoing federal-provincial talks dealing with a wide array of topics, from pensions to health care to constitutional reform.

Amidst this fray, the Royal Commission on Bilingualism and Biculturalism began its work in 1963. As the commission's inquiries progressed, its co-chair André Laurendeau would grow ever more convinced of the crisis in English-French relations that was wracking the country. Together with the other commissioners, he would try to develop proposals that could ease, if not resolve, the crisis. Once they were released, it would then fall to politicians and bureaucrats to respond to them and take action as they saw fit. Seven years after the commission first met, Ottawa and the provinces launched what eventually became known as the Official Languages in Education Program. Reaching this agreement would require a willingness to compromise and deft manoeuvring amidst a sea of competing ideologies and interests. This chapter will first look at the B & B

Commission's attempt to come up with solutions to the Canadian language problem of the 1960s, a process that was itself fraught with division and dispute. It will then look at what emerged from political discussions surrounding the reports of the commission and at how the federal government managed to assume a key role in the promotion of official languages through this process, despite intense constitutional haggling and increasingly adversarial provincial governments.

THE ROYAL COMMISSION ON BILINGUALISM AND BICULTURALISM

The members of the B & B Commission spent much of 1964 and 1965 on the road. Travelling from coast to coast, they held open meetings and special forums in cities and towns across the country, met with provincial premiers, spoke with advocacy groups and listened to "average Canadians" express their views on the nature of bilingualism and biculturalism in Canada. The commission's research team produced a deluge of research reports and collected boxes upon boxes of newspaper and magazine articles, while the commissioners sifted through literally hundreds of briefs submitted by groups from every province. Faced with this deluge of information, the commissioners may well have despaired at their Herculean task of recommending a course of action for the Canadian government.

Indeed, given the nature of Canadian federalism, the commissioners even had to decide which level of government, if any, they would deem best suited to taking action. Was promotion of bilingualism and biculturalism a national responsibility, or should it be left to local jurisdictions? The Quebec government, for one, seemed to be increasingly of the opinion that it should be given more powers to protect and promote the French language. Even the commission's objectives were challenged. Many groups representing Canada's "other" ethnic communities, particularly Ukrainian communities in the Western provinces, rejected the premise that Canada was a bicultural nation.

A contrary perspective was also forcefully presented to the commission. French Canadian and Acadian community organisations, who were facing the loss of their primary bastions of support, saw a potential godsend in the B & B commission's eventual recommendations. Dozens of these organisations, the more prominent including the Association acadienne d'éducation en Nouvelle-Écosse, the Société nationale des Acadiens (SNA), the Association canadienne-française d'éducation de l'Ontario (ACFEO), the Association des éducateurs canadiens-français du Manitoba (AECFM), and the Association canadienne-française de l'Alberta (ACFA), appeared at commission hearings and submitted detailed briefs. There was a unity in their message: official-language-minority education programs must be expanded if there was to be any hope of a future for their communities.[1] The provincial governments had proven hostile to this objective in the past, and several of these associations called specifically for Ottawa to take action to protect their language rights. While the provinces had constitutional responsibility for education, the federal government could theoretically be active in the area of language rights.

After sifting through the research reports, briefs, and proceedings from their meetings, the commissioners met several times to decide what they would recommend to the Canadian government. Prolonged and at times divisive discussions took place during those meetings, reflecting the diversity of strong opinions held by the commissioners. One of the first, and perhaps most fundamental, issues was the nature of the language régime they would recommend for Canada.

The commission considered a number of international models that could potentially have been used to craft a Canadian language policy. However, none of the countries studied provided a particularly close parallel to Canada's demographic realities. South Africa, with its evenly dispersed populations of English and Afrikaans speakers, offered government and education services uniformly throughout the country. But Canada did not have nearly as high a degree of individual bilingualism as South Africa, and its bilingual population was not evenly spread across the country. Moreover, because Canada's minority-language populations were more narrowly concentrated, the commissioners believed a policy along South African lines would be excessive and politically unfeasible. Language policy in Switzerland, on the other hand, was territorially determined: the language of government services was determined by each canton, most of which were unilingual German or French. Belgium had a similar set-up, with Flemish and French halves and bilingualism restricted mainly to the capital city. These models were also considered unworkable for Canada, given both the mobility of the Canadian population and the broader distribution of the minority-language populations. Moreover, the commission did not accept the redefining of Canadian duality from one based on language and culture to one based on a territorial division between Quebec and the rest of Canada. Applying this type of principle along provincial lines in Canada, the commissioners argued, would lead to "the recognition of only the majority's rights and to oppression of the official language minorities ... depriv[ing] minority groups *en bloc* of essential language rights."[2]

The closest workable model was the one employed in Finland, which offered government services to its Swedish minority in a series of bilingual districts. This appealed to some of the commissioners, since it would provide a more comprehensive structure for the minority language communities' rights. Accordingly, the commissioners decided to take this approach, adopting the guiding principle of "the recognition of both official languages, in law and in practice, wherever the minority is numerous enough to be viable as a group."[3] Protecting individual language rights, they hoped, would make it be possible to ensure the survival of small minority-language communities. Yet the commissioners did not believe that individual language rights were absolute. To make the policy viable, these rights could be exercised only where the minority language populations were concentrated.

In line with this principle, in the first volume of its report the commission recommended that the provinces of Ontario and New Brunswick become officially bilingual and that they join with the federal government and the other provinces, including Quebec, to create a series of bilingual districts in which government services would be offered in both official languages. It called for an official languages act, the main aims of which would be

a) to ensure that Canadian citizens can deal with federal administrative and judicial bodies in the two official languages;
b) to provide for the appointment of a high state official, independent of the government, with responsibility for inquiring into and reporting upon the implementation of the federal Official Languages Act;
c) to give the Governor in Council the necessary authority for negotiating with the provincial and local authorities involved – in the latter case with the consent of the province concerned – to widen the opportunities for Canadian citizens to deal with the branches of government in both official languages.[4]

This act would establish the right of every Canadian citizen to deal with central government offices and regional offices in bilingual districts in the official language of their choice, with a commissioner of official languages to oversee this process. The federal act would also provide for bilingualism policies addressing such issues as government publications, federal statutes, and court proceedings. A similar set of provisions was envisioned for the provincial acts.

Although several of Canada's "other" ethnic communities had submitted reports, the commission's report largely overlooked these groups. The exception was the inclusion a separate statement from Commissioner Jaroslav Rudnyckyj. While recognizing the importance of a policy aimed at the two dominant language groups, he was concerned by the failure to recognize languages such as Ukrainian and German and Native languages. He argued that the government should recognize the "regional bilingualisms" where other language groups were significantly concentrated.⁵ While his concerns would not translate into action in the federal government's language policies, they nevertheless represented an important current of thought on multilingualism, one that would become important in the 1970s, particularly in Western Canada and in the Trudeau government's multiculturalism policy.

THE B & B COMMISSION AND THE EDUCATION QUESTION

While a national policy of two official languages was the overarching policy recommendation from the commission, in terms of concrete action the members believed that the future of Canada's language communities would be determined in the education systems. As they noted, "the future of language and culture, both French and English, depends upon an educational régime which makes it possible for them to remain 'present and creative,'"⁶ They also were persuaded by the briefs of the French Canadian community groups stating that it was "the responsibility of the federal government to contribute to the additional costs involved" in providing this education.⁶ Fleshing out these beliefs into an acceptable policy was a more difficult task.

A first quandary for the commission was to determine what types of schools would be needed to support this "present, creative" régime. The most pressing issue was how to develop schools for the minority-language populations, particularly the French-speaking ones. In some countries with bilingual education systems, children of the minority-population were obliged to attend school in that population's language. Commissioner Gertrude Laing was strongly opposed to following this lead and called for Canada to instead adopt a principle of "freedom of choice," one that would allow parents from the minority-language community to send their children to majority-language schools if they felt that doing so was in a child's best interest (for economic reasons, for example).⁸ Her views prevailed, and the commissioners agreed to let parents determine the language of instruction for their children.

In a related vein, the commissioners acknowledged that parents from the majority-language community might wish to have their children educated in the minority language. We should note here that these discussions took place before the advent of French-immersion programs in Canada, which were better suited to these needs. While Commissioners Gertrude Laing and Frank Scott were supporters of freedom of choice, they also believed that the integrity of the French-language minority educational system needed to be protected.[9] The situation was further complicated by the significant number of parents of French origin, particularly in Western Canada, who had been assimilated into the English-language majority yet wanted to educate their children in French. The position adopted by the Commissioners was to avoid stressing cultural homogeneity and recommend that the minority-language schools accept students as long as they could follow the curriculum without slowing down their classmates. Their response to parents from the majority-language community who wanted their children instructed in the minority language schools was that their "right to do so must be respected, but special measures will be required to ensure that the language problems of their children do not interfere unduly with the education of the children whose mother tongue is the language of instruction."[10]

The commissioners recognized that minority-language schools would not be established by virtue of good wishes and permissive legislation alone, since they would entail costs over and above the cost of a single-language education system. The commissioners identified several different costs, ranging from smaller class sizes and additional administrative costs to purchasing new textbooks and audio-visual materials to training and hiring new teachers, but they differed over who should pay for these costs and over the type of arrangements that were necessary to ensure that minority-language education would be provided.

Since it was desireable for the commission to put forth a concrete proposal to resolve the problem of minority-language education, Professor Blair Neatby, the B & B Commission's research director, supported by Commissioner Laing, chair of the education study group, proposed that the federal government provide funding for official-language programs in education.[11] The main alternative floated in commission meetings was to propose a constitutional amendment obliging the provinces to provide minority-language education; Commissioners Laing and Scott supported this type of amendment.[12] However, Commissioners Royce Firth and Paul Lacoste argued that such a proposal could provoke a worse crisis in federal-provincial relations and that there was not enough public support for such a change at present.[13] Moreover, André Laurendeau noted that Quebec would probably not accept this type of proposal.

Opting, therefore, to propose federal funding for minority-language education, the commissioners had to decide how this policy would operate in practice. Neatby and Laing envisioned a universal federal funding formula applicable to all provinces. Other commissioners, notably Davidson Dunton, Paul Lacoste, and Frank Scott, wanted the federal money to be targeted specifically at minority-language education in the "unilingual" provinces, to enable them to catch up to Quebec, Ontario, and New Brunswick. However, this position was rejected by the majority of the commissioners, particularly given André Laurendeau's assertion that this proposal would be unacceptable in Quebec, which would get no funding. Blair Neatby and Jaroslav Rudnyckyj also noted that it would be unwise to exclude the "bilingual" provinces from a new funding program, since there would then be no incentive for them to improve their existing programs. Moreover, if the federal funding was merely rolled into an equalization grant, as had also been proposed, provinces such as Ontario could then divert the funds into other provincial priorities, such as welfare.[14]

One notes the implicit acceptance by the commissioners of a role for the federal government in support of minority-language education. While the commissioners recognized that education fell under provincial jurisdiction, they believed that the confirmation of the bilingual and bicultural character of Canada required action by the federal government, a position that reinforced Ottawa's intrastate vision of Canadian federalism.[15] They believed that while the provinces had the responsibility for the basic costs of education, the Canadian government could, and should, reimburse them for the additional costs involved in operating schools for their minority populations. Recommendation 26 of book 2 of the commission's *Report* thus reads as follows: "We recommend that the federal government accept in principle the responsibility for the additional costs involved in providing education in the official minority language." The commissioners were not entirely sure what these additional costs would be and believed that it would be difficult to provide a precise measure. Consequently, recommendation 27 reads: "We recommend that the federal grant to each province be based on the number of students attending official-language minority schools in the province, and that the grant be 10 percent of the average cost of education per student within the province." The commissioners also recommended federal grants to minority-language universities, teacher training institutions, and exchange programs.

The commission did not limit itself to the question of minority-language education. Second-language instruction was also considered an important priority, especially given the higher receptivity of young children to language instruction. A national interest was also attached to knowledge of the second language, since the commissioners believed that this knowledge would foster a greater degree of cultural understanding and familiarity with the way of life of the other cultural group. It would also advance a more practical objective. Because, as the commissioners observed, an overwhelming proportion of bilingual people in Canada had French as their mother tongue, "Official bilingualism in Ontario and New Brunswick, for instance, and in the federal Public Service, will not be a reality unless there are sufficient numbers of Anglophones capable of conducting business in French as well as in English."[16] The commissioners thus recommended "that the study of the second official language should be obligatory for all students in Canadian schools."[17] They believed that this recommendation would not entail radical change to the existing structure of provincial educational systems, since second-language programs were already offered in most of these systems, albeit not by all local school boards and not at all grade levels. The B & B Commission, notably, did *not* make any recommendations about federal funding of second-language instruction.

While the commissioners produced some assertive and imaginative proposals to improve the state of English-French relations in Canada, they were not in a position to implement these proposals themselves. Indeed, Canadian history is filled with examples of issues that were sent to royal commissions with the intent of making them disappear and with the resulting reports left to collect dust on bookshelves. The Canadian government did not, however, dismiss the report out of hand. It would, however, cherry-pick the recommendations it wanted to follow. To implement many of them, it would also need the consent of the provincial governments – governments that were not always as enthusiastic about the direction proposed by the B & B Commission.

OTTAWA RESPONDS TO THE B & B COMMISSION

The recommendations of the B & B Commission provided federal politicians and bureaucrats with a justification to assert a new role as the champion of the beleaguered official-language minority groups. Doing so would enable them to counter the provincial push for increased decentralization and to reassert the federal government's role as the arbiter of diverse interests. At the same time, many in Ottawa hoped that a national policy of two official languages would serve as a tool of nation-building and national unity and counter the rising separatist movement in Quebec. The Trudeau government was thus quick to transform many of the recommendations of the royal commission into concrete action.

In many respects, the Trudeau government would find itself in wholehearted agreement with the B & B Commission. As we shall see, it would sometimes go even further than the commission's recommendations. However, it is important to highlight a key ideological distinction between the thinking of Pierre Trudeau and of André Laurendeau on the issue of duality in the Canadian federation. The wording of the royal commission's terms of reference, as set out in 1963, refers not only to bilingualism and biculturalism but also to the "develop[ment] of the Canadian Confederation on the basis of an equal partnership between the two founding races." The phrasing of this mandate owes much to the political thought of Henri Bourassa, widely acknowledged as the father of the double-compact theory of Confederation. According to Bourassa's conception of Confederation, the deal struck in 1867 was "between two races in Canada, French and English, based on equality and recognizing equal rights and reciprocal duties."[18] Thus, the English and French languages should have special status in the country owing historic compact. The corollary was that the province of Quebec, as the heartland of the French culture, had a special role to play to promote and protect the heritage of French Canadians.[19]

André Laurendeau generally agreed with this conception of Confederation. His introduction to the report of the commission, often referred to as "the blue pages," does refer to the "equal partnership of all who speak either language and participate in either culture, whatever their ethnic origin" and affirms that "an attempt to make every possible provision for cultural equality is primarily an attempt to make every possible provision for linguistic equality."[20] But he also saw Canada as a country in which there were "two principal cultures [whose] influence extends, in greatly varying degrees, to the whole country," and he described these cultures as being "embodied in distinct societies," one of which was the "distinct French-speaking society in Quebec."[21]

Pierre Trudeau, while a strong supporter of official bilingualism, did not agree with this conception of Canada as a bicultural country. Rather than seeing Canada as rooted in an English Canadian collectivity and a French-Canadian collectivity, he preferred to work towards a pan-Canadian identity rooted in the individual rights of its citizens. For him, official bilingualism drew its legitimacy from the demographics of Canada's large English- and French-speaking populations, rather than from abstract conceptions of founding nations.[22] For this reason, he would largely jettison the biculturalism aspects of the commission's work and instead create a policy on multiculturalism. The idea of special status for Quebec was completely anathema to Trudeau, and indeed he would spend much of his career battling those who believed in it.

Prime Minister Trudeau's first policy response was the passage of the Official Languages Act in 1969. The act made English and French the official languages of Canada and provided for bilingual government services at all central agencies and within the federal courts. Bilingual districts were not immediately established, although steps were taken to begin negotiations for creating them. The government also began to establish language training programs for unilingual civil servants. The Official Languages Act did not, however, make any reference to education programs. Nor did it mention a role for the secretary of state in promoting minority-language communities in Canada. Consequently, the subsequent programs introduced by the federal government were not covered by any statutory authority.

The Liberal government did indicate that it favoured the education proposals of the commission. Under the leadership of Trudeau's predecessor, Lester Pearson, the Cabinet decided that the B & B Commission's "recommendations relating to education are matters for the provincial governments, but that the federal government would be prepared to help provinces in an *appropriate* way in the implementation of these proposals, if *desired.*"[23] Steps were also taken to prepare the department of the Secretary of State to take on this responsibility. Succeeding Pearson in 1968, Prime Minister Trudeau appointed his close friend and colleague Gérard Pelletier as secretary of state and transferred the government's Secretariat on Bilingualism to his department. The secretary of state also received responsibility for the Official Languages Act, the commissioner of official languages, and official language programs. Four new branches were established in the department for this purpose.[24]

Establishing a framework for the new official-language education programs required the consent of the provinces and became a major discussion point during the mega-constitutional negotiations that took place from 1968 to 1971. To develop program proposals in between top-level meetings of first ministers, a continuing committee of officials was established to deal with issues of official languages. The federal government accorded top priority to the official-languages dossier and allocated a substantial amount of money to provinces that were willing to conduct studies of the costs of implementing the B & B Commission's proposals, an offer taken up by Ontario, New Brunswick, and Nova Scotia.[25]

Over the summer of 1969, the subcommittee on official languages examined technical proposals for federal assistance and forms of guarantees for language-education programs. Overall, the federal government's proposals were strongly rooted in the personal convictions of Pierre Elliot Trudeau, who had long believed in individual rights and bilingualism.[26] The federal government's proposals reflected Trudeau's personal ideology through their emphasis on individual choice and the addition of a proposal to fund second-language instruction, which was not recommended by the B & B Commission. Although heavily influenced by Trudeau's ideology, the official-languages policy of the federal government received support from a large cross-section of parliamentarians and civil servants. In particular, Secretary of State Gérard Pelletier, his deputy minister Jules Léger, and his assistant deputy minister Maxwell Yalden (who would later become the commissioner of official languages) were all firm supporters of federal government intervention. Trudeau's official languages agenda also received support from a wide swath of Liberal MPs and senators – particularly those from French Canadian, Acadian, and Quebec ridings – from a substantial proportion of the Progressive Conservative caucus led by Robert Stanfield, and from the New Democratic Party.[27] Indeed, the Official Languages Act passed the House of Commons unanimously.

The first public statement from the Trudeau government on the direction it intended to pursue with regard to official languages in education was tabled by Gérard Pelletier in the House of Commons on 6 November 1969. Pelletier announced his government's commitment to provide $50 million for the first year of a new program to promote official languages in education. The exact structure of this program would be determined by discussions among the federal and provincial officials, since the federal government was not certain if a universal application of the commission's recommended 10 percent formula would be an effective use of its funds.[28] Indeed, earlier statements from the federal government indicated that it was more inclined to link its aid to new costs and programs, as opposed to maintaining the status quo.[29]

Pelletier also elevated second-language instruction to a level of importance greater than had been accorded by the commission. The Canadian government took the view that this type of instruction needed increased promotion and was worthy of federal government subsidization. Consequently, Pelletier revealed the government's willingness to financially support second-language instruction. The specifics of this funding were discussed in subsequent meetings of the Ministerial Committee on Official Languages. In April 1970, Ottawa specified that the level of funding would be lower than that being considered for minority-language education, because the extra costs were not as high. The Trudeau government also insisted on the right of parents to choose the language of instruction for their children. In the committee meetings, federal officials also raised the issue of program evaluation, suggesting a joint federal-provincial committee to provide both a qualitative and a quantitative evaluation.[30] The Trudeau government was clearly taking the lead in establishing the main terms of the debate that would shape Canada's language-policy direction for the 1970s. But would the provinces fall in line behind Trudeau's vision? This would be the challenge faced by Pelletier's negotiating team over the course of 1969 and 1970.

QUEBEC

While the B & B Commission had been created largely to respond to changes in Quebec, the new education programs being developed over the course of 1969-70 were not going to have much impact in that province. Quebec already had a complete English-language school system, one that was better funded than its French-language counterpart until the provincial government assumed control over funding in the mid-1960s. The province also had the most advanced programs for second-language instruction.

The development of the OLEP coincided with the Quebec government's attempt to assert its jurisdictional prerogatives, particularly those over education, and its representatives on committees were thus active participants in negotiations. These negotiations also coincided with a major flap over bilingual schools in St-Léonard and attempts by the provincial Ministry of Education to develop a new language policy for education. In the fall of 1969, the Bertrand government introduced Bill 63, which affirmed the right of parents to choose the language of instruction for their children. It also created a requirement that students graduating from English-language high schools in Quebec demonstrate a minimum level of competence in French in order to qualify for their diploma.[31] The government also created the Gendron Commission (Commission of Inquiry on the Position of the French Language Rights in Quebec) to examine the language of work in Quebec.

Given the terms of Bill 63, the government of Quebec had no problem with Ottawa's recommendation that parents should have the right to choose the language of instruction for their children if both majority- and minority-language schools existed in a district. It also indicated a willingness to consider eliminating the traditional link between confessionality and language of education.[32] This, however, was as far as fundamental agreement extended.

Quebec was less sanguine about the prospect of Ottawa having a role in evaluating the success of the OLEP, arguing that a standard evaluation would not be appropriate to the widely varying state of language education in the provinces. However, it was open to the possibility of a third party being involved in evaluation, such as the Council of Ministers of Education, Canada (CMEC) – a body completely controlled by the provinces that would thus strengthen interstate federalism and moderate federal intrusions in education.[33] Quebec also insisted that evaluations be based on provincially furnished statistics, rather than allowing federal officials to compile their own data.

While they did not result in open conflict, there were also some tensions over the objectives of the new program and Ottawa's language policies on the whole. Bertrand's government had become increasingly committed to making French the working language of Quebec and had insisted that the provincial government must be granted the constitutional powers necessary to realize this objective. In discussions of the proposed Official Languages Act, Bertrand stressed that the provinces must be "perfectly free to deal with this language problem in a way which best suits their special circumstances,"[34] but he was generally content with the act as long as it was restricted to federal institutions. Bertrand did not, however, see his policy of promoting the French language in Quebec as conflicting with the federal objective of promoting bilingualism at the national level and in the other provinces.

As André Laurendeau had predicted, Quebec opposed any attempt to link federal funds to developmental projects. With the most-developed minority- and second-language education systems, Quebec stood to gain the lion's share of a funding scheme based on existing enrolments. Officials argued that it was unfair to penalise the province that had done the most for its minority, simply because it had acted first.[35] Moreover, there were indications that Quebec considered the funds to be a repayment for past and ongoing expenditures. Quebec's representatives inserted provisions in the OLEP agreement that defined French as the minority language for the nine predominantly English-speaking provinces and English as the minority language for Quebec. Consequently, FSL programs in Quebec's English-language schools, which had to be expanded in light of Bill 63, would not be explicitly eligible for federal funding. The provincial government made this explicit in the footnote to the preamble of regulation 6 of the Department of Education, which outlined the new French-language requirement:

This regulation has no connection with the federal provincial programme of cooperation in matters of bilingualism in the field of education. Amounts recovered by the government of Quebec by virtue of the agreement between the government and the federal government are so recovered, in fact, for instruction to be given in the English language and for teaching of the English language as a second language, English being in Quebec the language of the official minority, as French is the language of the official minority in the other provinces.[36]

Indeed second-language courses, both FSL for anglophones and ESL for francophones, were probably the only programs needing further development in Quebec. However, the province of Quebec did not intend to channel the additional federal funds to its minority-language education system, despite the influx of new funds that were being proposed.

While Quebec was rather resistant to Ottawa's new programs, or at least to being obliged to develop new programs in exchange for the federal dollars, the English-language-majority provinces were divided on the proposals. New Brunswick, Ontario, and Manitoba were perhaps the most favourable to the new initiatives, while Alberta and Nova Scotia, with much smaller minority-language populations, were decidedly less enthusiastic. The size of the minority-language populations, while clearly a factor in this division, only partly explains the different positions taken by the provinces; other ideological and financial concerns played roles as well.

NEW BRUNSWICK

New Brunswick, with a francophone minority accounting for a third of its population, was the most enthusiastic supporter of the B & B Commission's recommendations. Liberal premier Louis Robichaud affirmed that his province gave provincial expression to a national English-French partnership and moved quickly to give statutory weight to its bilingual status. The New Brunswick Official Languages Act was adopted in the spring of 1969, before the federal government enacted comparable legislation.

New Brunswick was also one of the most ardent supporters of allowing the federal government to play a role in promoting official languages. Robichaud's Equal Opportunities Program was proving to be very costly, and his province had to pump a great deal of money into improving the long-neglected Acadian schools: money that was in short supply in the economically depressed Maritimes. Robichaud couched his support for federal involvement by stressing the national dimensions of bilingualism, stating that the object of the official-languages agenda should be to make English- and French-speaking Canadians feel at home from coast to coast.[37]

While national programs were one option that New Brunswick would support, it was not wedded to this approach. Early in 1968, appealing to Prime Minister Pearson's desire for national unity, Robichaud's government had approached the federal government for financial assistance with the significant start-up costs associated with its educational programs. When Prime Minister Trudeau came to power in that year, he clearly saw New Brunswick as a very useful piece in the federal-provincial game of chess. He resisted an early commitment to grant Robichaud's request, replying in November that it would be better for the province to pursue these issues through the forum of the Constitutional Conference.[38] Following this advice, Robichaud lobbied hard for a federally funded program to promote bilingualism and biculturalism.[39] Throughout the 1970s and 1980s, New Brunswick would prove to be Ottawa's staunchest ally in promoting its language policies and defending the federal role in this sector.

During the negotiations themselves, Max Cohen, a McGill University law professor and New Brunswick's head representative at the Constitutional Conference, determined that New Brunswick's best approach to getting the funding it needed would be to stress the federal government's right to use the spending power, which would allow Ottawa to provide funding to the provincial educational systems. Cohen also argued that New Brunswick should stress that the language issue was one of national concern that transcended the boundaries of individual provinces.[40] His argument gave credence to the Canadian government's intrastate approach to federalism, granting legitimacy to its role as the government that could address issues that crossed provincial borders and were directly related to national unity.

New Brunswick not only supported the language education programs in theory and the federal government's sought-after role, but it also generally supported the form that Ottawa wanted its financial contribution to take. While its representatives wanted to have a certain amount of money available for ongoing language programs, they also argued that a distinction should be made between operational and institutional costs, to allow for more rapid development of its programs.[41]

New Brunswick did have an interest in expanding its second-language programs, but its top priority was to develop its French-language minority-language schools. This task was estimated to cost millions of dollars per year just to bring them up to parity with the English-language schools. Both Premier Robichaud and his successor Richard Hatfield were faced with a vigorous lobby from the Acadian communities, who had been campaigning throughout the 1960s for increased and equitable financing for the Acadian schools. The province was thus dismayed by proposals emerging from other provinces, particularly Ontario, that emphasized funding second-language instruction to the detriment of minority-language education. Such proposals would benefit provinces with small minority-language populations the most. Moreover, it appeared that English second-language programs in New Brunswick's Acadian schools would not be covered by the federal formula payments, since only one language group would be eligible for second-language instruction payments in each province.[42]

Finally, New Brunswick was an important ally for Ottawa because of its support for entrenching language-schooling rights in the constitution as part of a bill of rights. Given its strong support for Ottawa's position, education officials hoped that one way or another, the Canadian government would channel money to the province so that it could proceed with its official-languages agenda. Due to its financial straits and the extent of its development plans, New Brunswick desperately needed this type of financial assistance, particularly if it was to defuse the criticisms originating with the Loyalist Associations and the Orange Order, which were hostile to the entire bilingualism agenda.[43]

ONTARIO

Ontario Premier John Robarts, sponsor of the Confederation of Tomorrow conference, was deeply involved in the language debates of the late 1960s. Rejecting Quebec's pretensions to speak for all French Canadians, he believed that he had an obligation to speak and act on behalf of French Canadians in his home province. Moreover, he believed that positive action on the language front would lead to a healthier atmosphere for discussions of Canadian federalism.[44]

Like New Brunswick, Ontario had not waited for Ottawa's funding programs to kick in before taking action. In 1967, Robarts extended government funding to French-language public secondary schools, acceding to the Association canadienne-française d'éducation d'Ontario's (ACFEO) demand of the previous fifty years. He then commissioned a series of provincial task forces on bilingualism, began a French-language training program for the civil service, created new grants for its bilingual universities, and signed agreements with Quebec to foster co-operation in education.

This is not to say that Ontario was uninterested in the federal proposals for financial assistance. The question was how it could accept this funding, given its vocal opposition to new shared-cost programs at the Constitutional Conferences. While Robarts had taken significant steps to advance Franco-Ontarian education, his government was also very interested in developing French second-language instruction for its English-speaking population. Education officials wanted a unified approach to bilingualism that could be defended to the provincial electorate.[45] They were aware that funding for second-language programs was not recommended by the B & B Commission but nevertheless believed that Ontario could make a good case for its inclusion, as long as minority-language education was made the top priority.[46]

To avoid the shared-cost-program approach, Ontario considered asking for an unconditional federal transfer to the provinces to cover the costs of the language programs. However, officials soon realized that it was hard to estimate what these costs would be and thus supported basing the transfers on a proportion of the average cost of education per student. To promote new development of programs, Ontario's representatives wanted Ottawa to provide incentive grants for new initiatives. They even considered asking the federal government to cover the full cost of developing Ontario's French second-language programs but recognized that such a request might stretch Ottawa's magnanimity.[47] Based on this advice, education minister William Davis wrote to Gérard Pelletier asking for a formula payment of 10 percent for both FML and FSL programs, to allow for the development of new programs. Moreover, he asked that this funding be in the form of a fiscal transfer with no federal strings or objectives attached, retroactive to 1968.[48]

The question of the program objectives was a major concern for the province of Ontario, which was under pressure from the Association canadienne-française de l'Ontario (ACFO) and other francophone organizations to restrict access to its French-language schools exclusively to members of the francophone minority. This objective conflicted with the stance of the B & B Commission and the federal government, which were stressing freedom of choice for all parents.

Overall, Ontario was more reserved than New Brunswick about allowing Ottawa a free hand in funding and controlling the language programs it was proposing. Furthermore, Robarts had different priorities from Robichaud, supporting minority-language education but viewing second-language instruction as the key to national unity and bilingualism. The provincial government and the main voicepieces of the Franco-Ontarian community also did not concur with Ottawa's preference for open access to minority-language schooling, which could potentially cause conflict. Yet on the whole, Robarts' government was onside with the priorities of the federal government.

MANITOBA

Manitoba was less active in the realm of official languages than its neighbours to the east, but changes were afoot in this western province in the late 1960s. In the 1969 elections, Duff Roblin's government was ousted from power by Edward Schreyer's New Democratic Party, who merged forces with Larry Desjardins, the Liberal MLA for the heavily francophone riding of Saint-Boniface, to form a majority. The members of Schreyer's government were relatively young and strongly favoured legislation to promote minority rights, including those of the Franco-Manitobans.[49] Shortly after the passage of the Official Languages Act, the Manitoba government moved swiftly to undo the long-standing injunctions against French-language education.

The centrepiece of Schreyer's program was Bill 113, which amended the Manitoba Public Schools Act to allow French as the language of instruction for the entire day for grades 1 to 3 and for all courses except for a mandatory English course for grades 4 to 12. The act also provided for minimum enrolment thresholds above which French-language classes would be guaranteed.[50] Bill 113, developed in consultation with the Franco-Manitoban community (which would also play a role on its implementation advisory committees), passed the Manitoba legislature unanimously on 16 July 1970.

While Bill 113 was a major step forward, it still had some shortcomings. It did not oblige the government to promote enrolment in the French-language schools. While allowing for up to full-day programs, the bill did not set minimum levels of French instruction for these schools, leaving this up local communities to decide by consensus. As future experience with the development of French-language education in Manitoba would show, these were serious omissions. However, the legislation did indicate the Schreyer government's support for the federal direction in official languages, although his government would not play a leading role in the development of the federally sponsored programs.

ALBERTA

The further one travelled east or west from Ottawa, the less support the Trudeau government's official-languages policies received in the provincial capitals. This was certainly the case in Alberta, a province whose opposition to new federal programs made it the unlikely ally of Quebec. Of the six provinces being studied here, Alberta's minority-language and second-language programs were the least developed and subject to the strictest restrictions.

Yet even in Alberta restrictions on French-language instruction were weakening. By the late 1960s, schools could offer half-day programs in French to allow young Albertans to "play a role in their bilingual nation."[51] The province appointed an associate director of curriculum to encourage the development of French programs and steadily extended its French second-language programs down through the elementary grades. However, Alberta's children still had one of the lowest participation rates in FSL programs in the country: only 25.3 percent of elementary school students and only 41.2 percent of high school students.

Despite the changes, the Alberta government was not in favour of several aspects of the federal government's policy on official languages. J.J. Frawley, Alberta's representative on the Subcommittee on Official Languages, indicated Alberta's opposition to making French an official language of the province. Alberta was against the entire concept of bilingual districts and coercive statutes as a means of achieving bilingualism and national unity. Premier Ernest Manning went so far as to question the constitutionality of the federal Official Languages Act,[52] and his successor Harry Strom recommended that the act be referred to the Supreme Court to test its constitutionality.

At the root of Alberta's concerns lay Premier Manning's rejection of the theory that Confederation was rooted in two founding races. He saw Confederation as a union of provinces: a position that ran fundamentally counter to the biculturalism aspect of the B & B Commission's mandate. Moreover, as Premier Strom noted at the Constitutional Conferences, only six percent of Alberta's population was of French origin, and the province was made up of a "mosaic of many ethnic groups, all contributing to the richness of [the] nation. We want to provide opportunity for all groups to develop culturally and economically."[53] This theme of multiculturalism and multilingualism would often be repeated in Alberta's discourse concerning the OLEP over the next two decades.

While Alberta was willing to permit half-day programs in French, its top priority was ensuring that all students graduated with strong English-language skills. Alberta's requirement of a minimum of a half day of English-language instruction was one of the sources of its objections to the proposed federal programs. Ottawa's draft plan suggested that a minimum amount of time spent per day in the various forms of language instruction would be required to qualify for federal dollars, a minimum that was higher than the maximum allowed in Alberta. Department of Education officials argued that provincial preferences concerning school organisation and administration should not interfere with its entitlement to federal support.[54] Indeed, the *Edmonton Journal* intimated that the federal formulas could be perceived as blackmail to alter provincial programs against the provinces' best interests and to incite provinces to spend money in sectors that were not a priority.[55] As in Quebec, protection of provincial jurisdiction against an intrusive federal authority was of paramount importance in Alberta.

Given the position of the provincial government, the Association canadienne-française de l'Alberta (ACFA) had to be careful with how it pursued its lobbying efforts. There were about twenty thousand students in the province who might be eligible for French-language schooling, a relatively small minority. ACFA, aware that even the Franco-Albertan community would want its children to be fluent in English, was thus careful to stress that new French-language programs would provide a means for all Albertan students (not just Franco-Albertans) to become bilingual. To this end, it called for legislation similar to Manitoba's Bill 113, including minimum thresholds for

French programs, transportation programs for students in remote areas, and French-language teacher training at Collège St-Jean. ACFA made a point of reminding the provincial government of the potential federal funding, which would be a means of offsetting the cost of these initiatives.[56] Its strategy also targeted the federal government, which seemed keen to bolster French-language minorities, and it asked Ottawa to provide core funding to its organisation, to replace the funding that had previously come from Quebec. If French-language programs were to take off in Alberta, federal funding and intensive lobbying would be required to bolster ACFA's stance vis-à-vis a very reluctant provincial government.

NOVA SCOTIA

Nova Scotia was not as resistant to French-language education as Alberta. Indeed, education minister Gérard Doucet, of Acadian origin himself, indicated a desire at the Confederation of Tomorrow Conference to create Acadian schools where all subjects could be taught in French.[57] Such an initiative could have proved to be costly; costs were estimated at $1.75 million for the first year of a program to serve the four main Acadian regions, and $770,000 for each subsequent year.[58] Doucet's officials indicated that the province should approach the federal government for financial help with these programs.

The rest of the Nova Scotia government was not as open to Trudeau's plans for official languages. Premier George Smith indicated that Nova Scotia's actions would be limited to the creation of a small translation bureau and rejected the notion of bilingual districts. The province further indicated that it believed that changes in attitudes towards official languages must come from education, not from statutes, echoing Alberta's position.[59] Moreover, the government did not intend to take leadership in this matter and opted to leave decisions concerning the teaching of subjects in the French language to local authorities. Consequently, Nova Scotia was unlikely to build in official recognition for Acadian education or guarantees for this type of instruction, as Manitoba had done.

Premier Smith considered other issues to be of greater importance at the constitutional bargaining table. The province was in financial straits similar to those of New Brunswick. Accordingly, H. Stevens, the head of federal-provincial fiscal relations, wanted the province to push for regional-disparity compensation payments and suggested that Nova Scotia make its participation in the Official Languages in Education Program a bargaining chip to be played in exchange for these payments.[60] Smith followed this advice.

Despite Nova Scotia's reluctance to forge boldly ahead with the development of French-language education programs, officials in the Department of Education worked through the possible implications of the OLEP. Since they believed that the federal government was likely to be more sympathetic to requests for start-up program costs than for long-term administrative costs, their funding proposals were couched in these terms.[61] While Nova Scotia had planned on standing back from official-languages programs and letting local communities take the lead, by the time that final negotiations were taking place in Ottawa, requests for financial assistance to French programs had created such an avalanche that there was heavy pressure on the government to enter into an agreement for federal funding.[62]

Premier Smith's speeches at the Constitutional Conference reflected the financial straits of his province. Like Premier Robichaud, he continually stressed the national dimensions of language issues and the need for a strong central government to fund programs that would address these concerns (his position, not coincidentally, would support a strong central government that could promote equalization to cope with regional diversity). One thus notes a commonality in the positions of the Maritime provinces, who were willing to countenance federal participation in education if it would result both in funds for their education systems and in a stronger Canadian government that could provide them with regional equalization payments.

NEGOTIATING AN AGREEMENT

While the proposals of the Royal Commission on Bilingualism and Biculturalism were the starting point for the Bilingualism in Education agreements, formal discussions among the various governments did not officially begin until the Constitutional Conference of December 1968. At the conference, the first ministers decided to have their officials meet in an ongoing forum in between the top-level conferences. To this end, a subcommittee of officials on official languages was established where many of the technical aspects of the program could be worked out. To handle the more politically sensitive aspects of the program, the Ministerial Committee on Language Rights was formed in February 1969.

Initially, both committees focussed on Ottawa's Official Languages Act, 1969. In May 1969 the subcommittee turned to the recommendations contained in volume 2 of the B & B Commission's report. The committee was instructed to prepare proposals on technical and financial aid from the federal government that could be agreed upon by the provinces. It was also charged with studying existing provincial policies and the cost of implementing the new proposals.

While the committee prepared its reports, the federal government developed its starting position. On 6 November 1969, Secretary of State Gérard Pelletier announced the federal proposals for the Federal-Provincial Programme of Cooperation for the Promotion of Bilingualism in Education, three days in advance of the second meeting of the Ministerial Committee on Official Languages.[63] Pelletier noted that Ottawa would commit itself to $50 million for the first year of a new agreement. He indicated, however, that the Canadian government was not wedded to the 10 percent formula proposed by the commission and that it was open to considering Ontario and Alberta's proposals for second-language instructional funding.

Over the following months, provincial reactions to Pelletier's proposals began to surface, and counter-proposals were floated. The Canadian, New Brunswick, and Ontario governments all suggested constitutional entrenchment of de facto language rights to accompany the financial aid. This suggestion met with resistance from the other provinces. Quebec demanded that its existing English-language programs be eligible for federal grants as well, so that it would not be financially penalized for having been a leader in official-languages education.[64]

By 1970 a program framework had emerged that diverged somewhat from the recommendations of the royal commission. The 10 percent formula was dropped in favour of a 9 percent formula for minority-language education, coupled with a 1.5 percent formula for the administrative costs of operating minority-language education programs. This change was intended to respond to pressures from the provinces for federal aid to cover costs linked to the development of new programs. Manitoba and Alberta remained concerned that these formulas would be inadequate for the cost of transporting students, which was a key issue in their vast school districts.[65]

The 1970 proposals also included a 5 percent formula to cover second-language instruction, which had not been recommended by the B & B Commission. The proposals also did not refer explicitly to the reports of the B & B Commission. The 5 percent formula responded to the proposals from Ontario and Alberta, although at a lower funding level than they had requested. (It is significant that the subcommittee of officials on official languages had not examined the costs and implications of federal funding to second-language instruction.) The formula was incorporated into the Bilingualism in Education Program as part of a package deal to secure provincial consent.

Pelletier and the federal delegation entered the 25 May 1970 meeting of the Ministerial Committee on Official Languages intending to reach provincial agreement on the objectives of the new program. The secretary of state also hoped to impose a time limit on the program: four to five years for second-language programs and ten to fifteen years for minority-language programs.[66] The federal government recognized that the provinces would not accept an agreement under which Ottawa paid solely for the development of new programs. It was thus willing to pay for ongoing costs but wanted payment to be linked to the concept of "extra costs," although it acknowledged that the definition of "extra" was likely to vary by province.[67] Moreover, by the May meeting, Ottawa was willing to proceed without the consent of all the provinces, although Pelletier hoped that unanimous consent could be reached.

The Trudeau government also hoped to avoid the formalities of a signed agreement, pressing instead for an exchange of letters that would start the program. This format was motivated partly by a desire for flexibility in the implementation of the program. It was also preferred because negotiations were continuing at the Constitutional Conference, where the use of the federal spending power was being discussed, but Trudeau did not want action on the bilingualism and national unity files to be held up until all the constitutional negotiations were completed.[68] Indeed, had this course been followed, there would have been no agreement, since this round of discussions died along with the Victoria Charter of 1971. A more informal financial arrangement, it was thought, would permit concrete action using methods employed in the past for joint federal-provincial programs, without creating a new, formal shared-cost program, a format that several provinces hoped to eliminate through the constitutional negotiations.

Over the summer of 1970, the federal government exchanged letters with the provinces confirming their agreement on the basic principles of the new arrangements for official languages in education. Finally, after twenty months of negotiations, the Federal-Provincial Program of Cooperation for the Promotion of Bilingualism in Education was officially announced on 9 September 1970. The agreement, although its terms had largely been defined by the Canadian government and the B & B Commission, incorporated a number of elements that had been demanded by various provinces and interest groups but left several questions unresolved. Some of them could not be readily resolved outside a formal agreement, and they would cause no end of headaches for officials over the decades that followed.

The only formal documents attesting to the existence of the new administrative program are a series of press releases jointly agreed to by the secretary of state and the premiers. The main press release that spelled out the details of the program, which would cost the federal government over a billion dollars in the 1970s alone, was a mere three pages long.[69]

Under the terms of the agreement reached, Ottawa committed itself to spend $50 million for the first year of a four-year program, during which it intended to spend a total of $300 million. These funds were to pay for the supplementary costs incurred in providing minority-language education and second-language instruction. How these costs were to be calculated was based on the concept of a full-time equivalent (FTE) student. FTE students were defined as students who received 75 percent of their instructional time in the minority language at the elementary level and 60 percent of their instructional time in the minority language at the secondary level. Accordingly, if three students received 50 percent of their instructional time in the minority language at the elementary level, they would be counted as the same as two FTEs. Conversely, three students receiving 100 percent of their instructional time in the minority language at the elementary level would be considered as four FTEs. Consequently, the formulas paid more as instructional time increased.

The Canadian government would pay for a percentage of the average cost of instruction for a full-time student enrolled in official-language programming. Three formulas were established under the program. The first paid 9 percent for FTEs enrolled in minority-language educational programs. On the assumption that costs of providing second-language instruction were "different and proportionately lower" than those for minority-language education, the second-language formula was set at 5 percent. Recognizing that provincial education departments would have increased administrative costs associated with expanding their bureaucracies to deal with minority-language education, the formula provided 1.5 percent of teaching costs based on the total number of children in the minority-language group. The federal funding was retroactive to 1 January 1970.

While the formula payment structure did refer to "supplementary costs," no mechanism was put in place to ensure that Ottawa's dollars would be used for increased development of official-languages programs. A province could theoretically continue to operate its existing programs as it had before 1970 and still receive federal funding. An avenue was, however, opened to additional funding for developmental projects. The press release made reference to "special projects" for which additional federal funding would be made available to enable provinces with less-developed educational systems to catch up to the others. In 1970, the nature of the special projects was not yet agreed upon.

Several provinces and francophone community organisations had made representations concerning the need for student exchanges and teacher training institutions in order to bolster the minority- and second-language education programs, a theme that also appears in the reports of the B & B Commission. A means of addressing these issues had not yet been agreed upon in 1970, although the federal and provincial governments kept the subcommittee of officials active to continue discussions on those matters.

The question of access to minority-language education programs had been a particularly thorny one to resolve. In the text of the agreement, the program's objectives were defined as follows: "to ensure that, insofar as it is feasible, Canadians have the opportunity to educate their children in the official language of their choice and that children have the opportunity to learn, as a second language, the other official language of their country." While Ontario had protested against permitting open access to its French-language education programs, the wording of these objectives implied a right of all Canadians, regardless of mother tongue, to choose the language of instruction for their children. For most provinces, this right implied access to minority-language education schools, since French-immersion programs, which had debuted in a few communities, were still considered to be highly experimental and were not mentioned in federal-provincial discussions.

Two more provisions of the initial agreements deserve special mention. The press release specified that the arrangements were designed to make federal support of these objectives possible without infringing on provincial jurisdiction in the field of education. This was of fundamental importance to appeasing provinces who were jealous of their prerogatives in this sector. While the issue of program evaluation had been raised by several participants in the negotiation process, the only mention of this issue was a brief reference to a reexamination of the formulas after eighteen months. No formal evaluation mechanism was mentioned, nor, indeed, any qualitative evaluation of how well the program was attaining its objectives. Admittedly, in the flush financial era of the late 1960s, program evaluation was not the major concern that it is today. Moreover, financial constraints that would make accountability for expenditures so important had not yet arisen. However, as these constraints closed in during the late 1970s, there would be no evaluation mechanism for the Canadian government to fall back on.[70]

THE PRESS CORPS REACTS

In addition to the official content of the press releases of 9 September 1970, Canadian newspapers provided details about the intentions of the program's framers. The *Globe and Mail* noted that the minority-language education program was intended to continue indefinitely, whereas the second-language programs were to last only for five to ten years. Both the *Globe* and *Le Droit* also stressed that the program was not intended to continue funding the status quo but was meant to fund extra costs and additional development.[71] The *Montreal Star* and *Le Devoir* observed that the program was a compromise between Ottawa's desire to fund minority-language education and a strong push from the Western provinces for second-language instructional funds.[72] Newspapers from the minority-language communities, such as *Le Droit* and *Évangéline*, also noted that the program took so long to establish in part because of difficulties in establishing a formula that would deal equitably with the diversity of minority-language populations in the country.[73] While these observations give us a good sense of the direction that Ottawa intended for the OLEP, these provisions were not written in stone or even in the official text of the jointly written press releases. Some of these "original intentions" would be conveniently forgotten by the participants as time wore on.

How stories about the OLEP were constructed in the various newspapers is also telling about the reception that the program was likely to receive in the provinces. In Alberta, the announcement of the program was buried deep within the *Edmonton Journal* and the *Calgary Herald*.[74] Both papers' headlines stressed that over one-half of the federal grants would go to Quebec: hardly an enthusiastic response. Ontario's emphasis on second-language instruction was mirrored in the focus of the *Toronto Star*'s article on the new program.[75] In Quebec, in contrast, the French-language dailies emphasized the amounts that the province would receive for the English second-language programs in French schools, downplaying the amount that would go to its English-language minority system.[76] Interestingly, the *Fredericton Gleaner*, in bilingual New Brunswick, failed to mention the program at all. In both Winnipeg and Halifax, the major newspapers simply ran a standard Canadian Press story outlining the details of the program. The program received front-cover play in the *Globe and Mail*, the *Winnipeg Free Press*, *Évangéline*, *Le Droit*, *Le Devoir*, and *La Presse*. While this placement can be attributed to some extent to the ideology of the publishing houses involved, the importance of the program for the two major French-language minority community papers, as well as for the French-language Quebec dailies and the national newspaper, is nevertheless significant.

CONCLUSION

The Bilingualism in Education Program (as it was known in 1970) was developed in the midst of a major transition period in Canadian federalism. The era of mega-constitutional discussions of the late 1960s indicated a shift in federal-provincial relations towards executive federalism. While the tenor of these discussions testified to the increasing strength of the provincial governments, the era of cooperative federalism and strong central government had clearly not yet ended. Although the Bilingualism in Education Program did not take the form of a formal, signed, shared-cost agreement, the federal government was still able to use its spending power, even when this power was being challenged by the premiers of Ontario and Quebec. The intrastate vision of federalism also still had a good deal of influence, as many provincial premiers, including Ed Schreyer and Louis Robichaud, defended the Canadian government's use of the spending power on issues critical to national unity.77 Moreover, the provisions of the final agreement were primarily those proposed by federal politicians and bureaucrats, drawing on the recommendations of the B & B Commission, while adding new components that they felt were needed.

Yet there were signs that Canadian federalism was in transition. Although the federal government was using its spending power, it was counterbalanced both by the qualifiers asserting provincial jurisdiction over education and the informal nature of the agreement. While the program's main provisions were based on federal priorities, the provinces had managed to secure a significant amount of funding both for second-official-language instruction and for preexisting programs. Nor was Ottawa able to prescribe an evaluation mechanism in advance. Although the provinces did not negotiate as a united block, the Council of Ministers of Education, Canada (CMEC) had been formed in 1967, and a possible role for this interprovincial council had been floated in discussions concerning evaluation of the program. However, the fact that the CMEC did not play a major role in the negotiations indicates that the provinces' interstate vision of Canadian federalism had not yet been fully developed. Thus, the Bilingualism in Education Program of 1970 is best seen as one that straddled the two conceptions of Canadian federalism. Efforts by advocates of each vision of federalism to pull the program into their sphere of control would come to shape its evolution, as we will see over the next few chapters.

A wide range of opinions and positions went into the formation of the first Bilingualism in Education Program. It aimed to address the official-language concerns of a wide variety of communities. Not all governments or communities were satisfied with the provisions of the initial agreement, and many would work to modify its structure. Nor was it entirely clear whether the formulas would be effective at meeting their objectives or whether the provinces would all "buy in" to the program. As we shall see, although it was a single agreement that bound the provinces together into the program, it had to be implemented in diverse contexts and serve many different objectives. Once it came into effect, provincial interest groups and minority-language communities would begin their efforts to mould the program to serve their interests. To see how this occurred, we must now turn to the manner in which the program evolved from these beginnings.

CHAPTER THREE

Growing Pains and Intergovernmental Squabbles, 1970–1976

In 1970, after two long years of wheeling and dealing, the Bilingualism in Education Program (BEP) was born. As we saw in chapter 2, Ottawa had agreed to provide $300 million to the provinces over the next four years in support of their minority-language education and second-language instruction programs. The program rested on a rather shaky base of guesswork and assumptions, and several aspects, ranging from evaluation to implementation, had been left deliberately vague to appease all the parties concerned. The early years were thus crucial ones for determining the future contours of the infant program. This chapter provides, first, a broad overview of the BEP in terms of federal-provincial relations and the launching of new annex programs and language-policy initiatives. The bulk of the analysis will be devoted to how the BEP was implemented at the level of individual provinces, how interest groups in the provinces responded to this new initiative, and the extent to which governments and bureaucrats fostered the development of new educational programs. As we shall see, the provinces responded very differently to the BEP right from the outset, and their reactions would have a significant impact on the success of Ottawa's language-policy agenda. The story picks up in the fall of 1970, when the first agreements were reached, and carries on through the program's first renewal in 1974. It concludes with the election of the Parti Québécois in November 1976, an event that shook the firmament of Canadian political life and bore directly on language debates in the country.

FLESHING OUT FEDERAL LANGUAGE POLICIES

After the successful negotiations that formed the Bilingualism in Education Program, the Canadian government turned its attentions to other aspects of the B & B Commission's reports. In 1971 the secretary of state launched the Official Language Minority Groups (OLMG) program to fund minority-language community and pressure groups in the various provinces, filling the gap left by the Catholic Church and the Quebec government's virtual abandonment of this role. The OLMG program was key to Ottawa's efforts to shape the embedded state, since the organisations it funded would actively support its bilingualism agenda, including the BEP.[1] Moreover, the Canadian government was again asserting a new role as defender of group interests that were being overlooked by the provinces and thus bolstering its defence of intrastate federalism.

While the Trudeau government actively supported the bilingualism aspect of the B & B Commission's work, it rejected its second tenet: biculturalism. Instead, over the course of 1970 and 1971, the federal government created the Multiculturalism Directorate to foster the concept of a multicultural Canada with two official languages, a Canada in which the citizenry, rather than the state, would determine the nation's culture. The shift from biculturalism to multiculturalism was welcomed in many of Canada's "ethnic communities," who resented the marginalization of their cultures implied by biculturalism. Western provincial governments were also favourably inclined to this direction, as it more accurately captured their demographic realities.

Multiculturalism was less enthusiastically received (to put it mildly) in French-speaking Canada, especially in francophone Quebec. French Canadians believed that it would threaten their quest for language rights, because it undermined the concept of a pan-Canadian cultural and linguistic duality.[2] Despite these fears, Ottawa's main priority lay with bilingualism, not multiculturalism, and it would back this priority up with substantially more financial resources over the following decades.

Together with the provinces, the Canadian government also expanded the BEP to respond to other recommendations of the B & B Commission. The Subcommittee on Official Languages held additional meetings in 1971 to flesh out supplementary initiatives, which were launched on 20 January 1972. The 1972 arrangements were subsequently referred to as the annex programs.

Annexes A and B were targeted at postsecondary education. Annex A provided between $7 and $8 million per year to universities offering minority-language education programs, particularly to those with teacher training facilities. Annex B provided minority-language students with travel bursaries to allow them to study in their own language at postsecondary institutions elsewhere in Canada. Annex C provided grants of one hundred thousand dollars per province for the construction or improvement of language training centres. Annexes D and E were intended for second-language learning, respectively providing five thousand bursaries per year for short-term training programs for second-language teachers and three hundred fellowships for students specializing in their second official language to undergo special immersion sessions.[3]

Annex F dealt with the "catch-up" programs concept by creating the special projects grants, which were intended for short-term programs (one to three years) targeted at very specific objectives related to the development of bilingualism in education. Provinces could propose programs that, if accepted by the federal government, would be paid for on a shared-cost basis: 50 percent by the federal government and 50 percent by the province. They would then be subject to formal evaluations. Special projects could range in scope from French-immersion pilot programs to library acquisitions to curriculum-development projects. Most of the annex programs, with the exception of the special projects, would not be contentious over subsequent years, but they nevertheless played important roles in fostering the expansion of minority- and second-language instruction in Canada.

The Canadian government also created two programs related to official languages in education outside the BEP umbrella. The Summer Language Bursary Program was launched in 1971 to provide grants to postsecondary students who wanted to undergo a short-term intensive training program in their second-language during the summer months. In 1973 this was followed up with the Official Language Monitors Program, under which students from either official language would work together with a teacher in a school where their language was the minority-language. These programs were funded completely by the federal government and administered by the Council of Ministers of Education, Canada (CMEC).[4]

The BEP was evaluated by the provinces after eighteen months, and the results released in 1973. Table 3.1 indicates the aggregate data collected on the development of minority- and second-language instruction from 1970 to 1972/3, using 1970 as the baseline (100) to calculate the level of student participation in the programs. The data suggest mixed results. All programs in the Prairie provinces experienced growth over the period, particularly minority-language education programs. Enrolment in minority-language programs also increased at the secondary level across the country, although elementary-level development was uneven. Second-language instruction was also beginning to grow at the elementary-level in Ontario and the West, reflecting the

Table 3.1
Student Participation in Minority-Language Education and Second-Language Instruction, 1970–1973 (1970=100)

	Atlantic	Quebec	Ontario	Prairies
Elementary MLE	95.41	105.32	97.05	132.90
Secondary MLE	104.69	124.46	105.15	115.60
Elementary SLI	93.85	95.16	107.53	105.30
Secondary SLI	93.85	108.46	96.74	102.14

Source: PAA, 88.88, Advanced Education – Program Support Branch, box 5, file: Regina Conference April 1973, Federal-provincial programme of cooperation for bilingualism in education at the pre-university levels. A working summary of the provincial reports, 1973. A summary report was prepared with student participation calculated by region. Breakdowns by individual province in the Atlantic and Prairie regions were not given.

priorities of the governments there. On the whole, however, secondary-level participation in second-language instruction was falling off. Part of this decline could be attributed to the change in university requirements, but other factors were also playing a role, including a continuing shortage of second-language teachers and a wider range of options from which students could choose.

Some qualitative observations were also made in the provincial reports. Minority-language education programs were discovered to cost more than the formulas provided for, largely because of the geographic distribution of the minority-language communities, which led to high transportation costs and schools with below-average enrolment.[5] With regard to the second-language instruction sector, the twenty-minute-per-day core French programs in existence in most provinces were found to be not very effective, if not counterproductive. Because a new approach to core French was needed, the provinces set up a joint task force under the CMEC to share their learnings about second-language teaching and to develop more effective French-language textbooks.[6] Finally, immersion programs were attracting increased interest from English-speaking parents, and provinces were beginning to introduce FSL programs at an earlier stage of the child's education.

Demographic shifts were beginning to act as a major constraint on all the provinces. School enrolments had begun to drop off, making it more difficult for the provinces to afford new programs. Consequently, the special projects, which offered 50 percent federal funding for small initiatives, looked increasingly attractive to the provinces with less-developed programs, who began to take a more active interest in this aspect of the program.

The federal government was also actively monitoring the manner in which the BEP was unfolding. Concerns had been raised by organisations such as the Société nationale des Acadiens (SNA) and the Fédération canadienne-française de l'Ouest (FCFO) over how the grants were being used by the provinces. In the Western provinces, there were concerns that too much of the money was going to English-speaking students and that the grants were being used to reduce local tax rates.[7] Accordingly, the federal government began to step up efforts to gain accountability for the use of BEP funds and made public its concerns over the possibility that these funds were being diverted to other purposes.

Ottawa's take on the early evolution of the BEP was generally positive. Secretary of State Hugh Faulkner stressed how this program was beginning to open lines of communication between English and French Canada: "malgré le chemin qu'il nous reste à parcourir, il y avait au moins lieu de se réjouir du fait que les communications avaient été rétablies, et de ressentir à juste titre une certaine fierté devant le progrès déjà accompli."[8] The federal government nevertheless understood that it needed to clarify the program's objectives to the public. Canadians had to be made aware that basic FSL programs would not produce fully bilingual children in the span of five to ten years but that they could provide the foundation for those who chose to become bilingual. Federal bureaucrats also wanted to increase the visibility of Ottawa's role in the program.

This positive attitude towards the progress accomplished to date was a strong factor in the Cabinet's decision to renew the BEP for another five years. Cabinet did, however, stress that more accountability and more evaluation were needed.[9] This decision was strongly supported by MPs and senators representing French Canadian, Acadian, and Quebec ridings, including Jean-Robert Gauthier and Roméo Leblanc, who pressed the government to maintain its involvement in the defence of minority-language education.[10] Moreover, the BEP's school-based programs were perceived to be a better long-term approach to bilingualism in the country than the eleventh-hour approach with middle-aged civil servants that was also being attempted.[11]

With the approval of the federal Cabinet, officials from the Secretary of State department met with their provincial counterparts in Halifax to determine the parameters of a renewed agreement. The program had changed somewhat since its inception in 1970, most notably with the addition of the annex programs and the participation of the territorial governments. But in large measure the BEP renewal process maintained the status quo.

On 1 April 1974 the BEP began its second five-year run. The formula payments were largely left untouched, as were the annex programs.

There were some minor modifications: provinces were allowed greater flexibility in their use of annex program funding, and the 9 percent formula was expanded to cover some French-immersion programs. The Canadian government (and the provincial bureaucrats) assumed that the annual average of $70 million in expenditures would continue to hold. While there had been some rumblings in Ottawa about the need for stricter evaluation and accountability provisions, no such provisions were included in the renewal.

A significant change did occur in the program's objectives, which now read as follows: "To ensure that, insofar as it is feasible, Canadians of either official language have the opportunity to educate their children in their own language, and that Canadian students have the opportunity to learn, as a second-language, the other official language of Canada."[12] The original objectives of the first BEP agreement had been described with slightly different terminology: "To ensure that, insofar as it is feasible, Canadians have the opportunity to educate their children in the official language of their choice and that children have the opportunity to learn, as a second-language, the other official language of their country." While at first glance these objectives seem to be fundamentally similar, if worded slightly differently, the reality was quite otherwise. Although federal officials would later claim that the change in wording was simply for the sake of clarity, the program's target groups had in fact been modified. The replacement of "Canadians" with "Canadians of either official language," and "official language of their choice" with "their own language," restricted access to the benefits of the program quite markedly. Canadians whose mother tongue was other than English or French were no longer covered by the program objectives. Thus, a provincial decision to deny them access to minority-language schools would not contravene the new BEP objectives. Similar restrictions could also be applied to members of the majority-language community, such as English-speaking Ontarians or French-speaking Quebecers, who wished to send their children to the minority-language schools of their province.

While newspapers did report on the renewal of the BEP and even included the text of the new objectives, no comment was made about the change in the wording of the program objectives. For the most part, officials tried to dismiss this change as one made for the sake of clarity. There were, however, pressures lying behind the change. Jane Dobell, the director-general of the Language Programs Branch of the Secretary of State from 1975 to 1977, noted that there had been complaints from French-speaking parents who believed that their children's progress in French was hampered by the presence of English-speaking students in the classroom.[13] As we shall see in our discussion of Quebec during this period, the Bourassa government was also crafting legislation to restrict access to its English-language schools and would thus have favoured the rewording of the objectives.

The 1974 renewal was generally heralded by parliamentarians, and press coverage included quotes from Conservative and NDP members of Parliament who hailed the program as promoting a bilingual Canada and as being a more effective means of reaching bilingualism than language training for MPs and civil servants. This consensus was crucial, since the 1974 renewal occurred during the brief Liberal minority government. The one criticism levied at the program came from Créditiste MP René Matte, who decried the fact that anglophone Quebecers were eligible for the grants under the program. For Matte, this was a waste of funds, since this community was already well established and funded and was not fighting a battle for survival as the francophone minorities were.[14] Matte must have been oblivious to how the BEP funds were used in his home province. As we now turn to a discussion of how the provinces implemented the BEP, we shall see that Quebec was quite distinct in how it used the federal grants: not to develop new initiatives but to pad the provincial treasury.

ALBERTA

At the outset of the first Bilingualism in Education agreement, Alberta's language programs were among the least developed in the country. Ernest Manning's Social Credit government had demonstrated serious hostility to the Official Languages Act, 1969, and had questioned its legality. However, Alberta had taken some tentative steps to soften its approach to French-language education, including the acceptance of half-day French programs. It was not, however, about to make a 180-degree shift, even with the advent of federal funding.

Alberta's approach to the BEP was outlined in the brochure "Federal Assistance to French Education in Alberta," which laid out the laissez-faire path the government intended to follow.[15] It stated that Alberta was fulfilling its obligation to the minority-language objective of the BEP by permitting the 50/50 programs and to the second-language objective through any board that chose to offer FSL programs. Federal dollars from the 9 percent and 5 percent formulas would be passed directly along to the school boards, while the Department of Education retained the 1.5 percent formula payment to administer the programs. School boards were given the autonomy to decide both how they wanted to spend the additional federal dollars and whether they wanted to introduce new programs. This hands-off strategy was characteristic of Alberta's global approach to education, which raised a substantial portion (over 40 percent) of school board funds through local taxation and allowed local boards a great deal of autonomy.[16]

While many school boards in Alberta were slow to take advantage of the federal funds, others were less reticent. Responding to the wishes of parent groups, school boards in districts such as St Paul, Bonnyville, Edmonton, and Falher began offering French-language instruction and French second-language programs shortly after Alberta relaxed its restrictions on French programming in 1968.[17] The federal grants provided an immediate influx of funding to enable the survival of these schools, which had been in doubt given the declining private-funding base of the 1960s. The Edmonton Catholic School Board was among the first of the traditional boards to begin to develop bilingual schools, which offered increased French-language instruction, some up to the 50 percent maximum permitted under the Public Schools Act.[18]

French minority-language schools in Alberta did not develop rapidly, however. Because many Franco-Albertan parents who had experienced the repressive policies of the past were concerned primarily with the preservation of their children's English skills, not all schools took full advantage of the 50 percent maximum.[19] The Alberta programs also made no distinction between children with French as their mother tongue and those with English as their mother tongue. While some districts were almost homogenous in this respect, official government policy was not to distinguish between the two. Thus, both groups had full access to the minority-language programs – a useful tactic, given Alberta's high rates of assimilation of the French mother-tongue population. However, this made it difficult to determine what proportion of the federal grants was going to minority-language education for Franco-Albertans and what proportion to French immersion for English-speaking Albertans. Teachers also had to cope with a student body with a diverse range of language backgrounds.

French second-language instruction also began to develop in Alberta in the early 1970s, when new programs were adopted in communities such as Red Deer and Lethbridge. Second-language instruction was still not viewed as particularly important for Albertans, and it attracted only a minority of students, although enrolments did increase from 25.3 percent to 36.5 percent of elementary students and from 32.1 percent to 39.2 percent of secondary students from 1970 to 1971, a significant jump for one year.

The Bilingualism in Education Program was a major support in the Franco-Albertan quest for improved education services. In 1972, the Association canadienne-française de l'Alberta (ACFA) called for the elimination of the 50 percent restriction on minority-language education and began to call for a more francophone atmosphere in the bilingual schools.[20] Franco-Albertan educational leaders, such as Joseph Moreau, the president of l'Académie Assomption's advisory board and a member of ACFA's Edmonton branch, also stressed the positive aspects of the BEP for all Alberta students, particularly the benefits of second-language skills for jobs. This strategy aimed at reducing the perception that the BEP was solely about the language rights of francophones and emphasized, rather, that it benefited broader segments of Alberta's student population.[21]

The other major development in language education in Alberta in this period was the report of the Worth Commission on Educational Planning, which had been established in June 1969 to develop priorities for public education in Alberta for the next decade. The nine-member commission examined all facets of education in the province, including French-language teaching, about which it made some key recommendations. It called for improved French minority-language education, so that Franco-Albertans could have a genuine choice between integration and assimilation. Moreover, it called on the government to give French-language education a higher priority than education in other languages, because even though Alberta had a multicultural population, it was in a bicultural country. True to its provincial realities, the commission also called for expanded programs in languages other than French to respond to the multicultural heritage of the province. Overall, the commission urged the province to stop "playing around with language study and make it possible for children and adults to become truly fluent in the language they wish to learn."[22]

Despite the recommendations of the Worth Commission, Alberta continued its hands-off approach to language education through the mid-1970s, noting in an annual letter to school boards that the Department of Education "is simply acting as an agency for transferring Federal funds to schools in which the French language is taught. Should the Federal Government decide at any time to terminate these funds for the teaching of French, such support will not be replaced by amounts from the Alberta Provincial Treasury."[23] It did, however, take advantage of the new annex programs. A bilingual-education research project was launched at the francophone Collège St-Jean, and French-immersion programs were developed and expanded in Edmonton, Calgary, and Lethbridge. As far as Ottawa was concerned, the provincial government was a model of accountability, providing clear statistics on how it was disbursing its funds.[24]

While there were positive signs for the improving state of bilingual education, Alberta's politicians still adhered to a multilingual model, and a 1976 reexamination report argued that the province should consider other programs that recognized the multilingual and multicultural nature of the province.[25] Given this ideology, ACFA remained cautious in its approach to demanding further change from the government. The Association canadienne d'éducation de langue française (ACELF) noted that in Alberta parents "are showing some weariness. The constant battles have weakened them."[26] ACFA nevertheless continued its campaign for expanded French-language programming, calling on the University of Alberta to purchase Collège St-Jean with the federal funds and make it a public institution. It also recommended that Alberta join with the other Western provinces to create a collaborative Office in French Education. Moreover, ACFA continued to work to gain acceptance for a right to French-language education in the province and for the elimination of the bilingual program's 50 percent ceiling on French-language education.[27]

This last campaign, conducted over the course of 1974 and 1975, was laying the groundwork for the association's fiftieth anniversary conference, scheduled to be held in October 1976. This conference would end up heralding a new era for French-language education in Alberta. Speaking to the conference delegates, Minister of Education Julian Koziak announced that his government was going to overturn the 50 percent cap: the upper limit was raised to 80 percent under regulation 250/76.[28]

This change was a major step towards expanded French-language instruction in Alberta, but Manitoba's experience with Bill 113 (and indeed Alberta's own experience with the acceptance of the 50 percent programs) had proven that the passage of permissive legislation did not necessarily lead to rapid expansion of programs. ACFA moved to adopt a plan of action on education and to hire a coordinator for this initiative. The association resolved to make education its top priority for the next three years and to adopt a persuasive political approach to secure government support for French-language education.[29]

The plan of action had three main objectives. The first was to seek provincial recognition of a legal right to French education, which would require concrete nonconfrontational political action, so as to avoid stirring up the latent hostility to French education in Alberta. The second was aimed at the Franco-Albertan community, which had to be convinced to send their children to the 80 percent programs. The third targeted teacher training, to ensure that there were sufficient numbers of qualified French-speaking teachers and that they had the necessary supports for their task.

Moving into 1977, ACFA was faced with an enormous task. It had been given provincial sanction to pursue 80 percent French programs. However, the Department of Education was unlikely to take a leading role in developing them, given its past performance with French-language instruction. The three-pronged task for the newly hired education coordinator of ACFA was a daunting one indeed. Careful manoeuvring would be needed to realize the plan, and allies would also be required.

MANITOBA

Manitoba's entry into the BEP agreements coincided with the passage of Bill 113, which guaranteed Franco-Manitobans access to minority-language education if a minimum number of students could be gathered to form a class. The influx of BEP funds sparked a flurry of activity in Manitoba, which quickly applied these funds to the new programs permitted under Bill 113. As had been the case in Alberta though, the Manitoba government was not initially proactive in its approach to French-language programming.

To a certain extent, the Schreyer government believed that Bill 113 fulfilled all its obligations to the Franco-Manitoban community.[30] With the legislation passed, the government was content to let the programs evolve as they might, but the Franco-Manitoban community was quick to indicate that this was not sufficient. The Société franco-manitobaine (SFM) published brochures on the details of Bill 113, including information on the federal grants. It also offered to organise meetings and local committees to pressure school boards to implement the provisions of the amended School Act and to fulfil the objectives of the BEP. The SFM called on the Manitoba government to take an active role in preventing the further assimilation of the Franco-Manitobans, to direct federal funds into the *Français* programs, and to establish French-language administrative units within the Department of Education.[31]

The government of Manitoba was not unsympathetic to the concerns of the Franco-Manitobans, once it was made aware of the community's needs. A French section of the Department of Education was established to determine the best method of distributing the federal grants and to develop programs to improve the quality of French teaching in the province.[32] While the federal formulas specified a certain percentage of additional costs for minority-language education and second-language instruction, Manitoba's education officials did not believe that these formulas reflected actual costs. Nor did they think that second-language instruction needed major additional development, aside from in-service teacher training. Conversely, there were major additional costs associated with the French minority-language program, which ranged from starting up classrooms, to hiring thirty new minority-language teachers per year, to transporting students to schools where French classes were offered.[33]

The Manitoba government quickly began to experiment with different ways of allocating its BEP grants to favour the development of the *Français* programs. Initially funds were allocated on a per-student basis, providing $2 per student in FSL programs, and $28 per student in FML programs, but this was quickly shifted to $25 per full-time equivalent (FTE) in FSL programs and $75 per FTE in FML programs. This shift heavily weighted funding towards the minority-language stream, which the province had identified as its top priority.³⁴ Initially, the province did not require rigorous accounting from school boards on how these grants were spent, and there were rumours of misallocation of funds, but the government's clear intention was to use the BEP funds for French minority-language education.³⁵

In May 1972 a committee was struck to investigate the state of French education in the province. The resulting report, the *Rapport Frechette*, called for research into the achievement of students in the French schools and for research to determine how best to establish an administrative structure to implement Bill 113.³⁶ Under an agreement with Quebec's Department of Education, Manitoba seconded Olivier Tremblay to create a plan outlining how to proceed with the development of its French-language programs. Several key problems were already evident in Manitoba, including the fact that 40 percent of French mother-tongue students did not take any French courses. The split between urban and rural access to the French programs offered under Bill 113 was also a major concern.

Olivier Tremblay worked with the planning and research staff of the Department of Education's French section from the fall of 1972 to June 1973 to assess the state of the province's French-language programs and to make recommendations to improve them. The Tremblay report identified eight major issues that were hampering the development of French-language education. The attitude of Franco-Manitoban parents was a key obstacle, since many were reluctant to enrol their children in FML programs. They were concerned about student achievement in these programs, which was perceived to be lower than in the English stream. The small size of schools in the province, particularly in rural areas, was seen as a limiting factor, especially when administrators were trying to organize multiple programs (FML and English) in the same school. Limited enrolments in the minority programs often meant that children did not receive instruction in the language of their choice. French-language students were seen as operating in cultural and intellectual isolation from the French Canadian culture, in part because the teachers in these schools often lacked the training needed to give them an adequate mastery of the French language and knowledge of the French culture. On a practical level, French-language teaching materials were in short supply. Finally, valid statistics on the different varieties of language instruction being offered in the province were hard to obtain.³⁷

Faced with this litany of problems, Tremblay recommended major changes. First and foremost, he asserted that the French section of the Department of Education was too small to deal with the responsibilities assigned to it. He argued that a clear administrative policy to put

Bill 113 into effect was needed. In order to implement this policy, a separate francophone unit should be created under a French-language coordinator with responsibility for the federal programs, policy development, and budget preparation. The budget of this section needed to be heavily weighted towards the *Français* priority, and the funding from the federal government should be only a supplement to a concentrated provincial funding program.

The initial response of the Manitoba government to the Tremblay report was the passage of Bill 71, which allowed students to travel to other school divisions to receive French-language instruction. It also began to study the feasibility of funding transportation for this purpose.[38] Planning for an expanded French-language division was also started. On 11 April 1974, shortly after the BEP was renewed, Tremblay was appointed as head of the French Language Education section of the Department of Education, to head the implementation of his plan. He envisioned a rapid expansion of French-language education and was supported by his deputy minister, Lionel Orlikow. In June of 1974, Orlikow recommended to his minister, Ben Hanuschak, that the Bureau de l'éducation française (BEF) be created in the department.[39] The BEF would be responsible for addressing declining *Français* enrolments and for providing technical and financial support to French-language education programs. It would also conduct research studies to support the expansion of these programs, prepare budgets, and develop and support services related to FML programs. Hanuschak accepted the proposal.

The secondment agreement with Quebec for Olivier Tremblay's services ran only until June 1975, and thus his team had to move quickly to solidify the BEF. To achieve its aims, the BEF needed a supplementary budget from the department, which was granted in August 1974. An action plan was quickly developed to address the fact that 40 percent of Franco-Manitobans were not in any *Français* programs and that 82.9 percent of the students in *Français* programs followed them for less than 50 percent of the day.[40] A solid French-language program for francophone students, at the maximum level of 80 percent, was made the top priority of the BEF.

Drawing on the federal funds, the BEF commissioned studies at the Collège universitaire de St-Boniface (CUSB) on the performance of students in French programs. As had been the case in other provinces, these studies demonstrated that students in full-day French programs did not lag behind their peers in core subjects such as mathematics and English and that they did have superior French-language capacities.[41] It was hoped that these studies could be used to overcome parental fears about student progress in the French programs.

The BEF also began to reconsider Manitoba's use of the federal grants. Under the first agreement, they had been administered in a rather disjointed fashion, and about 35 percent of the program's funds had not been passed along to school districts.[42] Moreover, Ottawa's money had largely been used to fund the status quo, rather than to incite new development. The department thus began to look seriously into how the BEP grants could be used to encourage innovation. A new system was developed by May 1975 under which the base grants (i.e., the $846,000 received annually before this point) would continue to be passed along to boards for the maintenance of existing programs. Any additional funds, which in 1975 amounted to $438,000, would be diverted into developmental grants, which were set up as $10,000 unit grants for schools, to be spent on textbooks, library and reference works, teacher training, and transportation costs. These block grants were only for a one-year period and were to be used only for new expenses; strict accounting of their use was required.[43] Additional tinkering was conducted in 1976. The new grant formula, which, it was also hoped, would spur the development of French immersion, provided $190 per FTE for students in FML and French-immersion programs. Out of a federal grant of $1,565,000, only $300,000 was spent on FSL programs, clearly indicating the emphasis of the bureau on FML programs.[44] Moreover, the BEF entered into a five-year special project agreement with the federal government to develop *Français* education.

The development of the grant formula and funding of research projects that supported French minority-language education fed into the third, and perhaps most dynamic, part of Manitoba's approach to French education. Olivier Tremblay created an *équipe d'interlocuteurs*, a team of five community-development officers under the jurisdiction of the BEF. The team divided the province into five regions, each containing a predominantly Franco-Manitoban school district and a number of other districts. The officers were assigned the task of going into these communities to rally support for French-language education, working with parents to pressure school boards to pass motions in favour of French classes and French schools.[45] They used research studies from the CUSB, in addition to those produced at the Ontario Institute for Studies in Education (OISE) by Professor Stacy Churchill, to convince parents that these programs would not harm their children's education or English-language skills. The grant formulas were used as *la carotte* to convince school boards and sympathetic trustees that there were financial benefits to introducing the programs. This approach was highly unconventional for a government department and not entirely trusted by the civil service, but it was vigorously defended by Orlikow and Tremblay. However, even defenders of this approach generally accepted that this type of activity could not go on indefinitely. Thus, the community development officers also worked to create a parents' group, the Fédération provinciale des comités de parents (FPCP), to continue its work in conjunction with other Franco-Manitoban organisations, such as the SFM.[46]

The early actions of the BEF and its community development team led to significant increases in FML registrations, which were up 14 percent in 1976.[47] However, if long-term progress was to be made, the BEF would need a formal, permanent status in the department. Formalization was supported by a network of Franco-Manitoban superintendents, teachers, and community activists, who together produced "Pour un réseau d'écoles françaises au Manitoba" in November 1975.[48] This coalition wanted the unilingual French schools to continue to develop and the BEF to assume permanent status in the Department of Education. Under pressure from the coalition and guided by the work of Tremblay, the provincial Cabinet granted the bureau a formal Cabinet mandate in June 1976. Tremblay, whose term had been extended for a year by the Quebec Department of Education, was replaced by the first assistant deputy minister of the BEF, Raymond Hébert. Over the remaining months of 1976 and into early 1977, Hébert worked to normalize the operations of his section, transforming contract positions and secondments into full-time positions and streamlining the functioning of the BEF.[49] Part of this normalization entailed phasing out the community development program, but by this point the FPCP had been established to continue this important work.

By the end of 1976, the Bureau de l'éducation française had taken over all responsibility for Manitoba's participation in the Bilingualism in Education Program. The previous three years had borne witness to a remarkable development in Manitoba's commitment to French-language education programs. The grant formulas used in the province were held up as a model by federal civil servants. Overall, the community development model used by the BEF had proven to be quite effective. Despite its successes (or perhaps because of them), the BEF under Olivier Tremblay had ruffled a number of feathers with its unconventional approach and was not well liked by the Conservative opposition in the province. However, by the end of 1976, Tremblay and Hébert had pushed through several important changes to the administration of Franco-Manitoban education and had secured permanent status for the BEF.

ONTARIO

The government of Ontario had been one of the most active participants in the negotiations of the BEP, and it is thus not surprising that the province was quick to develop its own approach to using these funds and to target them to specific priorities. In 1971, William Davis, who had been the education minister during the negotiations, took over as premier. Davis continued John Robarts' French-language services policies and was committed to continuing the expansion of French-language government services in areas where this was feasible. Davis' policy fell short of complete guarantees, but it was a practical approach nevertheless.[50]

A fair amount of progress took place in Ontario in the first years following the passage of Bills 140 and 141, which amended the Education Act to provide government funding for French-language public high schools. By 1972, 28,000 Franco-Ontarian students were enrolled in publicly funded French-language high schools, a threefold increase over a period of three years.[51] Of these students, 17,600 were in French-only schools, twenty of which were operating across the province. The remaining Franco-Ontarian students were enrolled in so-called bilingual schools, which either offered a portion of the school day in each official language or operated both an English-language and a French-language program in the same facility. Franco-Ontarian community leaders, particularly those of the Association canadienne-française de l'Ontario (ACFO), were quite critical of the bilingual schools, where the school administration and general atmosphere tended to be English.[52] This was a major concern for ACFO, which was fighting for separate schools (in the physical, not confessional, sense) for Franco-Ontarian students.

The Davis government took ACFO's concerns seriously and appointed the Ministerial Commission on French-language Secondary Education, headed by T.H.B. Symons, to investigate the issue of bilingual schools. The commission held its hearings in the midst of a crisis in the Northern Ontario community of Sturgeon Falls, where the school board refused to open a separate French-language high school, even though 87 percent of the community was French-speaking.[53] While the local community was predominantly Franco-Ontarian, the school board was centred in North Bay, and most of the school commissioners were anglophones.

Submitting its report in February 1972, the commission came down on the side of the Franco-Ontarian leaders, arguing that the "mixed or so-called bilingual school is a one-way street to assimilation for the French-speaking student," and recommended that the bilingual schools be phased out. It further recommended that a francophone assistant deputy minister be appointed to chair a permanent committee on French-language schools.[54] The Department of Education complied with this latter recommendation, creating the Council on French Language

Schools, under the chairmanship of Dr Laurier Carrière. The commission's recommendation to phase out bilingual schools was not adopted immediately as departmental policy, but it was dealt with on a case-by-case basis. Failure to adopt this policy would plunge the province into a long series of battles with the Franco-Ontarian leadership over separate facilities for French minority-language education.

Although Ontario kept its commitment to expand French minority-language education, its top priority was the expansion of French second-language programs, which directly benefited a broader portion of the electorate. Since the elimination of the university requirement for FSL, enrolment in secondary FSL programs had fallen sharply, dropping from 45 percent to 37 percent of all high school students between 1970 and 1972.[55] The provincial government wanted to increase participation and use the federal funding to offer a wider range of FSL programs, but it could not do so easily, since the province had imposed spending caps on educational programs in the early 1970s and BEP formula grants flowing through to the school boards were in many cases insufficient to begin new programs. Nevertheless, there was some expansion of FSL programs, facilitated by the granting formula developed by the province in 1972.

The 1972 formulas were neither internally consistent in their application nor consistent with the federal formulas. *Le Droit*, the major French-language newspaper in the province, conducted a study of the use of federal funds by the Carleton Catholic School Board in 1973. It found that the board received only a 5 percent formula payment for its minority-language students, rather than the 9 percent the province received from Ottawa. This translated into a $164,000 shortfall for the board, which would translate into a $4 million shortfall if repeated across the province.[56] Probing a little deeper, the Franco-Ontarian associations determined that of the $47.5 million received by the province by 1973, $36.4 million was earmarked under the federal formulas for French minority-language education, and yet only $17 million was sent to the school boards for this purpose. A further study conducted in Carleton in 1974 determined that the board was receiving a standard grant for all its students, on a per-student basis, for French-language education, rather than being pro-rated on a 15:1 basis for the FSL programs.[57] This outraged ACFO and the other Franco-Ontarian education associations, who demanded an explanation from the provincial government.

To the credit of the Ontario government, it did not try to dissemble on this issue. Minister of Education Thomas Wells admitted that the province was not strictly abiding by the federal formulas. He explained that the major additional costs for the province under the BEP stemmed from itinerant teachers who taught FSL courses at the elementary level and thus that the province was using its funds to cover these costs. Wells viewed the federal grants as broadly intended to encourage all forms French-language education and pointed out that all the funding was being used for this purpose.[58] Indeed, the total additional cost of Ontario's FSL and FML programs in 1972 was $17 million dollars, while the province received only $15 million from the federal government.

The other major recommendation from the Symons Commission was for an investigation of ways to meet the English-speaking population's desire for bilingual education. Indeed, one of the main reasons why the mixed schools had been maintained, aside from costs, was that English-speaking parents saw them as providing a good method of teaching their children French. Ontario was thus fertile ground for the French-immersion programs that had been pioneered in Quebec's Protestant school boards, and fifteen school boards had introduced these programs by 1972. They were often quite small and rudimentary, and some boards, particularly the Ottawa Public School Board, wanted to develop more comprehensive ones. It would take a substantial investment to accomplish this, far above the current granting levels.

The federal government took a keen interest in Ottawa's French-immersion programs as a test drive for the special projects it was launching under the BEP. While the province was reluctant to give additional funding to only one board, it was persuaded to participate in a pilot project for the school boards of the National Capital Region. In the end, all the boards in the region, public and separate, on both sides of the Quebec-Ontario border, participated in a special immersion project, which would result in a lasting French-immersion system in the Ottawa region. Significantly, the province was also able to secure agreement from the federal government to treat its French-immersion programs as equivalent to the French minority-language programs for formula purposes, which thus became eligible for the 9 percent grant.[59]

By the mid-1970s, the Franco-Ontarian lobby to change Ontario's use of federal grants began to achieve results. While the provincial government did secure Ottawa's agreement on the principle that the distribution of federal grants between the two main priorities was a matter for provincial decision, which technically permitted the province to use the various formula grants as it saw fit, it recognized that the Franco-Ontarians had a legitimate case.[60] Thus, in 1975 the province established a new grant formula for distribution of BEP funds to the school boards that significantly increased funding to minority-language schools and gave incentives to school boards that set up new French-language classes.[61] This grant structure reflected the province's emphasis on French minority-language education at the secondary level and French second-language courses at the elementary level. It was also designed to devote an increasing proportion of the federal grants to the FML stream, although additional expenditures from the province's own coffers were allocated almost entirely to FSL projects.

Overall, the Bilingualism in Education Program was not the main concern of either the provincial government or the Franco-Ontarian associations in the early 1970s. The battle over separate facilities for French-language secondary schools was continuing to rage across the province. While the Sturgeon Falls crisis was resolved in 1972, a new debate, over the establishment of a separate French high school, arose in Essex County in 1974. The debate, which was particularly vicious, attracted most of the public attention given to French-language education. Essex County Franco-Ontarians would eventually succeed in their quest for their own school when the province agreed to pay for construction costs. Nevertheless, the issue was highly contentious and overshadowed issues of federal-provincial relations on Bilingualism in Education.

NEW BRUNSWICK

A change of government did not alter New Brunswick's steady march towards official bilingualism. Richard Hatfield's Progressive Conservatives, who replaced Louis Robichaud's Liberals in 1970, were strongly committed to the idea of a fully bilingual province and a full range of services in French for the Acadian population. New Brunswick would lead the other provinces in its commitment to the official-languages policy emanating from Ottawa and would remain a key ally for the federal government, particularly when other provinces were more obstructionist.

By 1970, New Brunswick was still in the process of implementing the Equal Opportunities Program, which entailed a major revamping of the province's administration and funding of its school boards, the primary focus of which was bringing the French-language school boards up to parity with the English-language boards. Funding for the school boards had recently been transferred from local property taxes to a provincial taxation formula. Since the province was paying the full cost of the public school boards, English and French, the federal formula payments were deposited into the consolidated funds of the province, from which all departments, including education, received their funding. Accordingly, while the province was spending money to improve the Acadian school boards and schools, the BEP grants were not earmarked in such a way as to be seen to be flowing directly to the boards.

This lack of clear visibility in the transfer of federal funds to the school boards created problems similar to those experienced in Ontario. Even before ACFO and *Le Droit* were investigating the use of federal funds in Ontario, the Société nationale des Acadiens (SNA) and the French-language newspaper *Évangéline* were conducting inquiries into New Brunswick's use of the federal BEP grants.[62] The inquiries began in March 1971, and Acadian leaders and journalists continued to badger the government on this issue over subsequent years. The SNA went so far as to lodge an official complaint with the commissioner of official languages over the use of the federal grants.[63] The commissioner was unable to intervene, however, since education was a provincial matter not under the commissioner's jurisdiction, but this episode nevertheless indicates the levels to which the SNA would go to fight for Acadian education rights.

The SNA's ultimate objective was to have the province transfer the federal grants directly to school boards, which would then decide how to allocate the funds, an objective supported by a number of the English-language boards. But provincial authorities considered it best to use a system-wide approach to bilingualism, (rather than a piecemeal approach through individual boards), which paralleled Ottawa's national approach to official languages.[64] While the government did not cave in to the SNA's demands, its lobbying efforts and those of its successor organisation, the Société des Acadiens du Nouveau-Brunswick (SANB), did convince the province to better demonstrate its use of the BEP funds. Soon after, the government began providing figures about its spending on minority- and second-language education in the province. Over time, the provincial government would also develop better accountability procedures to satisfy both the Acadian organisations and the federal government.

While the federal programs did attract the attention of the SNA and the SANB, the Acadian groups were not only concerned with the administration of federal funds; they were seeking far more radical change in the Department of Education. In 1971, the SNA called for the department to be reorganised into two sections divided on a linguistic basis, each with a deputy minister, to improve the representation of Acadians in the department.[65] By 1973 the New Brunswick government began to respond to these demands, appointing the McLeod-Pinet Commission to propose methods of reorganizing the Department of Education.

Recognizing that this commission's recommendations could have long-lasting effects on Acadian education in New Brunswick, the SNA submitted numerous briefs calling for a complete reorganisation of the educational system. At issue was not only the question of duality within the Department of Education but, as in Ontario, the elimination of the detested bilingual schools. They had been viciously attacked in an editorial in *Évangéline*, as the following extract shows: "Un système scolaire bilingue est une utopie et un instrument d'assimilation. Sciemment ou non, c'est fonder une génération de jeunes qui ne seront ni francophones ni anglophones. Bravo, diront certaines personnes bien pensantes, enfin nous aurons des Canadiens. N'allons-nous pas plutôt former des monstres qui n'auront plus d'attache avec leur héritage culturel dans le sens large du mot."[66] Since the mid-1960s, the Acadian leadership of New Brunswick had begun to adopt an increasingly assertive position. New and younger leaders, committed to the full participation of Acadians in the political, social, and economic life of the province, came to the forefront of the Acadian associations. After decades of bilingual public schools, which had led more to assimilation and weak French-language skills than to bilingualism and a strong Acadian culture, unilingual French-language schools were viewed as essential to the preservation of the French language and Acadian culture in New Brunswick. While the Acadian leaders recognized that English-speakers in New Brunswick might want their children to become bilingual, they did not believe that putting English-speaking children into Acadian schools would be the best way to accomplish this goal, particularly given the detrimental impact this approach would have on Acadian children.

Unlike the situation in Ontario, and more like the situation in Manitoba, second-language instruction took a back seat in New Brunswick's approach to the BEP. A fairly comprehensive mandatory second-language program was built in to the education curriculum, but its implementation had been very uneven. A study conducted in February 1974 found that FSL teaching in the province varied widely across the province, ranging from 40 to 150 minutes per week, depending on the school. Moreover, there was a major shortage of qualified teachers. Of the teachers currently working in the FSL programs, 40 percent lacked a university degree, 50 percent had never taken a theoretical course on second-language teaching, 74 percent had never taken a methodological course on second-language teaching, and 30 percent had not spent any time in a francophone milieu.[67] Despite calls from anglophone parents, French immersion was still in the early phases of experimentation, and demand far outstripped class space.

Second-language instruction was even worse on the French side. ESL programs operated on the assumption that Acadian students would merely "pick up" English through cultural influences. The major weaknesses of this approach became abundantly clear through evaluations. The province was not, however, receiving any federal funding to deal with the ESL issue.

In late 1973, the McLeod-Pinet Commission submitted its report, "Education of Tomorrow." The commission called for an end to the system of two deputy ministers of education and wanted it replaced with one of a single, bilingual deputy minister. This recommendation provoked outrage and concern in the Acadian community, which pushed hard for the separate francophone deputy minister to be retained. The government did not reply to the commission's recommendations until the spring of 1974. Far from eliminating the two deputy ministers, Premier Hatfield announced a major reorganisation of the Department of Education along the lines demanded by the Acadians. It would be henceforth divided into three major sections. The first would deal with the English-language schools in terms of curriculum, teachers, and related issues; the second with the same issues, but for the French-language schools; the third with finance and administration common to both languages.[68]

While the reorganization was a key first step, other aspects of linguistic duality were sought by the leaders of the SANB. Their vision for New Brunswick centred on collective dualism rooted in the two official-language communities, each with its own autonomous institutions, rather than on mere bilingualism.[69] By the mid-1970s, numerous bilingual school boards and bilingual schools were still scattered across the province. While the utility of personal bilingualism was recognized by the Acadians, they no longer wanted their schools to be bilingual. As an editorial in *Évangéline* aptly put it: "Francophones do not want to repeat the error of many Anglophones by limiting themselves to learning only one language. They see the necessity and value of bilingualism, but they also do not want to drown in assimilative schools."[70] Throughout the mid-1970s, the districts of Campbellton, Bathurst, and Dalhousie, among others, were targeted by the SANB, as it lobbied for unilingual schools and school boards.

Until the mid-1970s, the overwhelming focus of the New Brunswick Department of Education had been on bringing Acadian schools up to parity with the English-language schools and on trying to rectify the past neglect of French-language curriculum and teacher training. Meanwhile, French second-language programs had largely taken a back seat. French immersion had been developed on an experimental basis, and two thousand children were enrolled in these programs by 1976, but there was no departmental policy to guide their future development.

By 1976, however, Acadian schools had caught up to a sufficient extent for the department to take stock of the situation in FSL programs. A new coordinator was hired to administer all the second-language programs in the province, signalling the beginning of a new phase in the development of New Brunswick's language education, one with an emphasis on French courses for English speakers. Thanks to the efforts of the Acadian leaders and supportive governments, the foundations for a modern Acadian education system were now in place, and more attention could be paid to the other priority of the Bilingualism in Education Program.

NOVA SCOTIA

Nova Scotia lagged far behind its Maritime neighbour in all aspects of its official-language education programs. In 1970 it had practically no FSL programs at the elementary school level, and French minority-language education existed in a quasi-legal manner in isolated regions. A single person at the Department of Education handled all language education matters. In many respects, Nova Scotia bore a close resemblance to Alberta, despite having a French-speaking population that was on par with Manitoba or Ontario.

Like Alberta, Nova Scotia transferred the federal grants almost in their entirety to the school boards on the basis of FTEs, while the Department of Education remained passive. Regions such as Clare County, with large Acadian populations, were able to develop new programs and libraries for their existing Acadian schools. The system was not as favourable, however, for areas where francophones in a minority position wanted to develop brand new programs.

For example, in Halifax a group of francophone and Acadian parents who sought to develop French-language classes ran into numerous obstacles from their local school board. Their numerous proposals were rejected on the basis of excessive costs, a lack of available classroom space, and a lack of local interest (after they failed to publicize the program); they were also rejected for trying to serve two objectives with one program (when the parents proposed a joint immersion/minority language school), for propagating separatism (when the parents proposed separate programs) and on the basis that language programs were unnecessary because Nova Scotia was not officially bilingual.[71] The parents started their battle in 1969, but it would not be until 1976 that Halifax got its first French-immersion program.

Minority-language education in Nova Scotia had an uphill battle to fight, not only with the provincial government and the anglophone population but with Acadians who were leery of a homogenous French-language school system. A position taken by the Fédération francophone de la Nouvelle-Écosse (FFNE) in favour of unilingual schools in 1970 "had only provoked mistrust and many concerns among the population."[72] Nova Scotia's Acadian leaders had to begin at home with an information campaign targeting Acadian parents and children about the need to preserve and develop the Acadian culture in Nova Scotia. The first step for the FFNE was a campaign outlining how

French-language schools could promote bilingualism in Nova Scotia. The federation was supported by the Acadian committee at the Department of Education, which called for the Acadian schools to adopt a policy of all-French teaching for the first three grades, a French atmosphere in the classes, and 50 percent of the school textbooks in French.[73]

A steady lobbying effort aimed at the Department of Education was also needed. The FFNE sought the appointment of a departmental official exclusively responsible for Acadian schools and the legal recognition of Acadian schools under the Education Act.[74] Their efforts bore fruit in 1973, when the department created a special consultative committee on French-language instruction, curriculum, and community interests. The committee was composed largely of representatives from Acadian regions and institutions and worked in consultation with the Committee on Acadian Studies to make recommendations to the Department of Education, including recommendations on all issues related to the BEP.[75]

Nova Scotia's progress with other aspects of the BEP was uneven. While predominantly Acadian boards invested their grants in new books and teachers for extended French programs, the predominantly English-speaking boards tended to concentrate on audio-visual materials.[76] While some of these purchases, such as audiocassettes and filmstrips, could be linked directly to the French programs, others, such as tape recorders and film projectors, had a more tenuous connection. Many boards were more scrupulous and invested in the development of new elementary-level FSL programs, which were approved by the department in 1973. FSL enrolment at the elementary level tripled over one year.

As in New Brunswick, Ontario, and Alberta, a government commission on education was active in Nova Scotia in this period. The Graham Commission (the Royal Commission on Education, Public Services, and Provincial-Municipal Relations) held inquiries from 1971 to 1974. The Acadian associations were optimistic that it might hold the key to achieving a number of their goals and submitted briefs outlining their concerns, including the French school in Halifax, the deteriorating state of Collège Ste-Anne, the anglicization of the Acadian population, and the lack of policy direction on French-language education.[77]

The Graham Commission did not disappoint the Acadians with its 1974 report. In its chapter dedicated to Acadian and French-language education, the commissioners sympathized with the Acadians' desire to preserve their language, culture, and identity and expressed the opinion that Acadians should enjoy full recognition of their linguistic rights.

While stressing that fluent bilingualism and full competency in English were essential for the Acadian population, the report recommended that the right of Acadians to be educated in their own language should be enshrined in law.

Some of the recommendations of the Graham Commission bear specific note, since they would provide the basis for the Acadian drive for additional language rights over the remainder of the decade and onwards. The first two recommendations are particularly important:

Recommendation 53-1: The Education Act should provide that French speaking children residing in communities in which 10 percent or more of the inhabitants are French-speaking have the right to receive from the time of their commencement of school, school programmes and instruction in the French language, such programmes being designed to provide them with a firm basis for mastery of communication and conceptualization in French.

Recommendation 53-2: The Education Act should also provide that these children have a right to receive, throughout their school careers, programmes and instruction in the French language designed to provide them, to the extent of their capabilities, with mastery of the skills of communication in French.

The commission also believed that second-language learning should be further developed but noted that vague concepts of national unity were poor motivators for students. Recognizing that it was unlikely that all students would wish to become bilingual, the commissioners believed that the emphasis of the second-language program should be on providing outstanding opportunities for those who did wish to learn French.[78]

The Fédération acadienne de la Nouvelle-Écosse (FANE) saw these recommendations as a useful start, and its 1976 action plan placed a great deal of emphasis on the need to push the government to implement them, particularly the recommendations calling for legal status for the Acadian schools.[79] The Association canadienne d'éducation de langue française (ACELF) was also generally positive, although it considered the 10 percent threshold of recommendation 53-1 to be too low for metropolitan areas such as Halifax. Moreover, the ACELF was concerned about shared facilities for the English and French streams.[80] The strongest negative reaction came not from within Nova Scotia but from neighbouring New Brunswick. *Évangéline*'s editors believed that the proposed changes would be a step towards assimilation rather than towards better protection of the French language, deeming the proposals to be "minces droits" and wondering why the commission would not propose full duality in the education system, as had recently been implemented in New Brunswick.[81] However, for Nova Scotia, which was not nearly as advanced as its neighbour in matters of minority-language education, these rights would be a major advance, and Acadian leaders were determined to fight for them.

The Nova Scotia government was slow to respond to the proposals. In 1975 a new assistant director of curriculum was hired to deal with French-language education programs, bringing the number of Department of Education staff responsible for French-language programming up to two. Some new curriculum plans for French-language social science and language-arts courses were also drawn up, but no steps were taken under Gerald Regan's Liberal government to bring about legal recognition for the Acadian schools of Nova Scotia.

Despite the glacial pace of the provincial government, local school boards continued their work in the mid-1970s to expand their French-language programs with the assistance of the federal grants. The Richmond County board created a French-language resource centre for its FSL and Acadian teachers. The Inverness board, encompassing the Acadian community of Chéticamp, created a French-only program for grades P (pre-kindergarten) to 6 and moved to make FSL a mandatory course all the way to grade 12, rather than for the single year (grade 7) mandated under provincial guidelines. Outside the main Acadian counties, schools in Kings County experimented with introducing FSL courses at the elementary level. However, their scattered approach resulted in an overly wide range of language skills at the grade 7 level, which led to great frustration for both teachers and students. Lacking provincial direction on a common starting point for FSL, the program was disjointed and in disarray.[82]

The complaint of the King's County board was echoed by FANE and by Acadian teachers. The government of Nova Scotia had done little since the introduction of the BEP to provide direction to the development of French-language education. While special projects had made sporadic development possible, a full network of legally recognized Acadian schools was still needed for the Acadians,[83] and a more structured FSL program including the option of French immersion was sought for the anglophones. While the situation of French-language education in Nova Scotia had improved somewhat in local communities since 1970, the government had done little by the end of 1976 to satisfy Acadian leaders by implementing the recommendations of the Graham Commission.

QUEBEC

For the first few months of its operation in Quebec, the BEP was the furthest thing from the mind of Robert Bourassa's newly elected Liberal government. In October 1970, the Front de libération du Québec (FLQ) kidnapped the British trade commissioner and the Quebec labour minister, plunging the province into chaos. The kidnappings made the new provincial government very sensitive to the separatist threat and to the charges of federal interference that erupted as a result of the Trudeau government's response to the October Crisis.

Of all the provinces, Quebec had the most developed system of both minority-language and second-language education. The official provincial position was that the federal grants were meant to reimburse the province for the work it had already done, as a form of "thank you" for its good work. For ideological reasons, it refused to make any linkage between these funds and a federal role in the management of the provincial education system and placed the federal grants into its consolidated educational funds. Provincial grants were not increased to school boards that offered the programs targeted by the BEP. As officials in the Department of Education stated, "Quebec simply wants more money and for the federal grants for this program to remain as unconditional as possible."[84]

One might be tempted to assume that the government was justified in this approach and that school boards were not trying to develop any new programs that would entail new costs. But this was not, strictly speaking, the case. The recently passed Bill 63 required additional French-language capacities of all graduates of the English-language school boards, and French as a second language was now required from grade 1 until the end of secondary school. No additional funding from the province was granted to cover the costs of these changes, and the regulation governing this requirement specifically denied the boards federal funds for this purpose. Quebec's English-language school boards had also begun to pilot French-immersion programs, starting with the South Shore Board in 1965 and the Protestant School Board of Greater Montreal (PSBGM) in 1967, and the Conseil des écoles catholiques de Montréal was also looking into developing French-immersion programs for its English-language schools.

These new programs required the expenditure of additional funds for textbooks, audio-visual materials, and the hiring of new teachers, yet no additional money was forthcoming from the Quebec government. This shortfall was a great concern to anglophone parents, who saw these new requirements taking financial resources away from other programs. Accordingly, the Quebec Federation of Home and School Associations (QFHSA) began to pressure the federal and provincial governments. It passed a series of resolutions at its 1973 annual general meeting calling for action from the commissioner of official languages and for the distribution of the BEP grants directly to the boards offering language programs.[85] Representatives of the QFHSA met with officials of the Department of Education, only to be told that there was no relationship between the federal grants and the provincial formula for school board grants,[86] an explicit refusal of intrastate federalism and a federal role in education.

The QFHSA routinely updated to its membership on the status of its lobbying campaign through its regular newsletter. The executive also engaged in direct lobbying of individual parliamentarians. Federal members of parliament were asked to help out with the QFHSA's quest for provincial accountability to the House of Commons and the public. They achieved some success in convincing MPs, particularly MPs from the opposition parties, to raise these issues during question period.[87]

The Quebec government was not responsive to the pressures of the QFHSA, believing its provision of English-language education to be more than sufficient. As regards the federal programs, Quebec was more interested in collaboration with the other provinces to strengthen *their* minority- and second-language programs through development of instructional materials and exchange programs.[88]

The major priority of the Quebec government in terms of language issues was not connected with the federal government or with promoting a stronger English-language program. The Gendron Commission (Commission of Inquiry on the Position of the French Language and on Language Rights in Quebec), which had been commissioned in 1969, finally submitted its report in 1972. It noted the predominance of the English language in the Quebec economy and the clustering of francophones in lower-level jobs. It considered the promotion of the French language in Quebec's economy to be the key to improving the status of francophones and to attracting immigrants to use the French language. Its members reasoned that since educational choices were being made to prepare workers for the economy, a French-speaking economy would provide the necessary incentive for immigrants to send their children to French schools. The commission further recommended that French be declared the official language of Quebec.[89]

The Bertrand government's response to the French-language issue, Bill 63, had not been popular in francophone Quebec. If the French-speaking majority was to be satisfied, Robert Bourassa's Liberal government had to develop a response to the Gendron Commission's report that would transform the operating language of the province, particularly of its economy, into French. Although the commission had focused on the economy, rather than on education, Bourassa placed a significant emphasis on the province's education system in his response, since it was most likely to bring about a revitalisation of the status of the French language in Quebec.

Bill 22, the Official Language Act, was introduced in the provincial legislature in 1974. Its main provisions did, in fact, stress the role of French in the economy of Quebec, employing a number of incentives to encourage businesses to undergo a process of francisation.[90] It also made French the only official language of the province, although it did not abrogate the right to use English in the courts and the legislature, which was protected under section 133 of the British North America Act, 1867. But in the education sector, the legislation went significantly beyond the Gendron Commission's recommendations. Bill 22 decreed that admission to English-language schools would be limited to children who had a "sufficient knowledge" of English,[91] which would be determined by language tests. In effect, Bill 22 was intended to limit access to English-language schools to children of the anglophone minority in the province and to coerce allophone parents into sending their children to the French-language schools. Supporters of Bill 22 hoped this would stem the tide of allophone assimilation into the anglophone community.

Bill 22 pleased nobody. The Québécois nationalists it was intended to appease argued that the provisions were too vague and easily circumvented by tutoring or by noncompliant school board officials. Indeed, experience would prove the nationalists correct, as allophone Quebecers who wanted their children educated in English found numerous ways to circumvent the legislation and its complex regulations.

The coincidence of Bill 22's introduction with the modified objectives of the Bilingualism in Education Program was not lost on supporters of Quebec's English-language school boards. The Quebec Federation of Home and School Associations was quick to realize the implications of the new objectives for Quebec. While the QFHSA was told by the secretary of state that the change in wording was merely for the sake of clarification,[92] it was clear that the objectives no longer implied any support for nonanglophone students in the English-language schools of Quebec. The QFHSA joined the multitude of organisations decrying the language tests of Bill 22, and urging the federal government to disallow the legislation. In this respect, it was disappointed when the Trudeau government announced in October 1974 that it would not challenge the bill.[93]

While the quest to overturn Bill 22 had ended in disappointment, the QFHSA continued to lead the fight for changes to the application of the BEP in Quebec. At the root of its concern was the fact that the government did not transfer any of the additional grants to the school boards, while at the same time it was imposing new requirements on the boards for the expanded provision of FSL and language tests at graduation. No such expansion of ESL was required of the French boards, and indeed expansion had been resisted by francophones on the grounds that it would harm programs such as art and physical education, precisely the impact that the FSL requirements were having in the English schools.[94] At a minimum, if the province was not going to pass along additional funds for the English-language program, the QFHSA hoped to at least secure funding for the new FSL programs.

The QFHSA continued its multipronged lobbying efforts. Its leaders met with senior officials of the Department of Education, demanding that the English-language boards receive a share of the BEP grants, particularly if they were to be forced to provide more FSL.[95] They also began another letter-writing campaign to federal MPs in the winter of 1975 outlining their concerns about the use of the federal grants. In April 1976 the QFHSA passed another series of resolutions aimed at gaining accountability for the BEP grants. To put these resolutions into action, the federation produced a brief for the federal and provincial governments outlining how the BEP had been implemented in the province.[96] The brief stressed the decline in funding and falling enrolment in the Protestant boards and how the new FSL programs were leading to a decline in their ability to hire specialists for programs such as art, music, and physical education.

The QFHSA's actions soon attracted the attention of the Protestant School Board of Greater Montreal (PSBGM). The PSBGM commissioners were upset that the Ottawa-Hull district boards were receiving additional funding for French immersion, while their board was not eligible for it. Moreover, school boards were not permitted to submit special-project proposals directly to the secretary of state, since federal guidelines stipulated that they must go through provincial channels.[97] They were unlikely to be successful using these channels, however, since the Department of Education was resisting providing additional funds for FSL. Led by trustee Winifred Potter, the past editor of the *QFHSA News*, the PSBGM decided to support the efforts of the QFHSA to get accountability for the BEP grants, and it passed a unanimous motion in July 1976 in support of the QFHSA resolutions.[98] The Quebec Association of Protestant School Boards also noted this work and supported these efforts.[99]

The QFHSA campaign had mixed results during the final years of the Liberal regime of Robert Bourassa. The letter-writing campaign aimed at federal MPs did attract some response. Ian Watson, MP for Laprairie, was one of the first MPs to respond to the campaign, and he asked questions in the House about the use of the bilingual grants.[100] Conservative MPs from outside Quebec also took an interest in the QFHSA's concerns. Harvie André, MP for Calgary Centre, noted that "there appears to be a great injustice perpetrated on the English speaking students of Quebec through the implementation of this programme in the province of Quebec. He said he would bring QFHSA's "view to the attention of the Commission of Official Languages." Joe Clark, MP for Rocky Mountain, indicated that he "had not appreciated the discrimination against English-speaking students in Quebec who wish to have help in learning French."[101] While the federal government did not actively press the government of Quebec to provide FSL funding directly to the English-language boards, it did indicate that it was free to spend the grants on this purpose if it so chose and, that it was not bound by the agreement to spend funds only on ESL and EML programs. This effectively put the ball back in Quebec's court.[102] The campaign also raised increased awareness and concern within the federal government about how Quebec was using the grants. Officials from the Secretary of State noted that Quebec was not sufficiently acknowledging the grants and called for an evaluation of how Quebec was using the funds.[103] If nothing else, the campaign put the BEP into the public eye and exposed it to greater scrutiny by politicians.

While the QFHSA campaign did lead to more visibility and questioning of the program, its main objectives were left unattained. The federal government refused to provide the federation with copies of the provincial accountability reports tabled in the House of Commons, on the grounds that this required the consent of all ten provinces. While the federal government was willing to use the QFHSA concerns as leverage with the Quebec government, it was unwilling to be completely open with a lobby group. By the mid-1970s, the Quebec government had adopted a very hard-line approach to the Bilingualism in Education Program. In meetings with the QFHSA, Assistant Deputy Minister Claude Beauregard claimed that the provision of English education was all that was required of the province.[104] Regarding the FSL provisions, he argued that they were a priority set by the "collectivity" and that additional funding did not always follow new educational priorities. Furthermore, according to Beauregard it did not cost the province more to provide English-language schools, and thus it should not provide them with more funding. If the anglophone community of Quebec wanted to have education in the English language, they must be prepared to make sacrifices. In the view of the Quebec government, since the education was being provided, the QFHSA had nothing to complain about.

This hard line was taken vis-à-vis the federal government as well. Strategy documents produced by the Quebec government stressed the unconditional nature of the payments and stated that the province should resist any initiative that would reduce payments to it.[105] The province also wanted to push for greater flexibility in the special-projects annex, so as to reduce the evaluation required of these projects. Officials proposed a set envelope of money for each province to spend as it pleased, a proposal that would have significantly weakened Ottawa's control in the only part of the BEP over which it had significant priority-setting input.[106] Quebec rejected outright any talk of federal involvement in pedagogical evaluation, and Department of Education officials were wary of the federal government using proposed evaluation mechanisms as a means of controlling the special projects.[107] The province also rejected the federal premise that the BEP was intended to cover additional costs, which, as mentioned, it believed did not exist in the province. Moreover, Quebec began to take a very legalistic approach to the BEP agreement, noting that nowhere in the 1970 or 1974 objectives were the words "extra costs" or "supplementary costs" used. Although this was technically true, the study presented above of the context in which the BEP was created clearly indicates that the program was intended for these purposes.

By the end of 1976, the government of Quebec had staked out a very obstinate position, resisting any federal intervention through the BEP into Quebec's educational system. The QFHSA's resistance to Bill 22 and its awareness campaign surrounding the BEP had served to politicize both the BEP and English-language education in the province more broadly. The already palpable tension between the Ottawa and Quebec City governments on issues of education and the nature of Canadian federalism was about to grow much worse: in November 1976 the Bourassa government fell to the Parti Québécois, a party committed to sovereignty-association.

FURTHER DEVELOPMENTS AT THE NATIONAL LEVEL

While the election of the Parti Québécois would herald the start of a harder line taken by the provinces towards shared-cost programs such as the BEP, the federal government was reconsidering its approach to its language agenda by the mid-1970s. Lobby organisations, which were also in a period of transition, were beginning to develop longer-term strategies to secure the language programs they believed were critical to the future survival of their communities.

Throughout the early 1970s, a wide range of French Canadian and Acadian minority-community groups had received grants from the Official Language Minority Groups Program to support their core operations. These funds helped to rescue a number of these associations, which otherwise would have become moribund. Moreover, with the advent of the OLMG, new provincial organisations such as the Fédération acadienne de la Nouvelle-Écosse were formed. Others were reorganized to take advantage of the granting provisions, which until 1975 targeted provincially based organisations, a key reason for the reorganisation of the SNA and the creation of the SANB.

In 1975 the major provincial francophone associations joined together to create the Fédération des francophones hors-Québec (FFHQ).[108] This federation was intended to serve as a nation-wide umbrella group through which minority francophone communities could lobby for the establishment of language rights as fundamental rights in Canada. It would also coordinate the activities of the provincial francophone organisations and facilitate the transfer of information between these groups. Ottawa was quick to modify the OLMG to provide funding to the new organization.

The FFHQ began to investigate how the federal government exercised control and evaluation over its grants to the provinces, and it was publicly critical of the provinces for their lack of administrative structures for French-language education and of separate French-language school classes, schools, and boards. It was critical also of the continuing scourge of bilingual schools and of the provinces' diversion of federal funds to other purposes.[109] Hubert Gauthier, the executive director of the FFHQ, lashed out in the media at provinces such as Alberta and Ontario for misallocation of the federal grants.[110] The FFHQ also coordinated the major provincial associations – ACFA, ACFO, the SFM, SANB, and FANE, for example – in the creation of the strategy document entitled *Les Héritiers du Lord Durham* (The Heirs of Lord Durham), which laid out the strategy of the FFHQ and its member associations for developing francophone rights at the provincial and national level, a strategy in which greater control of the federal BEP grants was a key element.[111] Over the following years, the FFHQ would become a major player in the debates over the renegotiation of the BEP.

While the FFHQ and the provincial associations were questioning how the federal government administered the BEP, officials from the Secretary of State were also contemplating new directions for the program. Early in 1975, Secretary of State Hugh Faulkner indicated that the current format of the Bilingualism in Education Program was not sacred; only the principle of the equality of the two language groups was. He mused publicly about the possibility of spending more money on special projects, rather than continuing to fund the status quo. Indeed, the federal government was concerned about the extent to which the formula payments provided an incentive for real developments in provincial language programs.[112]

The federal government was also considering a shift towards bilateral agreements with individual provinces, rather than continuing with multilateral negotiations. It was believed that in this manner federal dollars could be targeted more effectively at programs needing development in each province. For example, federal officials wanted to cease their heavy subsidies to Quebec's English-language education system and target the FSL and French-immersion programs, which could benefit more from this assistance.[113]

A major driving force behind these considerations was the fact that the federal government had simply guessed at the cost of the BEP at the outset and had not initially tried to track expenditures on the program.[114] By 1975–76, the annual cost had more than doubled, rising from about $50 million in 1970–71 to over $110 million. Consequently, the federal government wanted to ensure that this money was being effectively used by the provinces.

The federal government also wished to test its estimates of the additional costs against practical experience. Bureaucrats from the Secretary of State were sent on a cross-country tour in 1975 to try to determine the real value of additional costs, and letters were sent to provincial departments of education asking for their feedback.[115] Politicians also began to take an interest in issues of accountability. The BEP came under government scrutiny in an April 1976 meeting of the Canadian Government Committee on Broadcasting, Film, and the Arts. Questions from MP Serge Joyal to the secretary of state and his officials revealed that although accounting from the West had generally been clear, Quebec had provided no data, data from the Maritimes had been fuzzy, and Ontario had been spending the funds on its own priorities.[116] Both politicians and civil servants were becoming increasingly attuned to the need for more accountability for the BEP.

Not only did the federal government want to know how its money had been spent, it wanted to know how effective the program had been, so that future renewals could be based on actual experience. The provincial response was mixed. Nova Scotia, New Brunswick, and Ontario all indicated their support for cost-effectiveness studies. Manitoba, on the other hand, believed that the conclusions of such studies merely reflected the preconceptions of the investigators. The entire concept of supplementary costs and evaluation was challenged by Quebec, which resisted any notion that "supplementary costs" were involved, since the term was not in the text of the agreement.[117] All the provinces resisted any attempt by the federal government to impose its own priorities or direct involvement on the evaluation process, although the provinces that intended to conduct evaluations were willing to share their results.

This stonewalling created frustration for the Canadian government. As long as the BEP continued to operate as a predominantly interstate program, with the federal government acting as merely the funder of provincial programs, the provinces would be able to dictate the terms of both accountability and evaluation. It was thus becoming clear that in order to have significant input into a substantive evaluation of the BEP, the Canadian government would need to take steps to reorient the program along intrastate lines.

Through all these issues over program renegotiation and operations ran an important thread: the differences between bureaucratic and

Table 3.2
Provincial Spending on Special Projects, 1972/73 to 1975/76 (thousands of dollars)

Province	Minority language	Second language	Joint programs[1]	Total
Nova Scotia	343	73	6	421
New Brunswick	825	12	0	834
Ontario	636	5,217	0	5,854
Manitoba	462	98	242	804
Alberta	0	75	159[2]	234
Quebec	457	0	2,027	2,484
Total (all provinces)	3,215	7,296	2,753	13,271

Source: CRCCF, Fonds ACFO, FFHQ 1976–81, C2/463/3, Table of Expenditures on Special Projects, 1972–73 to 1975–76 (1977).
1. Some special projects funded both minority-language and second-language objectives, e.g., funding for the Bureau de l'éducation française in Manitoba.
2. Until 1978, Alberta did not report its spending on minority-language and immersion programs separately.

political conceptions of the Bilingualism in Education Program. Civil servants involved in the program described it as creating feelings of close collegiality across federal-provincial boundaries, feelings inspired by their work on a common objective, a sentiment that would augur well for increased intrastate functioning of the BEP.[118] But by the mid-1970s the program was exposed to a great deal more political scrutiny. Resistance to evaluation and accountability was rooted in political conceptions of constitutional jurisdiction and models of Canadian federalism. By the mid-1970s, federal civil servants committed to the program were expressing their concerns to provincial officials that they could not defend the BEP to federal politicians without solid data. They feared that without cooperation and accountability, the decision of whether to continue the program would become a political one.[119]

By the mid-1970s a divergence in how the provinces favoured certain BEP objectives over others was also becoming clear, as evidenced by which special projects were funded. Table 3.2 outlines spending on special projects for the period from 1972/73 to 1975/76. As the table demonstrates, the Maritime provinces and Manitoba had concentrated their efforts on minority-language education, which put them more or less in sync with the Canadian government's priorities. Ontario, on the other hand, had invested heavily in second-language programs, while Alberta had spent very little on special projects and what had been spent was split about evenly. Despite the booming French-immersion programs in its English school boards, Quebec had not allocated any special project funding to this purpose, other than the National Capital Region project. Clearly, the provinces had started to diverge in their priorities, and this divergence was being reflected by where they were investing their own money. For federal officials who saw minority-language education as the top priority, these trends were disconcerting.

EARLY PROGRESS INDICATORS

Although Ottawa had some concerns about accountability and the evaluation of the Bilingualism in Education Program, there were a number of encouraging developments from the program's first six years. Provinces such as Manitoba and Ontario had developed targeted granting formulas, although their effectiveness remained to be determined. A number of new administrative structures had also been established for French-language education, such as Ontario's Council on French Language Schools, Nova Scotia's Acadian Committee, Manitoba's Bureau de l'éducation française, and the linguistically organized New Brunswick Department of Education. But the provinces had yet to establish concrete evaluation and accountability mechanisms to track the federal funding, and thus this period was rife with accusations of misdirection of funds, accusations that were difficult to prove but nevertheless quite believable.

Francophone minority-language associations had taken an active interest in the new programs available through the BEP and were devoting substantial resources and energy to ensure that they were expanded and developed. Their capacity to engage in this lobbying had been strengthened by the advent of the OLMG, which gave them a more stable funding base for their activities. In this respect, the federal government was having some significant success in altering the parameters of the embedded state. Civil servants in all provinces who worked on BEP-funded programs were all also firmly in support of the program's continued success and were working behind the scenes to ensure that it would not fail due to political bickering. There were still significant challenges, particularly in the West and the Maritimes, where long-held internal fears of the francophone communities had to be overcome in order to build support for homogenous minority-language-education classes and schools. Lobby groups and civil servants alike (particularly in Manitoba) were, however, working to overcome these obstacles and making incremental gains in FML programming.

Second-language instruction was in flux in this period. While programs were being expanded to additional grade levels, there was more freedom of choice in the educational systems of the country, and many students were opting to drop FSL in secondary school. Although the second-language formulas were intended to last only for five to ten years, nobody mentioned the possibility of cancelling this funding at the 1974 renewal. In a more positive vein, immersion was proving to be a very popular experiment, as the initial studies of these programs showed that immersion students were significantly more fluent in French than their counterparts in core FSL programs.[120] Still, these programs were mostly pilot projects, and they had yet to produce their first graduating classes.

Most of English-speaking Canada was clearly moving towards improved language education for its official minority-language populations, and even recalcitrant Alberta had finally accepted full-day French programs. Such was not the case in Quebec. Language tensions were running high in the only province with a French-language majority. While English-language education organizations were fighting to improve the state of their language programs, particularly second-language ones, the provincial government was unresponsive. Indeed, the government had begun clamping down on access to the English-language stream, a trend that was making it difficult for advocates of bilingualism to promote improved French-language services elsewhere in the country. While the situation was tense under the Liberal government of Robert Bourassa, with the fallout from Bill 22, it would soon become much worse, as René Lévesque introduced the Parti Québécois' language reforms.

CHAPTER FOUR

Lévesque's Gambit Fails: A New English Canadian Consensus, 1976–1979

The months between the November 1976 election of the Parti Québécois and the March 1979 expiration date of the second five-year Bilingualism in Education Program agreement encompassed a crucial turning point in governmental discourse about language policy in education and a fractious period in Canadian federalism. The provincial governments were urged to take a much more aggressive posture in favour of interstate federalism by the government of René Lévesque: a government that lacked any inclination to compromise with Ottawa, *especially* on language issues. The Trudeau government was growing increasingly frustrated by the extent to which the Bilingualism in Education Program was merely funding the status quo in many provinces. It wished to reorient the program so that it could set new objectives and priorities and evaluate its outcomes. The federal government was also placing an increased emphasis on the BEP as part of its new "youth option" for bilingualism, as it reduced its emphasis on civil servant language training. These new directions would require provincial concessions, a state of affairs that put the two sides at loggerheads.

Given this polarization, could the Bilingualism in Education Program be expected to survive the next renewal process? This was a great concern for the French Canadian and Acadian communities that had benefited greatly from the federal grant programs. While new programs had been launched, most were not fully developed and remained heavily reliant on federal supports. Community groups were aware of the need to step up their lobbying efforts if they were to avoid having the gulf between the Canadian and provincial governments lead to the cancellation of the BEP. In the late 1970s they would be joined in their efforts by supporters of the French second-language programs, who rallied together as Canadian Parents for French. The efforts of these groups would help the Canadian government defend its intrastate conception of language policy in Canada, as they vigorously supported the nation-wide approach favoured by Ottawa.

While intergovernmental conflict would preclude the conclusion of a new five-year agreement before the March 1979 deadline, dialogue continued during this period. This chapter will demonstrate that the continuance of federal-provincial talks reflects a certain degree of the success both of the BEP and of the federal government's official-languages policy. While the premiers supported many of Quebec's demands for increased powers from Ottawa and its interstate stance on education programs, they were also faced with an altered embedded state. The new language programs had become commonplace and had built up expectations from parents that would be difficult to meet without federal financial aid. Cancelling the language programs was no longer a realistic option.

The other premiers were also opposed to Quebec's talk of secession. In this period they would attempt to forge their own language-policy direction, one that could meet their objective of greater provincial autonomy, while still expressing support for language rights in education. The English-speaking premiers would be responsible for a fundamental shift in the discourse of Canadian language policy, moving from language privileges into the realm of language-education rights. This shift would lay the groundwork for the next plank of Trudeau's intrastate strategy: the creation of the Canadian Charter of Rights and Freedoms, complete with official-language minority rights in education and a role for the Supreme Court of Canada in enforcing these rights. To understand how these developments occurred, we now return to the initial impacts of the election of the Parti Québécois in November 1976.

THE ELECTION OF THE PARTI QUÉBÉCOIS, BILL 101, AND RECIPROCAL AGREEMENTS

The election of the Parti Québécois on 15 November 1976 shook the Canadian political establishment to its core. While previous governments had demanded more power from Ottawa, never before had a provincial government been elected on a platform linked to separatism. The simple fact of the election alone did not bode well for a closer relationship between Quebec City and Ottawa, and the PQ's policies were about to drive an even wider wedge between the two governments.

One of the earliest pieces of legislation to emerge from the PQ government was Bill 101, entitled the Charter of the French Language, introduced in March 1977. Picking up where Bill 22 had left off, it included even stricter provisions to promote French as the working language of the province of Quebec, the most famous of which are its French-only sign provisions. Bill 101's ramifications for education were profound. Access to the English-language minority-education system was strictly restricted to "a) a child whose mother or father received elementary instruction in English in Quebec; b) a child whose mother or father lived in Quebec before the law came into force, who received elementary instruction in English outside of Quebec; c) children already legally enrolled in the English language system; and d) younger siblings of c."[1] In effect, migrants to the province of Quebec were barred from educating their children in English. This provision included migrants from English-speaking countries, such as the United States. More shockingly, Bill 101 used Quebec as its geographical reference for parental English-language instruction. Accordingly, children whose parents had been educated in English elsewhere in Canada or who themselves had attended English-language schools in other provinces were not eligible to attend Quebec's English-language schools. This highly controversial provision, which was pushed by Dr Camille Laurin, the architect of the legislation, was viewed with misgivings even by a large number of francophone Quebecers, reportedly including the premier himself.[2]

One section of the Charter of the French Language, section 86, did provide for expansion of access to Quebec's English-language schools: "the Government may make regulations extending the scope of section 73 to include such persons as may be contemplated by any reciprocity agreement that may be concluded between the Government of Quebec and another province."[3] Accordingly, if another province was willing to enter into a reciprocal agreement with Quebec that guaranteed French-language education to migrants from the province of Quebec, Quebec would allow children from that province access to its English-language education system. These provisions fell nicely in line with Quebec's interstate approach to Canadian federalism, as well as with its pretensions to act as an independent state. Not only did Quebec wish to deal with Ottawa on a state-to-state basis, but it also sought to craft agreements with other individual provinces on a similar basis.

On 21 July 1977, Premier Lévesque wrote to the nine other premiers to propose these reciprocal agreements.[4] The *Globe and Mail*'s Quebec columnist, William Johnson, predicted that their response would probably be negative. Indeed, René Lévesque was not expecting to gain support from more than two provinces.

Prime Minister Trudeau quickly urged the premiers to reject Lévesque's offer. He argued that minority-language education rights should not be considered a bargaining chip and that in fact they should be enshrined in the Constitution. Trudeau's response was an early indication of Ottawa's renewed contemplation of guarantees for minority-language education rights.[5]

To Lévesque's chagrin, the provinces who were leaders in minority-language education were quick to reject the reciprocal agreements. William Davis responded on 27 July 1977, noting that Ontario provided a full range of French-language education programs that were already open to Quebecers. While his province would immediately have qualified for the reciprocal agreements, he rejected them, claiming that this type of proposed agreement was a dangerous jurisdictional precedent in Quebec's move towards sovereignty-association. He further declared that his government's policies were rooted in the recognition that access to educational programs in their own language for Ontario's francophones was right and just. As he wrote in his letter, "I feel, however, that an issue as fundamental as language rights in education is not something that can be negotiated on a bilateral basis between provinces. Such rights should be accepted as a matter of fundamental principle and not be the subject of quid pro quo arrangements."[6] New Brunswick premier Richard Hatfield also rejected the interprovincial approach to language rights being proposed by Quebec. He supported Ontario's position and then took a step further by supporting Ottawa's call for the constitutional entrenchment of minority-language education rights, a position he had held since 1971.[7] Nova Scotia's premier, Gerald Regan, also rejected the Quebec proposal, arguing that issues of minority-language education rights were better suited to federal-provincial arrangements.[8] One by one, the remaining premiers rejected the Quebec proposal. Rather than coaxing the other premiers towards interprovincial approaches to education, as Quebec had intended, the proposed reciprocal agreements were having the opposite effect. Given the choice between appearing to support sovereignty-association and accepting Ottawa's financial aid and minority-language rights proposals, the premiers increasingly found themselves in Trudeau's camp.

THE ST ANDREWS DECLARATION:
AN ENGLISH CANADIAN CONSENSUS

Premier Hatfield was aware that no province wanted to play Quebec's game with the reciprocal agreements. But neither did the premiers want to be trapped by Trudeau's constitutional option or appear as if they were failing to improve the state of their minority-language education programs. Accordingly, Hatfield, who was to host a premiers' summit at St Andrews-by-the-Sea on 18 August 1977, decided to use the occasion to play statesman. He drafted a declaration calling for all the provinces to make their "best efforts" to provide minority-language education programs and for the Council of Ministers of Education, Canada (CMEC) to conduct a review of the state of minority-language education in each province.[9]

The weeks between Lévesque's proposal and the St Andrews conference were filled with activity. The Fédération des francophones hors-Québec (FFHQ), after initially trying to secure a role in any new agreement, made its opposition to Quebec's proposal known and voiced support for Trudeau's constitutional option.[10] The proposed St Andrews declaration grew in popularity among the premiers, who, one by one, rejected Lévesque's proposals, ending with the rejection by Saskatchewan's Allan Blakeney on 19 August.

At St Andrews all the premiers, with the exception of Lévesque, signed a declaration stating that the provinces would "make their best efforts to provide instruction in English and French wherever numbers warrant."[11] The CMEC secretariat was given a mandate to prepare a report on the state of minority-language education in the provinces. In agreeing to the St Andrews declaration, the provinces were seeking to set the terms of the language-education debate themselves, rather than simply agreeing to either Trudeau's or Lévesque's vision.

The declaration was a major unintended catalyst in the development of minority-language education rights in Canada. Lévesque's efforts to secure the agreement of the other premiers for reciprocal agreements and reduce Ottawa's role in language policy had backfired, forcing the premiers closer to Trudeau's camp. With the St Andrews declaration the nine premiers had come together for the first time to publicly declare support for minority-language education rights; the declaration would provide the basis for further development towards constitutional recognition of these rights.[12] Moreover, it marked a significant step for the CMEC in its involvement in the debate about the official languages in education, since it was to play a role in the study of these programs.

On 26 August 1977, Bill 101 was formally adopted by the government of Quebec, without any other province agreeing to the provisions of section 86. The government was concerned that the momentum had shifted in favour of Ottawa's intrastate, constitutional approach to language policy and recognized the need to reassert a provincially driven vision that would not open the door wider for Ottawa. Moreover, it still hoped that some type of agreement could be reached to satisfy section 86's requirement. Jacques-Yvan Morin, the education minister, hoped that the CMEC meeting in Montreal scheduled for February 1978 would produce better results, under the assumption that education ministers might be able to agree to proposals that the premiers, for political reasons, could not.[13] Regaining provincial consensus was a key priority over the intervening six months.

Quebec opted to remain a part of the CMEC and assume its presidency in September 1977, following through on a commitment by the previous Liberal government. Initially, it was uncertain whether Jacques-Yvan Morin should assume this position, given the PQ's intention to have Quebec secede from Confederation, or at least to reduce its participation in federal-provincial arrangements. However, a convincing argument was made that participation in the CMEC would give Quebec a stronger position from which to defend its position on educational matters, particularly with a renewal of the BEP coming up.[14]

Quebec also had to decide whether to participate in the CMEC study on minority-language education, to which the other nine premiers had agreed at St Andrews. The Ministry of Intergovernmental Affairs wanted to refuse participation and relaunch its bilateral accords proposal. However, the Ministry of Education successfully argued that participation would highlight the strong record of Quebec in minority-language education programs and enable the province to guide the study's structure.[15] Minister Morin hoped that by participating Quebec might revitalise talks for an interprovincial arrangement on minority-language education and bolster the CMEC's capacity to prevent further encroachments by the Trudeau government in this sector. Indeed, Quebec was able to guide the CMEC's report towards a bland statistical format, rather than one filled with concrete recommendations for new programs.[16]

The Montreal conference, held on 24 February 1978, did lead to a declaration upon which all the education ministers could agree. It stated that each "child of the French-speaking and English-speaking minority is entitled to an education in his or her language in the primary or the secondary schools in each province wherever numbers warrant. The implementation of this principle will be as defined by each province."[17] This declaration was more restrictive than St Andrews, limiting language rights to the official-language minority populations and leaving its interpretation and implementation up to individual provinces. Premier Lévesque hoped that provincial consensus on the Montreal declaration would stem federal government involvement in minority-language rights.[18] While Jacques-Yvan Morin believed that the declaration was a step in the direction of a multilateral accord and that it might suffice for the purposes of section 86, Claude Morin, the minister of intergovernmental affairs, disagreed. He urged his colleague to continue to press for the reciprocal accords through the CMEC. Quebec must not be seen, he argued, as failing in its attempt to secure the agreement of the other provinces on an issue this important.[19]

Given Claude Morin's decision that the Montreal declaration was not a sufficient alternative to formal reciprocal agreements, Quebec's English-language schools remained closed to migrants from other provinces. While the federal government did not support Bill 101, it did not disallow the legislation. It did, however, support the efforts of groups such as the Protestant School Board of Greater Montreal that were challenging the legislation in court and voiced its opposition to the coercive measures employed by the new laws.[20]

Prime Minister Trudeau was growing increasingly committed to a constitutional solution. Writing to the premiers in September 1977, he proposed "to inscribe in the Constitution a right in relation to language of education based on the declaration of principle and your own stated objectives that emerged from St Andrews." The preference of the federal government was "to have the constitutional right established in terms of the official language of choice. This could be done by inscribing in the Constitution a provision recognizing and declaring that, in Canada, every Canadian parent has the right to have his or her children receive their schooling in the official language of the parent's choice, wherever the numbers of children for whom one or the other official language is chosen warrant the provision of the necessary facilities."[21] This preference would be the cornerstone of the Liberal government's approach to minority-language education rights for the next five years. Trudeau vehemently rejected suggestions, such as those from the Pepin-Robarts Task Force on Canadian Unity, that these rights be left to the discretion of the provinces. The failure of Quebec to defend the rights of its anglophone minority was cited as a prime reason why this route would fail.[22]

The debates over minority-language education during the summer of 1977 brought the conflict between the visions of Ottawa and Quebec City into the open. Most of the nine premiers found themselves somewhere between the two extremes of constitutional guarantees and completely interprovincial approaches, and the St Andrews declaration attempted to stake out an independent position that preserved provincial autonomy over language. Yet this declaration forced the premiers to go public with a vague declaration of support for minority-language education rights, a declaration to which they would be held to account by the Trudeau government and the minority-language communities. The declaration would constrain their room for maneuvering in the future when Ottawa proposed guaranteed minority-language education rights: rights that in principle they supposedly agreed with.

THE YOUTH OPTION – NEW DIRECTIONS IN FEDERAL LANGUAGE POLICY

As noted, the Bilingualism in Education Program was only one component of a larger language-policy direction followed by the Canadian government in the 1970s. It also seemed to be the most productive of Ottawa's language policy initiatives, having increased opportunities for minority-language education and second-language instruction in the provinces. Accordingly, late in 1976 the federal government began to turn towards a "youth option" for bilingualism.

The youth option first appeared as government policy in the Speech from the Throne of October 1976, which called for "a better balance [to] be established between the money spent to introduce bilingualism in the public service and the money spent to enable more Canadians, particularly young people, to learn to communicate in both official languages." It was presented as an alternative to the concurrently pursued civil service training program and appeared regularly in speeches throughout the early months of 1977. Prime Minister Trudeau, speaking to the Canadian Association of Broadcasters, indicated his desire to shift to "greater support for teaching French in the schools – where it should be taught – rather than in crash programs for public servants."[23] The same sentiments would be echoed in the June 1977 policy paper "A National Understanding."

In a period when the costs of bilingualism programs were escalating rapidly, the federal government wanted to target its funds more effectively, and the civil service programs had proven to be rather disappointing in their results. The "youth option" originated with Commissioner of Official Languages Keith Spicer, who suggested it in his fifth annual report and in his representations to Treasury Board President Jean Chrétien and Prime Minister Trudeau over the summer of 1976.[24] Spicer had long been an advocate of education as the route to bilingualism, and his annual reports routinely stressed the greater effectiveness of language training for children.[25] With the poor results of the civil service programs, Spicer's proposals began to find receptive ears in the Trudeau government.

In addition to pedagogical reasons for stressing language training at an early age, Ottawa hoped that its language programs would "result in a healthy attitude" towards whichever language was being taught as the second language and a "sympathetic understanding of the people who speak that language."[26] Thus, the youth option was expected to also serve as a tool for fostering national unity.

Although the federal government was moving towards an increased stress on the youth option, it was not entirely satisfied with the current arrangements of the BEP. It wanted a cultural enrichment component added to the language education programs and perhaps included in the program objectives.[27] The secretary of state also wanted to eliminate some troublesome areas that created negative perceptions of the programs. Chief among them was the issue of accountability. It was increasingly difficult to justify a federal role in language education when provinces such as Quebec did not subscribe to the principle that additional costs were entailed by the provision of minority- and second-language education. John Roberts, the new secretary of state, further mused that perhaps it would be advisable for the federal government to end its funding of ongoing programs, wondering if a state of dependence was being created that ran counter to the spirit of the Constitution.[28]

In accordance with this desire to reshape the program, the federal government indicated in the spring of 1977 that it wanted to move from open-ended formulas to a series of bilateral agreements under an umbrella agreement that would lay out general principles. This arrangement would also permit Ottawa to deal with the provinces one on one, rather than as a united front. The secretary of state also raised some program alternatives, including continuing the existing formula payments with more accountability and evaluation and an increased emphasis on development; terminating the formulas completely and expanding developmental activities; shifting to fiscal transfers for maintaining existing programs and expanding developmental activities; and linking federal contributions to provincial performance, rather than costs.[29] As Ottawa's proposals evolved over the course of the following two years, they increasingly focussed on shifting the federal role into funding development of new programs, rather than maintaining existing programs through the formula payments.[30]

The federal government also sought to control the spiralling cost of the BEP. In September 1978 Ottawa announced that the program, which had cost over $222 million in 1977–78 (see table 4.1), would be capped at $170 million for the following year. By December 1978, the federal government had elaborated a plan to phase its involvement completely into developmental projects, shifting 20 percent of its contributions each year for five years.[31] This move would allow the federal government to exercise more control over the programs, provide a more demonstrable link to new developments and permit more substantive evaluation. It would also satisfy the concerns of the FFHQ and Quebec's anglophones about the lack of incentives for development and the need for accountability. The provinces' rhetoric concerning their jurisdiction over minority-language education, so touted by Lévesque in Montreal, was thrown back in their faces by the Canadian government, which argued that ultimately the responsibility for education was a provincial

Table 4.1
Federal Contributions for Bilingualism in Education, 1970–1983 ($)

Year	Formula	Nonformula	Total
1970–71	49,950,000	558,933	50,508,933
1971–72	73,257,873	1,350,417	74,608,290
1972–73	64,527,152	3,055,623	67,582,775
1973–74	80,741,361	9,273,313	90,014,674
1974–75	78,973,637	11,880,201	90,853,838
1975–76	97,421,639	14,072,668	111,494,307
1976–77	142,848,870	19,960,600	162,809,470
1977–78	195,077,445	27,442,327	222,519,772
1978–79	178,113,302	31,670,046	209,783,349
1979–80	145,515,826	29,861,642	175,377,468
1980–81	141,951,109	29,819,035	171,770,144
1981–82	141,748,213	31,776,451	173,524,664
1982–83	140,000,000	36,276,619	176,276,619
Total	1,530,126,427	247,009,251	1,777,135,678

Source: Canada, Language Programmes Directorate, Education Support Programmes Branch, Secretary of State, *Federal-Provincial Programmes for the Official Languages in Education – Supplementary Tables, 1970–71 to 1981–82* (November 1983), 119.
Note: Formula payments were OLEP payments that were linked to a fixed percentage cost of providing minority- and second-language education. Nonformula payments were for the annex programs, including special projects.

one![32] If they were to secure continuation of the federal grants, the provinces would have to compromise.

The switch from the civil service approach to bilingualism to the youth option was generally accepted by the provinces, aside from Quebec, whose education minister noted that the Trudeau government was advocating a "concept of federalism that has led the government to interfere more and more in areas having to deal directly with education."[33] However, the provinces had a different conception from Ottawa concerning how the BEP should evolve. They wanted a longer-term commitment from the federal government to the BEP, to allow for greater stability, and more flexibility in how they could implement the program. Rather than phasing out the formula payments, they wanted higher federal contributions. Ontario proposed a 15.8 percent formula payment for second-language instruction, based on its additional costs.[34] Quebec, eager to remove federal tentacles, pushed for a fiscal transfer option for provinces that did not want to be bound by the formulas.[35]

The provinces were not overly enthusiastic about Ottawa's proposals. Although Ontario and New Brunswick indicated that more evaluation would be a good idea, they preferred to carry out their own evaluations and then share the results. Manitoba indicated some support for increased linkages between dollars and developments, provided that the provinces were involved in setting priorities. The provinces were also vaguely supportive of a new cultural component of the program.[36]

There were also many criticisms. The federal government's move towards a rights-based model of language education was decried as meddling.[37] Several provinces, led by Quebec, stressed the need to maintain the unconditional nature of the payments in order to protect provincial jurisdiction over priority setting. The shift from maintenance to development was also widely criticized, since it would create the public impression that funding was available for new programs without a concurrent awareness that federal money to maintain existing programs was being cut.

The decision to cap the BEP was also denounced by the provinces as the "old federal trick" of getting the provinces to commit themselves to programs and then pulling the financial rug out from under them.[38] The provinces argued that since they had participated in a program that was in the national interest, the Canadian government should continue to support this program. Quebec in particular, stood to lose between $350 and $380 million over the next five years. Feeling specifically targeted by the federal government, Quebec refused to commit itself to future involvement in the Summer Language Bursary and Official Language Monitors programs (which were normally negotiated separately) until the BEP issue was settled, effectively freezing these two programs. (The Summer Language Bursary Program allowed university students to travel to another province to spend several weeks learning their second language in an immersion environment. The Official Language Monitors Program paid university students, usually from French-language communities, to work as teaching assistants with second-language teachers.) There were also province-specific reactions to the new federal directions, which will be discussed later in this chapter. On the whole, there was much doubt whether the gulf between the federal government and the provinces could be bridged.

THIRD-PARTY INVOLVEMENT

As Canadian experience with the language policy of the Official Languages Act era proceeded, a number of new organizations formed and took an active interest in the future of the BEP. Many operated at the national level, received federal funding, and had a direct interest in the continued development of minority-language education and second-language instruction.

From within the government itself, the Office of the Commissioner of Official Languages, created in 1969, was increasingly assuming the role of advocate for the new programs. Keith Spicer, the first commissioner, was quite critical of the manner in which the federal government and the provinces developed their official-language programs, and routinely used blistering language in his Annual Reports to describe the development of the BEP. His successor, Maxwell Yalden, while somewhat more reserved than Spicer, was also a vocal critic of the 1978 cutbacks to the BEP. Of greater significance than the commissioners' words, however, was the role that the office played in the formation of a new pressure group. At a conference hosted by Commissioner Spicer in March 1977, Canadian Parents for French (CPF) was born.

Canadian Parents for French was initially a very small organization formed by parents committed to second-language learning. However, with federal funding from the Secretary of State, CPF quickly developed into a nation-wide organisation with chapters in each province and a regular newsletter. Its primary objective was to urge the federal and provincial governments to devote money and effort to providing opportunities for Canadian children to become proficient in their second language. The group was also intended to act as an information liaison, informing parents and schools about available programs in each province.[39]

Canadian Parents for French was keenly interested in the Bilingualism in Education Program and wanted to ensure that its second-language funds were used to maximum advantage. The group quickly became an advocate for accountability, and as a group of voters it could demand answers from the provincial governments that Ottawa could not. The CPF called on the CMEC to clarify the grant structures of the BEP in the provinces and to institute legislation for the mandatory teaching of French as a second language. It believed that by clarifying the nature of the grants available, parents could more effectively lobby individual school boards for change. As it noted: "too often local school boards use lack of money as an excuse for not offering more or better French programs. Parents who can produce accurate figures will have a better chance of countering this herring."[40]

The federal government was very pleased with the CPF's efforts and urged it to continue looking into community-level accountability, which even provincial governments had been reluctant to do.[41] The CPF followed this advice and in 1979 called for concentrated action at the local level to prevent provincial and local governments from using confusion over the BEP as a smokescreen for not expanding their programs.⁴² In addition, it routinely updated its membership about language-education rights and the state of development of second-language instruction in each province.

While Canadian Parents for French was dealing with second-language instruction issues, the Fédération des francophones hors-Québec was taking the provinces to task on the issue of minority-language education. In its November 1977 missive, "Les gouvernements jouent avec les minorités," the FFHQ lambasted the provinces for their proposal to raise the second-language formula to 15.8 percent, while not doing anything to increase funding for minority-language programs. As it pointed out, "What good will it do to have anglophones in Canada understand French as a second language if francophones outside Quebec continue to be assimilated?"⁴³ The FFHQ continued to demand the establishment of minority-language education rights and called on the provinces to pay more attention to their francophone minorities.

The CMEC's January 1978 report on minority-language education was also the object of vivid criticism. In "De l'action, s.v.p.," the FFHQ criticized *The State of Minority Language in the Ten Provinces of Canada* as a waste of time that failed to develop any recommendations or action plans and that was prepared without consulting the minorities that it purported to be investigating.⁴⁴ This lack of consultation by the CMEC would become an increasingly sore spot for the FFHQ. In its September 1978 press release, "Premiers concernés, derniers consultés," the federation decried its continued exclusion from CMEC meetings that were being held to discuss the future of the BEP and attacked the federal government for its cuts to the program.⁴⁵ Frustration with the CMEC had been building for quite some time. The FFHQ had first attempted to meet with the CMEC in March 1978. Repeated overtures were met with the same response: the CMEC refused to meet peer-to-peer with their leaders and told them that the FFHQ's provincial component organisations should instead meet with provincial ministries of education. The CMEC claimed that it would be pointless for the FFHQ to meet with them, since the CMEC did not have the ultimate decision-making power; the provinces did.⁴⁶ To an external observer, it is clear that to have acceded to the FFHQ's demands for a peer-to-peer meeting would have been tantamount to conceding the national, pan-Canadian nature of official languages in education and would have undermined the provincial position that these issues could be regulated at the provincial level.

The FFHQ was cognisant that while final decisions were indeed made at the provincial level, the main forum for discussions and policy setting was the CMEC and thus that participation in this process would be extremely valuable. Indeed, the FFHQ had been created in part to have a national organisation to deal with other interprovincial and national bodies, such as the CMEC and the federal government. But the CMEC continued to refuse to meet with the FFHQ, and thus its lobbying efforts continued to be restricted to areas outside the official forums of the federal-provincial discussions.

DEVELOPMENTS IN THE PROVINCES

While federal-provincial negotiations about the future of Canada's official language policies were going on, the BEP continued to evolve in each province. Provincial governments, some of which changed political stripe, continued to develop and implement new language programs in education and to shape their responses to Ottawa's proposals. Lobby groups were also highly active in this period, seeking input into provincial decision making and trying to keep the new programs active and moving forward. Bearing this in mind, we now return to the six provinces to determine what was shaping their approach to the BEP between November 1976 and March 1979.

QUEBEC

Of all the provincial governments, Quebec's was certainly the one most changed since November 1976. The Parti Québécois quickly set about implementing its agenda, including the language legislation discussed above. The shift in government also had implications for the future participation of the province in the Bilingualism in Education Program and other national programs. While Quebec remained involved in the BEP, it qualified its participation in the following manner: "All new arrangements ... will necessarily be affected by Quebec's political evolution and, as such, must be considered provisional."[47]

René Lévesque was determined to ensure that the federal government would not be allowed to play divide and conquer with the provinces on the official-languages front. Thus, within the forum of the CMEC, an organisation whose importance grew significantly in the latter years of the decade, Quebec pushed for a united front in negotiations with Ottawa. It feared that a series of ten bilaterally negotiated agreements with each province would allow the federal government to intrude more significantly into education and reduce the amount of money that would flow to Quebec under future arrangements.[48]

From Quebec's perspective, Ottawa's new directions held the prospect of several new intrusions in education and were in direct conflict with the direction in which the PQ was heading with its language policy. The federal government was pushing for a definition of the program objectives that would entail open access to minority-language education, while the province wanted to make sure that access was limited to current Quebec citizens who were members of the official-language minority group, in conformity with Bill 101.[49] The secretary of state's thrust towards a developmental angle was likewise considered jurisdictional interference in education, with a completely arbitrary constitutional justification. Quebec reminded Ottawa that the decision to fund existing programs was a federal one, initiated as part of its language policy, and that it was acceptable only insofar as it did not interfere with provincial priorities.[50]

In a similar vein, Ottawa's insistence on linking the BEP payments to additional costs continued to be rejected by Quebec, which maintained that these costs were so integral to the province's education system that an analysis of which costs were additional would be impossible. However, in 1979 the province did attempt such a study, which tried to prove that minority- and second-language programs cost the province $117 million, which could be eliminated by phasing them out.[51] Oddly, this report was based on the assumption that the per-student cost of the per-student cost of the Protestant school boards was $117 higher than the per-student cost of the Catholic boards. This discrepancy was curious, since provincial grants to the Protestant School Board of Greater Montreal (PSBGM) were lower than provincial grants to any Catholic school board on Montreal island. Moreover, the province had long maintained that there was no reason to provide additional funding to the English-language boards, since they did not cost any more than their Catholic counterparts![52] Ottawa's accountability proposals were also viewed with suspicion. The term used for accountability in the French versions of these proposals was "responsabilité," which implied a greater federal role in education than the province deemed acceptable.[53]

The Parti Québécois was increasingly conscious that the federal government had never wanted to fund Quebec's fully developed programs and that the other provinces were similarly upset that Quebec received the lion's share of the grants. All the proposed modifications to the BEP would cost the province money. Indeed, its formula payments were going to decline anyway as Bill 101's provisions began to kick in, reducing English-language education enrolments. Quebec thus began to push for a fiscal transfer or an opting-out provision in the BEP that would allow Quebec to receive financial compensation.[54]

Quebec was also faced with Prime Minister Trudeau's attempt to parlay the St Andrews agreement into constitutional entrenchment of minority-language education rights. The Parti Québécois fought this development, which could further enshrine Ottawa's role as the protector of official-language minority communities. Indeed, anglophone organisations in the province, including the Quebec Federation of Home and School Associations (QFHSA) and the PSBGM were keen to see Ottawa take on this role and called for a constitutional entrenchment of the right to freedom of choice in the language of education.[55] Any federal document that appeared soft on Bill 101 was roundly criticized by these groups, who wanted to ensure that Ottawa was not sliding away from its commitment to freedom of choice. They also continued to lobby the federal government to ensure that accountability remained high on the agenda. Their campaign included briefs, letters, and targeted action aimed at cabinet ministers from Quebec.

The only nonfrancophone organisation in the province that seemed amenable to the PQ's policies was the Council of Quebec Minorities (CQM, formed in November 1978), which wanted to find ways for the minority communities to make the best of Bill 101 and ensure that the diversity of minority life in the province was protected.[56] Indeed, the council was careful to completely avoid the use of the word "English" anywhere in its constitution. However, the CQM was not nearly as activist or vocal as the QFHSA and the PSBGM, which continued to occupy the spotlight on the question of education rights in Quebec.

Clearly, Quebec was a critical player in the debates swirling around issues of bilingualism in the late 1970s. Between its language laws, its preparation for a referendum on sovereignty-association, and its central position in the debates on the BEP, it was at the centre of all debates on issues of language rights. By early 1979, it was not at all clear what role Quebec would have in the future of the BEP, but it was obvious that any solution to the controversies surrounding the program's future would need to accommodate its interests in one form or another.

ALBERTA

Alberta was sympathetic to Quebec's attempts to stave off federal "intrusions" in education, and Alberta's officials noted that their responses to CMEC and federal proposals were often similar to those of Quebec. Alberta strongly resisted federal attempts to impose its priorities on evaluation and to shift funds from maintenance to development, both of which were considered to have an unacceptable steering effect on provincial programs.[57] Its position was made more obstinate by its concurrent efforts to deal with Trudeau's interventionist energy and resource policies, both of which were viewed with great hostility by Peter Lougheed's government.

In other respects Alberta was not in accord with *la belle province*. For instance, it favoured a move towards a bilateral approach to the BEP, since bilateralism would permit changes to better reflect provincial needs. Education Minister Julian Koziak also wanted the formula payments altered to reflect true additional costs. Koziak called for an increase to the minority-language education formula so that the federal government would be paying for between one-third and two-thirds of the cost of these programs.[58] Ontario's proposed 15.8 percent formula for second-language instruction programs, however, was viewed as excessive for the province's needs.

Alberta's officials were tempted by several other proposals that were floated during this period. While concerned by the interference that a complete shift of Ottawa's funding towards developmental projects would entail, they recognized that this change would mean additional funding for Alberta.[59] A proposal from Manitoba to move to a per-capita funding model would also favour Alberta, increasing its annual grant by $12 million. Officials did not, however, come out strongly in favour of either of these proposals, because they believed that they would not meet with approval from other provinces and that voicing support for them could undermine Alberta's negotiating position.

English-French bilingualism in Alberta had never been a major priority for the provincial government, and its main role in the late-1970s BEP negotiations was to push for increased funding for multilingual education. It had already acted independently to develop language-education programs for its larger German and Ukrainian communities, and the Edmonton Public School Board also offered programs in Cree and Hebrew. Department of Education staff produced a number of proposals to the federal government and to the CMEC to see if funding for these other second-language programs might be feasible,[60] but they generally came to naught, lacking support from other provinces.

Although the Alberta government was interested in multilingual programs, it was also faced with a constant barrage of lobbying efforts to keep official bilingualism on its agenda. The founding of Canadian Parents for French had a major impact on Alberta; membership in CPF was particularly high in Western Canada. The CPF's Alberta wing engaged in a major push for the development of French-immersion programs that proved to be very successful, as pilot immersion programs in Calgary and Edmonton proved to be very popular and made the national news.[61]

The CPF also pooled its efforts with the Association canadienne-française de l'Alberta (ACFA) to work for French-language schools, both minority-language and immersion schools.[62] In much of the province, particularly in the south, Franco-Albertans were numerically insufficient to warrant the creation of French-language educational programs. The support of anglophones who wanted French immersion often created enough demand to warrant the establishment of French instructional programs, albeit not necessarily as French in cultural character as some Franco-Albertans may have wished.

The period from 1977 onwards was a particularly important time for ACFA. Having adopted a new action plan at the 1976 congress, education coordinator Alain Nogue began work in August 1977 to lobby the government and school boards for increased French minority-language programming. As he prepared for this task, the model of Manitoba's Bureau de l'éducation française (BEF) proved to be very useful. In addition to standard lobbying efforts on a personal level with the minister and deputy minister of education, a substantial community mobilization effort was undertaken. Research studies, including studies by Jim Cummins and Bruce Bain, were used to demonstrate the efficacy of French-language education to the Franco-Albertan communities. Nogue worked with local parent committees to lobby school boards and held community forums that debated the merits of minority-language education programs. In addition, the financial carrot of the BEP grants was regularly used as an inducement for the school boards.[63]

ACFA also continued to lobby for the constitutional right to French-language education, arguing that the St Andrews promise of a "best efforts" approach to minority-language education should include this right.[64] The association urged school boards to move towards the goal of 80 percent French programs and to create a French atmosphere in schools offering such programs. Furthermore, it called on the government to intervene in cases of school jurisdictions that were blocking transportation arrangements that would permit students to travel to districts where French-language education was offered.[65]

ACFA used arguments that were designed to appeal to the self-interested perspective of English speakers in Alberta. In defending the need for both minority- and second-language education programs, ACFA and the CPF pointed to the increasing need for bilingual applicants for new jobs that were being created in the federal government and elsewhere,[66] thereby arguing for bilingualism from a functional as well as a rights perspective. Moreover, ACFA noted that support for French minority language education, in the light of the Péquiste election, could be viewed as a key indication of support for national unity.[67]

The campaign by ACFA and the CPF had a significant impact on Alberta's French programs in this period. The province announced in February 1978 that it was going to chip in $2.5 million of its own funding to expand its French programs, tripling the support staff at the departmental level. The following month, Julian Koziak announced that his department intended to top up the federal grants with its own money.[68] This undertaking was fulfilled in November 1978 with the announcement of additional provincial grants to small schools in rural areas to offset the additional cost of running the programs.⁶⁹ In 1978 the province even gave a grant to ACFA to permit it to hire a support person for its educational coordinator who would work with local and regional French-education committees. Thus, while Alberta was still fighting to protect provincial jurisdiction in education and was resisting the constitutional option proposed by the federal government, by 1979 it was expanding its support for official-language programs in education and was finally beginning to commit some of its own funds to them.

MANITOBA

Of all of the provinces, Manitoba had by far the most advanced grant structure under the Bilingualism in Education Program in the mid-1970s, including special short-term developmental grants for minority-language education, on top of its regular grants for official-languages education. It was also the only province to require strict accounting from school boards for the use of these funds. In 1977 the province was already spending 35 percent of its federal grants on new developmental initiatives, a percentage that increased each year.⁷⁰ The BEF also entered into an agreement with the government of Quebec in 1977 to help with its pedagogical-development programs and to assist in the recruitment of new French teachers.⁷¹

The Bureau de l'éducation française, once a temporary section of the Department of Education, was moving towards a more standard bureaucratic model in 1976–77 and was aware that its survival depended on its ability to function as a normal division of the civil service. By 1977 it had withdrawn its staff from community-mobilization initiatives, the model that was now proving so useful in Alberta. Education Minister Ian Turnbull noted that it was not the intention of the bureau to promote one type of French-language program over another and that it was not the role of the government to assume an advocacy role in this sector.⁷² Senior bureaucrats in the Department of Education had been uncomfortable with the community-mobilization activities from the start, and the Conservative party was downright hostile to them. Indeed, the entire push for 80 percent French programming had created some significant unrest at the local level; a French-only school in St Vital was called an example of "separatism" when it opened in April 1977.⁷³ The process of normalisation had been completed by October 1977, when the Conservative Party, led by Sterling Lyon, came to power.

The election of the Lyon government was not a positive development for French-language education in the province of Manitoba. While the number of programs was not reduced and grant structures were left intact, there was no significant new growth under this government.

Within the first month after his election, Sterling Lyon called Ottawa's policy on bilingualism a failure and noted that Western Canadians did not share the Ottawa's "overwhelming preoccupation with linguistic and cultural affairs."[74] Lionel Orlikow, the deputy minister who had shepherded so much of the early development of the BEF, was fired almost immediately. The Lyon government adopted a policy direction towards increased local governance in educational matters. A proposed revision of Bill 113, dubbed Bill 22, would have restricted the pool of children that could be drawn upon to create a French-language school to the school level, rather than an entire district, a change that would have had a chilling effect on the creation of new programs.[75] The Lyon government era was also overshadowed by a constitutional challenge to Manitoba's Official Language Act. In March 1975, Georges Forest filed suit against the Manitoba government, claiming that the act violated the terms of the Manitoba Act, 1870. Throughout this period, as the Forest case was winding its way through the Manitoba court system, it was increasingly politicizing debates over French-language rights in the province and polarizing the population. In December 1979 the Supreme Court would rule in Forest's favour, declaring the Official Language Act of 1890 unconstitutional.[76]

The Franco-Manitoban community did not ease off its demands for improved programming. A great deal of progress had been made in the community-mobilization era. In 1974, 47 percent of French minority-language students were in programs that offered less than 40 percent of daily instruction in French, and only 28 percent were in programs offering 70 percent or more. By 1978 these figures were reversed.[77] The BEF now had fifteen full-time staff, compared to two in Nova Scotia and three in Alberta, which had comparably sized francophone populations. The Franco-Manitoban community called for the inclusion of a cultural aspect in the French schools and the elimination of mixed schools, which were called parts of "un système bâtard" that led to anglicization.[78] The community, supported by Canadian Parents for French, wanted a greater distinction between French minority-language schools and French-immersion programs and the development of separate pedagogical models and facilities for these two different objectives. Both the CPF and the Franco-Manitoban organisations also called on the government to improve transportation funding so that students could in fact get to the French-language schools.[79]

Regarding the Bilingualism in Education Program, the province was concerned that the current structure of the formula payments was very unfavourable to it. The province had 4.5 percent of Canada's population, 3.2 percent of the official-language minority population, and 4.2 percent of the majority-language population, and yet it received only 2 percent of BEP formula funding.[80] If formula payments were to be continued, Manitoba wanted them reoriented to better reflect the ratio of the province's population to that of the rest of Canada. Manitoba also supported linking federal funds to the progress that had been made since the inception of the BEP, an area where it had clearly been a leader.

Finally, it is noteworthy that while the Conservative government was not particularly supportive of bilingualism in the late 1970s, the staff of the BEF was strongly supportive of the aspirations of the Franco-Manitoban community. Indeed, the bureau provides an excellent example of the operation of the embedded state. Defending the BEP, it supported Ottawa's demands for accountability and its call to move away from formula payments towards bilateral agreements that more effectively met community needs.[81] In 1979 the BEF even came out in favour of enshrining Franco-Manitoban educational rights in the constitution, although Premier Lyon was opposed to doing so and to Trudeau's proposal for a Charter of Rights and Freedoms.[82]

ONTARIO

Ontario continued to be under fire for the manner in which it spent federal grant money. In April 1977 a *Toronto Star* report claimed that 65 percent of the federal grants received for minority-language education were in fact being spent on second-language instruction programs.[83] While the province had secured federal approval to use the BEP grants as it saw fit, pressure from the media and francophone organizations prompted the government to change its approach. Accordingly, in April 1977 Education Minister Thomas Wells introduced a new grant structure under which all grants had to be clearly linked to program spending and boards had to submit their plans for using the grants in advance in order to receive funding. In addition, minority-language grants were significantly increased, tripling at the elementary level.[84] The shift in the formula also paid for performance: second-language grants were increased as time spent in the programs increased, which would provide an incentive for immersion-style programs.

The province also increased its spending on capital costs. Ninety-five percent of the cost of constructing new French-language instructional units at the secondary level would be covered by the province, and the French-language learning-material fund was increased from $250,000 in 1975 to $2.5 million in 1978. Combined with the new grant formulas, this change had the cumulative effect of increasing minority-language education grants to school boards significantly, from $5.8 million in 1973–74, to $8.8 million in 1976–77, to $17.1 million in 1977–78.[85]

Some problems remained. There were conflicts at the local level over whether the school boards or the French Language Advisory Committees were responsible for the distribution and management of the funds, and there were allegations of abuse of power on both sides.[86] There was also concern about the accountability provisions built into the grants, which permitted up to 35 percent of the grants to be used on vaguely defined indirect costs. In the Carleton Catholic School Board, inquiries into the use of the provincial grants were beginning to turn up some disturbing revelations about the actual (not reported) use of the grants, controversies over which would come to a head in 1979–80.

The Franco-Ontarian community was also greatly angered by the Department of Education's proposed 15.8 percent formula for second-language instruction. ACFO saw it as denying the importance of minority-language education, which, it argued, should receive at least as much funding.[87] The issue of school management was also beginning to increase in importance, as a consortium of Franco-Ontarian organisations (ACFO and the Franco-Ontarian associations of educators, school commissioners, parents, and superintendents) called in 1977 for a homogenous French-language school board for the Ottawa-Carleton region.[88]

The persistence of mixed schools continued to preoccupy the Franco-Ontarian community; their concerns were echoed by education experts. A study conducted by Stacy Churchill at the Ontario Institute for Studies in Education (OISE) denounced the mixed schools as "an almost total denial of basic educational needs on a massive scale," and as a means of transferring students between languages.[89] The community was also not satisfied with the slow-and-steady French-language-services policy of the government. A bill to guarantee French-language services, introduced by Liberal MLA Albert Roy, was killed by the government because it was seen as going too far, given the current state of development of these services.[90] The government received three thousand letters between April 1978 and February 1979 from members of ACFO, all denouncing this decision.[91]

The Davis government also had to contend with Ontario's English-speaking majority, various elements of which were opposed to the government's bilingualism initiatives. The Alliance for the Preservation of English in Canada (APEC), which was formed in 1977 in reaction to the PQ's election, organised two thousand letters in opposition to any French-language services over the same period that ACFO sent its letter. Moreover, the government had to make sure that more moderate elements of its English-speaking majority saw the bilingualism grants as benefiting them as well. Its approach in negotiations with the federal government reflected this balancing act. Ontario's main contribution was the 15.8 percent proposal for second-language instruction, which was very expensive for the province.[92] This was the major priority of Ontario's language-education policy in this period, and one in need of more funds, particularly given inflation and dropping enrolments. Ideally, Ontario wanted the formula payments to continue to be unconditional, although it was willing to provide additional accountability and the results of its evaluations.

In 1978 the Department of Education realized that it had no contingency plan for funding French-language programs without federal money and that local expectations had risen to the point that cutting off these programs was not a viable option.[93] To avert the prospect of Ottawa cancelling the BEP, Bette Stephenson, the new minister of education, advised CMEC president Jacques-Yvan Morin to tone down his rhetoric concerning federal intervention in education, since it might give the Canadian government further excuses to withdraw from funding the maintenance of existing programs.[94] Ontario's officials were aware that the public did not know which level of government was funding the various programs and thus decided to support increased visibility for the federal government's contributions, so that the province could point fingers if funding was cut off; otherwise, programs begun with federal seed money would have to be funded by the province when the money dried up. Thus, as BEP negotiations were reaching a critical point in 1979, Ontario was playing a strategic balancing game, trying to satisfy both the Franco-Ontarian minority community and the English-speaking majority, while also attempting to increase federal funding without increasing federal intervention.

NEW BRUNSWICK

As New Brunswick headed into the late 1970s, the overall tenor of its programs remained fundamentally the same. In January 1977 the Department of Education rolled out a new policy on French-immersion programs that became eligible for increased provincial grants provided that 40 percent of instructional time was in French.[95] Increased grants were allocated to minority-language schools and bilingual districts in 1978. The province moved towards a 1,200-hour program for FSL in October 1978, up from the 750-hour program in effect before then. The establishment of a dual structure in the Department of Education also proceeded apace, aided by the federal grants.

Pressure groups in New Brunswick also continued to present their demands to the provincial government. Leaders of the Société des Acadiens du Nouveau-Brunswick (SANB), with the support of the Association des enseignants francophones de Nouveau-Brunswick (AEFNB), continued their campaign for a dual school-board structure, whereby a network of school boards, one French and one English, would completely cover the provincial map. The campaign had some success, as Bathurst moved to two unilingual school boards in 1978.[96] The SANB also pressed for a reorganisation of the use of BEP funds. On a more radical level, the Parti Acadien, which called for an autonomous Acadian province, ran candidates in the 1978 election and won 12 percent of the vote.[97] By the late 1970s, the word "bilingual" was beginning to take on negative connotations in Acadian New Brunswick, where it was increasingly seen as code for assimilation.[98]

Pressures were also levied on the provincial government from the other side of the debate. The New Brunswick Teachers' Association (NBTA) expressed concern over the perceived neglect of FSL programs to the benefit of French immersion. Amidst growing redundancy in its ranks, it was particularly concerned that anglophones were not being considered for the new jobs created in the immersion programs.[99] It called for an increase in the attention paid to the core FSL programs and improved teacher recruitment policies. Radicalism also existed in the English-speaking communities of New Brunswick. Anglophone militants organised a mail-in campaign to the government in the winter of 1978, with cards reading, "I STRONGLY OBJECT TO MY TAX DOLLARS BEING USED TO PROMOTE ENFORCED BILINGUALISM IN THIS PROVINCE BY MEANS OF FRENCH SCHOOLS AND IMMERSION CLASSES. *What can YOU do to have english declared the official language of this province?*" (emphasis in original).[100] Clearly, there was a wide range of opinion in the province over how best to address issues of official languages in education.

To cope with the growing tensions over community duality, New Brunswick increasingly pressed for a more global approach to bilingualism in the federal programs.[101] The province wanted to make sure that programs to promote bilingualism also increased understanding between the two linguistic groups and believed that this goal could be better achieved through a more holistic funding approach. In addition to diplomatic initiatives spearheaded by Premier Hatfield to foster understanding between language groups, such as the St Andrews declaration, New Brunswick also pushed for less rigid approaches to federal-provincial relations in the BEP negotiations. Deputy Ministers of Education Harvey Malmberg and Armand Saintonge proposed a funding model to address the systemic costs of bilingualism, rather than per-student costs, and supported both the developmental thrust proposed by the federal government and the increased accountability provisions.[102]

New Brunswick hoped that the next round of BEP agreements would give it increased funding to deal with the steep costs of making the provincial administration officially bilingual. It was willing to cozy up to the federal government and bend jurisdictional prerogatives in order to attain this objective. In this respect, New Brunswick was the polar opposite of Quebec and Alberta, as it moved decisively towards official bilingualism, a state of affairs that would make Quebec's vision of a united provincial negotiating front difficult to achieve.

NOVA SCOTIA

Following the federal-provincial conference in Banff in May 1977, Nova Scotia's government noted that it was generally pleased with the progress made to date on both Acadian and French second-language programming, particularly the programs in the Acadian regions. Ottawa's proposals for new cultural components of the BEP were welcomed. However, its officials did oppose any attempt to reduce funding levels, particularly given the province's plan to expand FSL at the elementary level. Federal attempts to link funding to performance were also resisted, since they were seen as overly open to subjectivity.[103] On the whole, Nova Scotia was not particularly adamant about any aspect of the BEP negotiations, aside from supporting increased federal funding levels, which were seen as quite important in a province without a particularly strong tax base.

The Fédération acadienne de la Nouvelle-Écosse (FANE) continued to lobby the Liberal government of Premier Gerald Regan and Education Minister George Mitchell. FANE denounced Lévesque's reciprocal agreements, arguing that it was nonsensical to make guarantees to a migrant Quebec population that were not yet in place for Acadians.[104] FANE was still trying to bring its rather conservative Acadian population around to the notion of increased French educational programming and to overcome distrust in the community.[105] Given Nova Scotia's historic treatment of French-language education, it is understandable that Acadian parents were reluctant to enrol their children in French programming. Even school commissions in largely Acadian regions, such as Argyle, were not in favour of homogenous French-only schools, preferring bilingual programs.[106] Parents believed that if their children were bilingual, they would be better able to compete for jobs. They also feared that a backlash from the province's English-speaking majority might result from linguistically divided schooling. Despite these community fears, FANE hoped to leverage Nova Scotia's support for the St Andrews declaration into more concrete action for French-language education.

Assimilation rates were continuing to increase in Nova Scotia, as was intermarriage with members of the anglophone communities, and the Acadian schools were taking on an increasingly English character as the assimilated student population increased in number.[107] To counter these trends, FANE targeted three main priorities: "the equality of the French language as a language of education; the protection of the francophone character of the Acadian communities; the control of Acadian institutions."[108] The federal programs seemed to be the best route to achieving these objectives. FANE was made aware of a number of local complaints about misallocation of BEP funds, including expenditures on audiovisual equipment and sewing machines, and began to demand explanations from the provincial government.[109] It called for accountability for the use of the funds and for more publicity about the programs to bring them into the public eye. As this pressure campaign continued, increasing numbers of special projects were targeted at the Acadian population. In the view of many Acadians, without the federal government, "many of our rights would be forgotten or ignored," and thus these programs were seen as critically important in the communities.[110]

The Liberal government did introduce some changes as a result of the BEP funds and FANE's pressure. Cost-sharing arrangements were worked out between school districts to enable students to travel for French programs, and additional staff were hired to work with the assistant director of youth education responsible for French education.[111] In September 1977 the first total-immersion classes were opened in Halifax: eight years after the first proposals for such classes were killed at the school board level.

In October 1978 a new premier, Conservative John Buchanan, was sworn in. Under Buchanan's government, the Acadian leaders began to make progress that had not been possible under the Liberals. Indeed, the government asked for FANE's input for the BEP negotiations in February 1979. In its first head-to-head meeting with the premier and Education Minister Terence Donahoe, held in March 1979, FANE won acceptance of the principle that French education was a necessity for the Acadian population and recognition that existing structures provided for this purpose were not sufficient to meet Acadian needs.[112]

Donahoe seemed open to real change for the Acadian population, and FANE seized on this opportunity to legally entrench French-language education. While meeting with the minister, the federation pushed for legal recognition for French education, the establishment of mechanisms for anglophones to participate fully in the Acadian programs, and the development of more French-immersion programs. As a first major step, they sought a curriculum that would be 100 percent French for grades kindergarden to 6, and then at least 50 percent French for grades 7 to 12, along with the establishment of an Acadian section in the Department of Education to provide curriculum direction.[113] The initial signs from the newly elected government were positive. Thus, there was a certain optimism among the Acadian leaders that the objectives they had been fighting for since the beginning of the BEP might in fact be realized in the near future.

CONCLUSION: MARCH 1979 – THE HAIL MARY PASS INTO LIMBO

As the second Bilingualism in Education Program agreements wound down to their close in the winter of 1979, little had been agreed upon. The federal government, faced with a mounting deficit and rising costs, slashed its funding for bilingualism programs. In February it announced its intention to cut bilingualism funding by a third. Rather than increasing from $455 million to $500 million, as had been predicted the previous year, funding would be cut down to $349 million.[114]

In the absence of an agreement with the provinces, the federal government also slashed the Bilingualism in Education Program, which had cost a whopping $209 million in 1978–79, back to a maximum of $170 million. Out of this total, only $140 million was to be made available for formula payments, and the rest was to be spent on the annex programs. With the hope that the next year would be more fruitful in terms of reaching a multiyear federal-provincial agreement, the BEP was renewed for one more year.

The future of Trudeau's approach to bilingualism was quite doubtful in March 1979. His government had been steadily slipping in popularity, and its future was far from secure. On 26 March 1979, an election was called for 22 May, an election that Trudeau was not certain of winning, given the rising popularity of Joe Clark's Conservatives. Moreover, the Quebec government was poised to announce a referendum date. The referendum had been promised to come before the end of the Parti Québécois' term, and Lévesque had now been in office for almost three and a half years.

The other provinces were deeply divided on their approaches to bilingualism. New Brunswick was firmly committed to becoming officially bilingual and stood alone among the provinces in this respect. Other provinces, such as Ontario and Manitoba, had made great strides towards increased French-language services but remained opposed to locking their governments into an obligation to official bilingualism. Still others, such as Alberta and Nova Scotia, had made gains in their French-language services but lagged behind in their willingness to guarantee these services or even to take leadership in their expansion. Quebec was most adamant in its rejection of official bilingualism and indeed had been moving towards French unilingualism and the rejection of all federal intervention in its jurisdiction over language and education. Moreover, the Parti Québécois had been trying to expand provincial jurisdiction at the expense of the federal government, and it was attempting to circumvent Trudeau's efforts to guarantee official-language-minority education rights. Quebec thus stood as a major roadblock in the federal government's efforts to steer the provinces towards an intrastate approach to minority-language education rights.

Despite these factors, not all signs pointed to the death of the Canadian government's official languages programs. While Ottawa was cutting back on the amount of funding it was willing to devote to the BEP, it had not cancelled the program outright, and cuts to the BEP were less deep than to other language programs. An increasingly wide network of organisations, including the CPF, the FFHQ, ACELF, and a wide array of provincial groups committed to minority- and second-language education were all working to ensure the preservation of these programs and strongly supported continuing federal involvement in this sector. Moreover, in many provinces the question was no longer whether such services would be provided but in what form: a critical shift of discourse. Finally, through the St Andrews and Montreal declarations, the nine anglophone premiers had all publicly committed themselves to the continuance and expansion of minority-language education programs. They had taken a key public step towards acceptance of minority-language education rights: a step that would play into the federal government's strategy for constitutional change.

The Trudeau government could cite some important successes in advancing its intrastate approach to official languages. While the provinces still resisted allowing the federal government to dictate the form of language-education programs and their evaluation, a decade of federal funding had locked the provinces into providing these programs for their citizens. Moreover, the PQ's language policy had forced the other provinces closer to Trudeau's conception of language rights in education. It remained to be seen, however, whether the federal government could capitalize on these gains, increase its role in crafting language programs in education, and perhaps secure provincial consent to establish official-language-minority education rights in a reformed constitution. To accomplish this, the Trudeau government would need to retain its hold on office, defeat the Péquiste referendum on sovereignty-association for Quebec, and somehow convince the strong advocates of interstate federalism, led by Quebec and Alberta, that Ottawa's approach to language policy was necessary. These tasks would preoccupy the federal government for the next four years, and it is to them that we now turn.

CHAPTER FIVE

The Constitutional Debâcle and the Rise of Language Rights, 1979–1983

At the beginning of spring 1979, the Bilingualism in Education Program agreements had lapsed, but had been provisionally extended for one year. The newly rechristened Official Languages in Education Program (OLEP) had a budget of only $140 million for formula payments, which were paid out at the reduced rates of 6.65 percent, 3.7 percent, and 1.11 percent for the 1979/80 fiscal year.[1] The program would be provisionally extended three more times before a new multiyear protocol agreement was reached in December 1983.

While negotiations continued between the federal and provincial governments on the future of the OLEP, there were several higher-profile issues dominating federal-provincial relations. Of these, the Quebec referendum and the constitutional patriation process bore directly on the future of Canada's official-languages policies. The Trudeau government was frustrated with the slow pace of change that funding programs had engendered in language rights during the 1970s. Seeking to solidify both official bilingualism in Canada and a role for the federal government in the defence of official-language minorities, Ottawa moved on the legal/constitutional front to enshrine the constitutional rights of official-language minorities to education in their mother tongue in the new Canadian Charter of Rights and Freedoms. This campaign was ultimately successful. Bolstered by the embedded state, the financial incentives of the OLEP, and the premiers' own declaration at St Andrews, Trudeau was able to convince the provinces to support the inclusion of minority-language education rights in the Charter.

While the constitutional debates of 1980–81 largely overshadowed the ongoing OLEP negotiations and in effect precluded the conclusion of a new agreement, their outcomes shaped the positions taken by Ottawa and the provinces. Once minority-language rights had been constitutionally guaranteed, the pace of negotiations to reach a new multiyear agreement accelerated rapidly. Alongside these developments, the provinces continued their implementation of their official-language education programs. These three major threads of official-languages development affected both each other and the protocol agreement reached in 1983. This chapter looks first at provincial-level developments in language policy during 1979–1983 and then turns to the development of the Charter of Rights and Freedoms and its ramifications for official languages. It concludes with an analysis of the OLEP negotiations and the impacts of these tumultuous years on Canadian federalism and the future of Canadian language policies.

ALBERTA

In July 1979, David King, who replaced Julian Koziak as Alberta's education minister, requested a review of all programs that were designed to encourage accessibility to French-language education. The review was intended to determine the extent of Alberta's support for the programs and to explore ways in which they could be improved.[2] In earlier years, Alberta's officials had taken the view that they were merely acting as disbursement agents for the federal grants, and they did not top up the federal contribution to official-languages programs. Nor did they take much interest in elaborating an independent language policy for education.

David King, a supporter of official languages and national unity, took a different approach. In May 1980 his department indicated that Alberta would top up the reduced federal grants for minority-language education back to the 9 percent level for all French-language programs covering at least 25 percent of instructional time.[3] The government also agreed to top up the second-language instructional grants to the 5 percent level until 31 December 1981. Alberta took additional steps to support French-language education programs. Transportation grants to school boards offering French-language or immersion programs were tripled in September 1980, and the School Act was modified to allow children to attend school in another jurisdiction where French-language instruction was offered.[4]

Despite these improvements, there was nevertheless some disappointment about results and resistance at a philosophical level to the French-language programs. The major shortage of qualified French teachers persisted, and the Alberta government was not willing to spend additional funds to recruit teachers from other provinces for this purpose. FSL enrolment had also continued to fall throughout the decade, from 28.9 percent to 22.7 percent at the elementary level and from 43.4 percent to 28.3 percent at the secondary level from 1972–73 to 1978–79, and the government was taking no major steps to reverse this trend.[5] Moreover, in the years leading up to the adoption of the Charter, Alberta reiterated its opposition to the constitutional entrenchment of language rights in education and to language rights in the School Act.[6]

Resistance also persisted within the Franco-Albertan community to homogenous French-language schools. The Association canadienne-française de l'Alberta (ACFA) largely left this issue to decisions at the local level, although it did begin to urge separate facilities for immersion and minority-language programs in the early 1980s.[7] Seventy percent of students in Alberta's French-language programs had English as their mother tongue, and Canadian Parents for French (CPF) was among the most important organisations in the province for the promotion of French-language education and a key ally for ACFA. On a practical level, the children of the CPF parents furnished the necessary numbers to open French-language schools in many jurisdictions. CPF was quite vigorous in advocating the right of parents to have their children educated in either official language and repeated this message regularly to the Lougheed government.[8] Other organisations in the province, such as the Alberta Teachers' Association, the Alberta Cultural Heritage Council, and the Canadian Council of Christians and Jews, also came to support this position.[9] Indeed, by the early 1980s, middle-class urban anglophones were proving to be very important allies in the Franco-Albertan quest for French-language rights and were beginning to have a moderating effect on the government's position. In this respect, the Bilingualism in Education Program had significantly altered Alberta's political culture as the province's leaders moved towards greater openness to bilingualism and French-language educational programming.

MANITOBA

By the late 1970s the Bilingualism in Education Program had slid into the background as far as most Manitobans involved with official languages were concerned. On 13 December 1979, ruling on the *Forest* case, the Supreme Court declared the 1890 Official Language Act invalid.[10] This decision forced the government of Sterling Lyon to develop a policy on bilingualism that would satisfy the requirements of the Manitoba Act, 1870. As political scientist Raymond Hébert describes this period, "From the beginning, it is obvious that the Lyon government was to be as miserly as legally possible in the recognition of French-language rights in Manitoba."[11] The Lyon government was also deeply opposed to the Trudeau government's attempts to enshrine the Charter of Rights and Freedoms in the Constitution. Thus, until the Conservative government was defeated by Howard Pawley's NDP in November 1981, a rather tense atmosphere reigned in Manitoba politics concerning issues of bilingualism.

While the Lyon government may not have been overly favourable to expanding French-language services, the Bureau de l'éducation française (BEF) was sufficiently ensconced by 1979 to operate without excessive governmental interference. Like other provincial government sections responsible for French-language education, the BEF acted as part of the embedded state, working in tandem with its federal counterparts to expand official-languages education. The BEF was supportive of Ottawa's youth option and continued to develop new language programs.

One such program was a pilot project in core French, begun in 1980, which offered incentive grants to schools that doubled daily French instruction to forty minutes per day. Immersion programs also continued to grow exponentially, to the point where their enrolment exceeded that of the French minority-language programs. In 1983 there were 9,100 students in French immersion, compared to 6,100 in the minority-language programs, and the gap continued to widen. The BEF also continued to support the development of new programs in both French minority-language education and French immersion. By 1981–82 the province was spending $1 million more on these programs than it received from Ottawa.[12] Under the Pawley government Ronald Duhamel (who had replaced Raymond Hébert as head of the BEF in 1979) was promoted to become the first Franco-Manitoban deputy minister of education, which sent a strong signal about the NDP government's commitment to French-language education.

A strong coalition of organisations had developed over the 1970s to support official languages in education. Working together with the CPF, the Société franco-manitobain (SFM) promoted the development of both the *écoles françaises* and immersion schools. They also argued that both types of schools should be guaranteed by law, rather than merely permitted, and that separate granting structures should be established for each type of program, a policy being pushed by the Fédération des francophones hors-Québec (FFHQ).[13] While expressing support for these objectives, in an interesting shift of the federal government's game, Duhamel suggested that the SFM divert more of its efforts into lobbying the federal government to restore the pre-1979 funding levels.[14] The embedded state method could thus work both ways. Thus, despite the

Lyon government's hostility to official bilingualism and entrenched language rights, a strong coalition existed in both the bureaucracy and the Franco-Manitoban population to ensure the continued development of official-language programs in Manitoba.

ONTARIO

Franco-Ontarian criticism of how the Ontario government handled its implementation of French-language programming had been escalating over the course of the 1970s. By 1979 the now-routine battles over French-language secondary schools had made their way to the community of Penetanguishene, on the Bruce Peninsula. Franco-Ontarian leaders had become increasingly frustrated with the piecemeal approach to minority-language education taken by the Davis government and were upset over the province's lack of control over local school boards that were supposed to implement provincial policy. To cite a prominent example, inquiries into the accounts of the Carleton Catholic School Board revealed that the board siphoned off money intended for minority-language programs for other purposes.[15] In response to these revelations, the Association des enseignants franco-ontariens (AEFO) called on the provincial government to rectify the problems.

The Franco-Ontarian investigations and pressures did not go unnoticed. However, the government was also concerned about a possible backlash, not only from the francophobic Alliance for the Preservation of English in Canada (APEC) but also from those whose support for French programming was less than firm. Thus, when the government increased incentive funding to help create more French-language instructional units (FLIUS) at the secondary school level in October 1979, it did not adopt a policy of separate facilities for all of these units and refused to build a French-language secondary school in Penetanguishene.[16]

Ontario did take additional steps to improve the state of its French-language schools. Supplementary grants were provided to small secondary schools that served a large geographical area and additional funds were provided to mixed schools to enlarge their French-language sections, with restrictions to prevent a mixed school from supplanting a French-language one.[17] The new grant structures developed by the government met with a certain satisfaction in the Franco-Ontarian community. However, calls continued for greater provincial controls on the school boards and an escalator built into the grant structure to cope with inflation. Moreover, Franco-Ontarian leaders were still concerned by the persistence of mixed schools at the elementary level and continued to demand that the Ontario government eliminate them.

Thomas Wells, who was now minister of intergovernmental affairs and responsible for francophone affairs, noted in May 1981 that the province's reputation among Francophones was still negative and that its commitment to French-language services was viewed with suspicion.[18] To combat this, he believed that the province needed to move towards a legislative framework that would guarantee French services in key functional areas. Indeed, Premier Davis was moving on the national front to support Prime Minister Trudeau's drive to enshrine minority-language education rights in the Constitution, which would help shore up his government's image in this community.

QUEBEC

In November 1979, with Joe Clark now prime minister, the Lévesque government presented its white paper on sovereignty-association, outlining its vision for the future of Quebec. Lévesque had been waiting for Trudeau to leave the PMO, so that he would be freed from his prime adversary during the referendum campaign. However, the Clark government fell on a budget vote in December 1979 and went down to defeat to the Liberals in the subsequent February election. Thus, once again the Trudeau government was in office, opposing Lévesque's referendum.

While the referendum on sovereignty-association occupied most of the attention of Quebec's Parti Québécois government during this period, the Department of Education continued to participate in the negotiations for the OLEP, in case the referendum failed. Two cabinet directives governed the negotiating stance adopted by the province: directives 78-409 and 79-88. They called for a continuation of unconditional payments, maintained at a minimum base level, with a provision that Quebec should negotiate a means of opting out should this approach fail.[19] Quebec was pushing hard for an opting out provision in the new OLEP agreement but continued to be a member of the Council of Ministers of Education, Canada's (CMEC) OLEP working group, to ensure that it could shape the agreement from which it would be opting out.[20] This strategy of maintaining ties with the CMEC during the referendum campaign was a wise one, since the referendum went down to defeat on 20 May 1980. Moreover, it meant that Quebec had maintained ties with the other provinces, which it would need to battle the constitutional proposals emanating from the Trudeau government that followed in the wake of this defeat.

The Quebec government's insistence on minimal accountability and its move to opt out of the OLEP continued to aggravate leaders in Quebec's anglophone community. Marcel Fox, executive director of the Protestant School Board of Greater Montreal, suggested that the federal government refuse to pass along its grants until the province agreed to be accountable and that it make public the reasons for this course of action.[21] MP Warren Allmand, a champion of the Montreal anglophone community and ally of the PSBGM, moved in the House of Commons on 31 October 1979 "that this house require the Secretary of State to delay the implementation of the new federal agreements on minority and second language education until there has been a complete examination of the manner in which former agreements were carried out and how the money was spent."[22] His motion failed to gain unanimous consent. Indeed, despite the best efforts of the anglophone community, grants continued to flow to Quebec through the interim agreements without trickling down to the boards in the form of additional funds.

In the meantime, Quebec continued to pare down its English-language programs. Between 1977 and 1980, English-language school enrolment fell by 17 percent, due to Bill 101.[23] In 1981 the Department of Education's new *régime pédagogique* called for the elimination of ESL classes in French-language schools for grades 1 to 3.[24] There would be, however, one small reprieve for the anglophone community. Following the passage of the Charter of Rights and Freedoms in 1982, the Association of Quebec Protestant School Boards launched a court challenge, supported by the federal government, to sections 72 and 73 of the Charter of the French Language. Although the Quebec government of René Lévesque opposed the Charter of Rights and Freedoms and Trudeau's constitutional renewal process, it was forced by a Supreme Court decision of 26 July 1984 to modify the Charter of the French Language, in accordance with section 23 of the Charter of Rights and Freedoms, to grant English-language education rights to children whose parents were educated in English elsewhere in Canada, thus ending the struggle over reciprocal arrangements.[25]

NEW BRUNSWICK

As had been the case throughout the 1970s, New Brunswick remained thoroughly committed to the cause of official bilingualism and continued its move towards increased linguistic duality and expanded language-education programs. OLEP negotiations were handled by the premier's office, which took a keen interest in the developments, including its plans to try to negotiate a separate agreement with the federal government. After the defeat of the Quebec referendum, cooperation with the federal government extended to New Brunswick's efforts to be declared officially bilingual under the Constitution.

Following the 1979 report of the Finn-Elliott Commission,[26] which had been mandated to study the organisation and borders of school commissions and make recommendations on how to modify them, the province moved decisively towards the creation of dual unilingual school boards across the province and the organisation of all schools on the basis of mother tongue. This policy was supported by Bill 88, An Act Recognizing the Equality of the Two Linguistic Communities, which passed in 1981. This act recognized the collective rights of the two language communities and gave each community its own institutions, including its own school boards.[27]

In addition to these legislative changes, the province did its utmost to maintain funding to the OLEP. New Brunswick was very concerned that the federal government might withdraw altogether from the OLEP and wanted to avoid the costs that withdrawal would entail for the province.[28] In addition to new costs stemming from its duality thrust, the Department of Education had also adopted a twelve-hundred-hour program in FSL, which it was spreading throughout the province. It also hired an immersion consultant in 1980 to direct the growth of this burgeoning program. Indeed, French-immersion enrolments were spiralling upwards faster than classes could be created, and communities such as Sackville had to turn away students.[29] By 1982–83 over 15 percent of all anglophone children in the province were enrolled in these programs, with even higher rates in Fredericton and Moncton.[30]

The growth of French immersion was not always viewed as a positive development, and it led to conflict in Grand Falls, where French-speaking children were being admitted to the immersion schools run by the English-language boards.[31] The SANB and local Acadian elites were aghast at this phenomenon, which they saw as undermining the spirit of Bill 88 and siphoning children away from the French-language schools. The SANB took the provincial government to court over the Grand Falls case, and its approach – dual unilingualism – defeated the local proponents of bilingualism.[32] Justice Richard ruled that although parents could choose to send their children to either the English system or the French system, children with a basic knowledge of French could not attend the French-immersion schools.

To cope with the heavy demand for immersion and the court ruling, New Brunswick introduced a policy in 1982 stipulating that immersion programs had to be offered by school boards when requested by a minimum number of parents.[33] The province completed its redrawing of school districts to ensure complete coverage of English- and French-language school boards for the province. Finally, under the revised

Constitution, the province was indeed declared officially bilingual, and Premier Hatfield was a key supporter of the Charter's new minority-language education rights.

NOVA SCOTIA

Despite all the progress that had been made with respect to Acadian education in the 1970s, Nova Scotia's legislation remained silent on the status of French-language education; by 1980 it was alone with Newfoundland in this respect. The Fédération acadienne de la Nouvelle-Écosse (FANE) was hopeful that the nebulous status of French-language education would be changed under the new Conservative government. Early indications from the education minister, Terence Donahoe, were quite encouraging. Donahoe himself was personally committed to the creation of Acadian schools as legal entities and announced in November 1979 that the province was now "attempting to develop appropriate regulatory authority to enshrine the concept that there will first of all be established ground rules for the maintenance for those that exist and the establishment, in areas where appropriate, of Acadian schools."[34] While he observed that it would be some time before a province-wide French school system could be established, he also stated that "it's a realistic expectation of the Acadian community and a right to come to this Provincial Government or any future government and say: You have a regulation which says that this is what an Acadian school is and the kind of area and community in which it should be established, so make sure that you fund it and have it built properly."[35] Thus, while Nova Scotia's finances did not make a province-wide system possible at the moment, the province was actively pursuing increased funding from the federal government to establish it in the future.

Crafting legislation that would meet with popular acceptance would be difficult for the government. Studies of the use of BEP funds discovered that Acadian parents were still largely opposed to the concept of unilingual French schools, even in 1980.[36] Moreover, given the cutbacks to the BEP, boards were having difficulty maintaining the programs that they had developed; additional program development was out of the question with the existing funds. Consequently, Acadian leaders were careful with the message they projected. Working together with Canadian Parents for French, they stressed the benefits of French immersion and second-language learning programs in the creation of bilingual students and called on the government to move towards formally legalizing Acadian education and to enshrine the right of parents to choose the language of their children's education.[37]

By April 1981 the Department of Education had finished preparing legislation for Acadian schools, and Bill 65 was sent to the legislature. Its most important feature was an amendment to the Education Act to include Acadian schools. It also laid out the requirements for the designation of Acadian schools, assigned responsibility for determining curriculum and textbooks, set ratios of instructional time in French to instructional time in English, and decreed that the principal language of administration in Acadian schools would be French. Essentially, the legislation made the status quo legal. The bill was introduced in the legislature on 16 May 1981 and passed with the support of all three parties on 24 June 1981.[38] Because some concerns remained about how the bill would be implemented in practice, a ministerial advisory committee was established to deal with issues of implementation.

In response to FANE's concerns, the boundaries for an Acadian school's catchment area were widened in 1982 to cover two adjacent school districts. Other new guidelines for the Acadian schools were released in 1983. Minister Donahoe allowed assimilated children to count towards the minimum number of students required to create Acadian classes. The Acadian schools were to have 100 percent French instruction for grades P to 6 (except for an English course introduced in grade 3), a minimum of ten credits in French (and at least three per year) for grades 7 to 9, and a minimum of eight credits in French (and at least two per year) for grades 10 to 12.[39] It is worth noting that these provisions did not provide for more than 50 percent French instruction as the base level for the Acadian high schools. Indeed, efforts to increase the percentage of the day spent in French led to fierce battles in Chéticamp in the mid-1980s. Acadian and English-speaking parents alike reacted with hostility towards any indication that the Acadian school would operate entirely in French.[40]

While the government had introduced legislation for Acadian schools, they were far from firmly entrenched in the mid-1980s and were about a decade behind their counterparts in Manitoba and Alberta. A new organisation, the Fédération des parents acadiens de la Nouvelle-Écosse (FPANE), was formed in 1984 to work towards implementation of Bill 65, to fight for school management rights, and to overcome the reluctance of the Acadian community vis-à-vis homogenous schools.[41] Indeed, this battle to overcome concerns about homogenous schools would prove to be a very long one, involving many court challenges under section 23 of the Charter and an arduous public-education campaign. As recently as 2000, FPANE was still fighting court battles for homogenous French secondary schools, and parental opposition to these schools had still not been completely extinguished.

NATIONAL DEVELOPMENTS: THE PATH TO LANGUAGE RIGHTS

A Conservative Interlude

When the Liberals went down to defeat in May 1979, Joe Clark's Conservatives assumed power with a minority government. David Macdonald was appointed secretary of state, and the provinces were not certain what to expect from the new minister regarding the OLEP. In the run-up to the election, Clark had emphasized his concept of Canada as a "community of communities" and seemed much more open to decentralized federalism. Early indications from the Clark government did seem to signal that it would continue to fund the OLEP, having expressed support for the Liberals' youth option. Moreover, Clark's government seemed more open to a flexible approach to the program and was not planning to insist too heavily on provincial accountability for the OLEP funds, since it did not want the federal government to become a shadow minister of education.[42]

The Conservative government did not survive long enough to have a significant impact on the OLEP, however. While there were some indications that the Conservatives may have been more amenable to provincial demands, this path was cut short in December 1979, and the February 1980 election of the Liberals returned the negotiations to their previous incarnation.

THE QUEBEC REFERENDUM

The first major challenge of the reinvigorated Trudeau government was to confront the referendum on sovereignty-association scheduled for May 1980. Some of the official-language minority groups, including ACFA, the SFM, and the SANB expressed some limited support for the Oui side in the referendum.[43] While none wanted Quebec to separate, sympathy was nevertheless expressed for Quebec's desire to secure additional powers and protections for its French language and culture. Moreover, the official-language minorities wanted to increase their bargaining strength and hoped that their governments would speed up the expansion of French-language services as a way of combating Quebec separatism.

Many provincial ministers were surprised by this position. They had believed that their efforts to date would be sufficient to win the support of the official-language minorities in the battle against separatism. Terence Donahoe had mentioned this as a good reason to support Acadian education,[44] and similar comments had been made by other premiers and ministers. Dick Johnson, Alberta's minister for foreign and intergovernmental affairs, was quite upset at ACFA's unwillingness to campaign for the Non side.⁴⁵ He had assumed that the association would be willing to attest to the improvements made in his province under its "best efforts" approach, even if the changes were not as rapid as may have been desired. It is striking how efforts targeting official-language minorities in many provinces were conceived as efforts to win over Quebec, rather than as efforts undertaken for their own sake.

Come referendum day, the Non side won by a margin of 59 percent to 41 percent. Pierre Trudeau, who in speeches leading up to the referendum had promised constitutional change, rather than a preservation of the status quo, immediately began his drive to patriate the constitution. This effort, which was accompanied by a push for a Charter of Rights and Freedoms including minority-language education, heralded the next major stage in Ottawa's move towards official bilingualism and minority-language education rights. What had begun with financial carrots under the Bilingualism in Education Program now moved towards the legal stick of the Charter.

PATRIATION OF THE CONSTITUTION AND THE CHARTER OF RIGHTS AND FREEDOMS

While Prime Minister Trudeau's desire to enshrine the rights of official-language minorities to education in their mother tongue long predated the creation of the Bilingualism in Education Program, the difficulties that Ottawa faced in cajoling the provinces to expand their official-languages programs brought the need for a constitutional solution to the official-languages issue into sharp relief. The funding programs had strengthened the hand of official-languages advocates, and the St Andrews declaration was a major step forward, but most premiers remained leery of making minority-language education a constitutionally entrenched right. In the early 1980s, it was far from clear how the Charter would operate in practice and how it might affect the future of the OLEP. Nevertheless, it was clear that the official-languages terrain was shifting, and senior officials continued to bear the funding programs in mind as they contemplated Trudeau's proposals.⁴⁶

Of the ten provinces, eight initially opposed the federal government's efforts to patriate the Constitution, for various reasons, many of which were entirely unrelated to the Charter and official languages. But some premiers, including Manitoba's Sterling Lyon, were vehemently opposed to the provisions for a Charter of Rights including official-language education rights. In the view of Premier Lyon, language rights should not be extended beyond national institutions, and the federal government should not be preoccupied with such issues.⁴⁷ And of course, Premier Lévesque, still stinging from the referendum defeat, was firmly opposed to the language-education rights being proposed for section 23 of the Charter.

Language rights were particularly important for Trudeau and the federal government. A decade of providing funding to the provinces for official languages in education had improved access to programs but produced very limited results in terms of language rights. By 1981 only New Brunswick offered unrestricted rights to minority-language education. Manitoba, Ontario, and Quebec offered limited rights, while the legislation of most other provinces was permissive at best. While the OLEP's financial incentives had resulted in changes, many provinces were less focussed on the federal priority of minority-language education and paid more attention to the politically popular immersion and second-language programs.

Trudeau did have two provincial allies for his reform efforts. Ontario supported both enshrining two official languages in the constitution and enshrining the right to an education in either official language, where numbers warranted. As Premier Davis noted, "In the interest of our future together, it is time to ensure that, anywhere in Canada parents of the official-language minority can have their children educated in the English or the French language, as the case may be."⁴⁸ However, he resisted imposing official bilingualism on the provincial governments and defended his incremental approach to bilingualism while continuing to reject demands that Ontario be made officially bilingual.

New Brunswick was even more welcoming of the federal proposals. Premier Hatfield wanted to have New Brunswick designated as officially bilingual under the Constitution, and he was a vigorous advocate of the constitutional entrenchment of minority-language education rights. Hatfield was not in favour of limiting the provision to "where numbers warrant," since doing so implied that the right would be abused. Rather, he argued that "We must ... continue to move forward the rights of Canadians to have, to be taught, to express, and to work in either of the two languages, and to do this by consent."⁴⁹

Numerous lobby groups lined up to express support for the federal government's constitutional proposals on minority-language education rights. The PSBGM and the QFHSA both called for the right of all parents to choose the language of instruction for their children, be it the majority or the minority language. They argued that this right should be based on the right of an individual to free choice, rather than on the collective right of a language group.⁵⁰ Canadian Parents for French supported the proposals of these Quebec groups, since such a broad definition of language-education rights would provide legislative support for French immersion programs as well.⁵¹ Francophone organisations called for the widest possible definition of section 23 language rights, and they too objected to the "where numbers warrant" clause. ACFA argued that "the two official languages of Canada must belong by right to all Canadians."⁵²

Despite these various lobbying efforts, in an effort to appease Quebec the constitutional agreement of 5 November 1981 continued to insist on the restriction of section 23 rights to Canadian citizens whose mother tongue was that of the official-language minority.⁵³ Moreover, section 59 of the Constitution Act, 1982 established that section 23(1)(a) of the Charter (which reads, "Citizens of Canada whose first language learned and still understood is that of the English or French linguistic minority population of the province in which they reside ... have the right to have their children receive primary and secondary school instruction in that language in that province") would come into effect in Quebec only if and when it was authorized by the legislative assembly or government of Quebec. In the interim, section 23 would only apply in Quebec to those citizens who had been educated in English in Canada or had children that had been educated in English elsewhere in Canada.

While the federal government did have its supporters for section 23, they too were wary of the implications the Charter might have for the OLEP. New Brunswick education minister Charles Gallagher noted that there had to be a linkage between enshrining language rights in the constitution and the provision of sufficient funds to make these programs real and meaningful. The Hatfield government was concerned that after constitutional entrenchment Ottawa would withdraw from using the spending power on official-languages education.⁵⁴ Withdrawal would be a disaster for New Brunswick, which therefore argued that the development of minority-language education would be much slower if its progress was left to the courts.

Ontario also noted that it would be funny to chop the OLEP at the same time that the federal government wanted to entrench minority-language education rights.⁵⁵ Minority-language education lobby groups, such as the PSBGM, joined in the chorus of voices calling on the federal government to continue to play a role in subsidizing a minimum level of minority-language education across the country. Clearly, although there were supporters for section 23, their support was qualified on the understanding that the federal government would continue to financially support minority-language education. Federal officials were aware of these concerns and, as we shall see, would continue to use the financial carrot of the OLEP to make minority-language education rights more palatable to the reluctant provinces.⁵⁶

The Quebec government did not consent to the constitutional agreement reached between the federal government and the other nine provinces, despite the inclusion of provisions built into the renewal package to appease it. Moreover, the Parti Québécois was furious at the Canadian government's decision to proceed with the new constitutional package despite Quebec's opposition. Accordingly, in November 1981 Quebec withdrew from all interprovincial meetings, which would make negotiating at the CMEC level difficult, since its consent was crucial to a new OLEP agreement.

The passage of section 23 of the Charter of Rights and Freedoms in 1982 and the establishment of a provincial consensus on minority-language education rights in the wake of the election of the PQ would strengthen the federal government's hand in the OLEP negotiations. With section 23, a key intrastate plank had been laid in Canadian language policy, one that legally obliged the provinces to provide minority-language education and established a recourse to the federally appointed Supreme Court as a fall-back position, should the OLEP negotiations fail. The Charter also strengthened the hand of official-language minority communities seeking to develop their education programs in the following decades.

However, the provinces still retained jurisdictional authority over education, including the power to determine which priorities they would emphasize and the extent to which they would facilitate the development of new official-languages programs. Although the federal government had managed to secure its primary objective – minority-language education rights – it could exercise only limited control over the pace of development of these programs. Moreover, the Charter did nothing to change the situation of immersion and second-language programs, which were also seen as important, if secondary, objectives for the Trudeau government. Accordingly, while these latter programs had gained a substantial foothold in Canadian education since the inception of the OLEP, they were still subject to interstate negotiations.

Although the Charter had been enacted, a new protocol agreement had not yet been reached, and it is to this negotiation process that we now turn.

Negotiating a Protocol Agreement – Four Long Years

In contrast to the first two BEP agreements, agreement on a new multi-year deal for the Official-Languages in Education Program proved to be exceedingly difficult. This is not to say that the participating governments had turned their backs on official-languages programs. Indeed, most were more supportive than they had ever been. However, the political and constitutional turmoil of the late 1970s and early 1980s in many ways precluded any agreement between Ottawa and the provinces.

While a relatively constant cast of political players were involved in the OLEP throughout the 1970s, the period from 1979 to 1983 witnessed heavy turnover of key cabinet ministers. Accordingly, most negotiations were handled by senior civil servants, who nevertheless had an interest in defending the interests and programs of their governments. To come to a protocol agreement, which would lay out the general principles and terms applicable to all bilateral agreements between Ottawa and the provinces, these officials were responsible for negotiating an acceptable compromise on a wide array of complex and politically sensitive issues ranging from financing to evaluation, from objectives to accountability.

The Funding Conundrum. At its core, the OLEP was a financial arrangement between the federal government and individual provinces whereby Ottawa contributed funds to programs that contributed to its objectives but that were designed and administered by the provinces. Thus, from the perspective of the provinces, the most critical issue was the amount of funding that they would receive under a new agreement. While some provinces, such as Quebec and Alberta, were concerned about some of the more theoretical aspects of the program, such as its objectives, others with less lucrative treasuries, including Nova Scotia, argued that they were "too poor" to have principles and basically were interested in increased funding.[57]

From Ottawa's perspective, all federally funded programs needed to be reexamined in the light of its spiralling deficit. The free-spending era of the late 1960s, which had spawned the open-ended BEP agreements had come to a close, and the Treasury Board wanted to impose some control over all cost-sharing arrangements. In the view of the Canadian government, it had expressed a commitment to the OLEP by chopping only 20 percent of its budget, versus the 34 percent that had been chopped from programs for bilingualism in the civil service. The provinces, on the other hand, believed that the funding cut from the civil service programs should be redirected into the OLEP if the federal government was truly serious about its youth option.[58]

Under the Clark government, the newly appointed Conservative secretary of state, David Macdonald, was first to confront the provinces' demands. Initially lending them a sympathetic ear, he argued to Cabinet that restoring the OLEP funding cut by the Liberals would go a long way to improving strained federal-provincial relations.[59] His suggestion was coldly received. Prime Minister Clark told Macdonald that if he wanted to find more money for the OLEP, it would have to be found within his own department, a position supported by Finance Minister John Crosbie.[60] Treasury Board president Sinclair Stevens was more blunt. Stevens cited the "unevaluated and doubtful effectiveness of the program" and questioned the belief that more funding would facilitate smoother federal-provincial relations. Furthermore, he questioned the appropriateness of any federal involvement in education.[61] Given this reception, it could be considered a minor victory for Macdonald that his government signed a second interim agreement with the provinces in February 1980.

The reelected Liberals initially showed no more willingness to restore the OLEP funding levels. Following the CMEC meeting of September 1980, the frustrated education ministers stated that "clearly, bilingualism is no longer a federal priority."[62] The provinces, Canadian Parents for French and the Association canadienne des enseignants de langue française (ACELF) continued to demand funding increases through 1981 and 1982. But facing a deep recession, the federal government remained unwilling to increase funding without a concomitant increase in accountability from the provinces. It would not be until early 1982, when the provinces had conceded to some of the federal government's demands for visibility and accountability and the Constitution had been repatriated, that the Trudeau government would agree to make its "best efforts" to increase the funding levels.[63] The new secretary of state, Serge Joyal, was committed to the OLEP's success and pushed within the federal government for an increased envelope of funding. Joyal managed to secure an increase to $190 million in March 1983, with the promise of an additional 5 percent (or $15 million) per year.[64] While this was a marked improvement over the interim agreements, it still fell well short of the high point of the BEP in 1977–78, when the federal government spent $222 million. Nevertheless, the provinces, recognizing that they were unlikely to secure more money than this, accepted the federal government's offer.

Fighting for an increased funding pool was easily agreed upon by the provinces. Agreeing on how to divvy it up was significantly more difficult. Lobby groups such as the CPF and the FFHQ had long criticized the formula payments as providing little incentive for development, since they gave the most money to provinces with the best-established and most costly programs while doing little to help the poorer provinces in need of the most development.[65] However, as a national program, any OLEP agreement would somehow have to satisfy all the provinces, including Quebec, which had benefited enormously from the existing arrangements and resisted any attempt to reduce its share of the funding.

Table 5.1
Average Cost of Education per Student per Year, 1977–78 ($)

Province	Elementary	Secondary
Alberta	1,567.92	2,064.90
Manitoba	1,547.33	2,039.37
Ontario	1,678.05	2,425.82
Quebec	1,590.00	2,728.92
New Brunswick	1,242.44	1,617.98
Nova Scotia	1,315.55	1,705.49
National Provincial Average	1,473.18	2,011.07

Source: PAA, 85.360, ACFA, box 28, file: Divers documents – Canadian Parents for French (Alberta Branch) 1977–79, *Canadian Parents for French Newsletter*, no. 4, September 1978.

A wide variety of proposals was floated by individual provinces to determine how the OLEP funding should be allocated. While most community organisations wanted to scrap the formula payments altogether, the provinces generally found them acceptable, if in need of realignment. The first challenge was to come to agreement on the starting point for funding allocation. In the past, the formulas had been based on the average cost per student in each province, multiplied by the number of FTEs in existing programs. Some provinces, favouring a developmental thrust, wanted to do away with this reliance on current enrolments. Manitoba proposed a redistribution of funds on a per capita basis, with the size of the minority-language community factored in.[66] However, both New Brunswick and Quebec stood to lose significant amounts of funding under the Manitoba proposal, and thus it did not meet with any great success.[67]

New Brunswick then proposed a system of block grants based on real additional costs, which would be increased according to inflation. Under its proposed Bilingualism in Education Support Transfer (or BEST) Program, the OLEP would be transformed along the lines of other established program financing arrangements, whereby each province would receive a block of funding for specifically targeted purposes: one grant for second-language instruction and another for minority-language education.[68] This proposal also met with little support from the other provinces, particularly given its lack of flexibility to redistribute funding between the two objectives.

In July 1980, Alberta developed a more successful proposal that would change the formula for OLEP funding from one tied directly to provincial costs to one based on a weighted national average.[69] Formula payments would be based on the average cost of education per student *in Canada*, rather than in individual provinces. As can be seen from table 5.1, the smaller provinces with the least-developed programs would benefit greatly from this redistribution. The Maritime provinces were already below the national average cost of education, even before this average was weighted for provincial populations. Once that adjustment was made, the Western provinces would also benefit from Alberta's proposal. To make the proposal palatable to Quebec, which could lose under this formula, Alberta argued that a floor should be established at level of the 1980–81 payments, to prevent Quebec's share from slipping further.

The Alberta proposal was greeted with a fair bit of enthusiasm and won the endorsement of Canadian Parents for French, which liked how it favoured the provinces in need of more development. In fact, the CPF had been developing a proposal along virtually identical lines. The CMEC adopted the basic premises of the Alberta program, accepting the weighted national average and an interim floor on payments while the new structure was gradually phased in.[70] The federal government was enthusiastic about the weighted national average suggestion, since it favoured the additional program development sought by secretary of state officials. Moreover, it favoured Ottawa's intrastate position, since it took all of Canada as its frame of reference and seemed to implicitly accept the need for a national solution to language questions. It was thus included in the protocol of 1983. Nor did Ottawa have a major problem with the idea of a floor, although the exact level and base year for this floor would prove problematic, as we shall see in the discussion below of the final phases of the protocol negotiations in 1983.

Some provinces remained less satisfied with the formula payment structure. Manitoba had been pushing for a block formula on a per capita basis, while New Brunswick had some reservations about the weighted national average, because it did not take into account some of the systemic costs of bilingualism in the provinces.[71] These two provinces, as we shall see, ended up being accommodated through a different arrangement than the others accepted.

Greater divisions arose on the question of the percentage levels of the formulas. Ontario had proposed a substantial increase in the second-language formula to the level of 15.8 percent, which was supported by a number of other provinces, eyeing a cash grab. However, in May 1980 Alberta rejected this level as unjustifiable, and Ontario's officials, facing criticism from the Franco-Ontarian community, backed away from their proposal.[72]

Other proposals for adjusting the formulas were floated in this period. In July 1980, Alberta proposed increasing the minority-language formula to 15 percent.[73] However, the federal government resisted any major increase in funding during this period. Moreover, by this point most provinces thought that any increases to the formulas were unlikely to meet with federal approval and thus focused on defining what types of programs would be eligible for formula funding.[74]

Immersion programs were at the centre of these funding discussions. They had not even been considered at the outset of the BEP and had been built into the program haphazardly over the course of the decade. However, French immersion had attracted significant public support and had led to the creation of the CPF. It was perhaps the most popular of the OLEP-funded programs and had by far the most impressive growth rates. Yet not everyone was pleased with the French-immersion craze. The Canadian Teachers' Federation (CTF) called for an increased emphasis on the core French programs, which it believed had been ignored due to the immersion boom.[75] The FFHQ was also very concerned about the growth of immersion programs, which were funded out of the same pool of money and at the same level as minority-language programs. The FFHQ argued that French immersion risked becoming the catch-all response of anglophones to demands for French minority-language education and wanted to ensure that immersion did not overshadow minority-language programming. It was also very concerned that the immersion programs were draining money that should be going to francophones and wanted separate pots of money established for French immersion and French minority-language education.[76]

A more precise definition of the role of immersion suited the needs of a number of provincial governments. Separate reporting of French minority-language and immersion programs had been a major priority of many lobby groups, including the CPF, ACELF, and the provincial affiliates of the FFHQ. Agreeing to this demand would allow the provinces to satisfy these groups.[77] Moreover, a uniform definition of what constituted immersion would enable a more equitable distribution of the federal grants. Ontario noted that some provinces claimed the 9 percent formula for programs with 25 percent French instruction, while many of its programs with 40 to 50 percent French instruction had been claimed only under the 5 percent formula.

In the final agreements, the formula for minority-language education did not increase, as had been demanded by the FFHQ, nor did the second-language formulas. However, in satisfaction of the FFHQ's demands, French immersion was reported and classified separately in the protocol agreements.[78] This institutionalisation of immersion and continuation of its higher levels of funding satisfied the CPF, while francophone community organisations would now be able to have access to more accurate figures concerning how the provinces were prioritizing immersion and FML programming, a useful tool in lobbying the provinces in this sector.

Duration of the Agreement. Past agreements on the Bilingualism in Education Program had been for a fixed length, four and five years respectively. In the years leading up to the end of the second agreement the Canadian School Trustees Association called for a longer agreement of ten to fifteen years, to allow for better curriculum planning. Other lobby groups suggested a more restricted period; Canadian Parents for French asked for a five-year agreement, for a program that would be expected to last at least another ten years. The provinces, for their part, sought an agreement of at least another five years.[79] However, the federal government, concerned about the open-ended nature of the programs, wanted even shorter agreements, preferably of three years.[80]

The issue of the duration of the new OLEP agreement is a particularly intriguing one, despite its innocuous appearance. At the outset, the program was not intended to last nearly this long. Second-language instruction was slated for only five years of federal funding, and minority-language education for ten to fifteen years. However, by the early 1980s the OLEP had become so woven into the fabric of federal-provincial relations that nobody was seriously considering cancelling it. With the Charter now obligating provinces to provide minority-language education, they were eager to receive federal funds to pay for it. For its part, Ottawa realized that continued OLEP funding would help to speed up the implementation of section 23. The program's continuation was no longer in question, only its details and how often the provisions could be altered by the participants.

Program Objectives. Discussions about the wording of the OLEP's objectives were the most politically delicate. The language used in this section held the potential to firm up either provincial or federal claims to jurisdiction in the official-languages sector. It could also advance either of their visions of what type of language policy Canada should have, who this policy should serve, and what kind of Canada they wanted to build.

One issue that was easily dispensed with was the federal government's proposal to incorporate a cultural component into both the minority- and second-language programs. This proposal aimed to give Canadians of the minority-language community a better sense of their own culture and members of the majority-language community an understanding of the culture whose language they were learning. The federal government hoped that it would reinforce national unity and understanding, and several lobby groups, including the CPF, the CTF, and francophone associations, also expressed their support.[81] General agreement was quickly reached on the principle that the OLEP should provide "opportunities for cultural enrichment though knowledge of the language and culture of the other language group."[82]

Most other elements of the objectives were significantly more complex. The governments returned to the highly contentious issue of who should be covered as the intended beneficiaries of OLEP-funded programs. In 1974, the shift in objectives to aim minority-language education solely at members of the minority-language community had passed largely without notice outside Quebec. By 1979, other organisations and governments were taking a greater interest in these definitions. Canadian Parents for French lobbied strongly for the right to choose either official language for education for all Canadian children.[83] The QFHSA, seeking a broader catchment pool for Quebec's English-language school boards, did not even want this right restricted to citizens. Some of the participating governments were also seeking a return to the 1970 wording, including Alberta and the federal government, which wanted to stress the access of "Canadians" to minority-language education, rather than restricting access to the minority-language community, as Quebec was demanding.[84]

The Quebec government proved to be a formidable adversary. The PQ believed that a broader definition of the program objectives would threaten its linguistic balance, which it was trying to solidify with Bill 101.[85] In the long run, satisfying Quebec proved to be more important than the principle of freedom of choice. While the federal government did believe that French Canada extended from coast to coast, it could not deny the importance of Quebec's francophone population in this equation and recognized that Quebec's participation in the OLEP was essential. This was the key limiting factor in Ottawa's efforts to devise intrastate solutions to Canada's language issues. The target group for minority-language education was therefore limited to members of the minority-language community. This principle was modified in one important way, however: both the anglophone and francophone regional minorities in New Brunswick were specifically included, whereas prior agreements named only the francophone minority.[86]

Both the federal and provincial governments were increasingly sensitive to questions of constitutional jurisdiction by the late 1970s. The provinces wanted to restrict Ottawa's role in education, while the federal government wanted to reinforce its justification for involvement in this sector. From the outset, the provinces declared that education was their exclusive jurisdiction and wanted wording to this effect included in the OLEP agreement.[87] They stressed the need to be able to set their own objectives and timetables in this sector and to be free from federal control. Quebec, in particular, was concerned that the federal government was trying to establish a beachhead in the control of educational programs through the OLEP.[88]

While the Canadian government did recognize that education was a provincial responsibility (and in fact had used this as justification for pulling out of the maintenance of existing programs), it argued that official languages and minority-language community rights were a national priority that had to be supported with federal funds, an assertion that was supported by the commissioner of official languages.[89] These claims were premised on the notion that issues of official languages in education were linked with issues of national interest such as the respect of fundamental rights and the "rapprochement entre les différentes régions du pays."[90] For its part, the federal government wanted mention of its program objectives, contents, and priorities in the OLEP agreement.[91] Ottawa was supported by the government of New Brunswick. Education Minister Charles Gallagher stated that the constitutional entrenchment of language rights must be linked to the continued provision of federal funding, arguing that provincial efforts in education contributed to national official-language objectives. Moreover, minority-language schools contributed both to geographic mobility within Canada and to the development of an equal partnership between the two linguistic societies, which were issues of national interest linked to national objectives.[92]

The CMEC recognized that it would not be possible to secure continued federal funding of the OLEP if the provinces did not recognize a federal interest and role in this sector. The two sides came to a compromise solution whereby the federal government recognized that the provinces were responsible for education. In return, since the provinces recognized that the official-languages policy and funding programs of the federal government contributed to Canadian goals and objectives, they permitted the federal government to contribute to the costs of providing minority-language education and second-language instruction. While the federal government was unable to establish a firm beachhead in education in terms of the language of the OLEP agreement, it did secure provincial recognition that funding of language education could be accepted as part of Ottawa's legitimate role in promoting the official languages and supporting the vitality of official-language minority communities.

The nature of Ottawa's future role in the OLEP was the most difficult issue to resolve. Dissatisfied with its role in funding the maintenance of basic education programs in the provinces, the federal government wanted to shift all its funding into the development of new programs, a move that had broad support among francophone minority communities and the CPF. The provinces were almost universally opposed to the developmental thrust. The three largest providers of minority-language education (Ontario, Quebec, and New Brunswick) all argued that this shift would unfairly penalise provinces with well-developed systems and, moreover, would have a chilling effect on the development of new programs, since they would have their federal funding pulled after a few years.[93] The notion of federal funding being intended to "increase opportunities" for language education was particularly problematic. The three provinces preferred to limit the role of the federal government to "assist[ing] in providing" opportunities.[94] Quebec believed that the agreements should be structured so that there were separate pools of money for the maintenance of existing projects and for the development of new projects, each of which should be guaranteed a minimum level of funding that was not less than what had been allocated under the current agreements.[95]

The provinces were largely able to wear down the federal government on its desire to move out of maintenance of existing programs. The one victory that Ottawa did claim was that funding would be broken down by categories in the protocol agreement, more clearly indicating what its funding was to be used for. Beginning with the 1983 protocol, federal funding was categorized into four sections: infrastructure support (which covered maintenance of existing programs), program expansion and development, teacher training and Development, and student support.

Additional Costs and Accountability. The initial justification for federal involvement in official languages in education had been based on the B & B Commission's premise that additional costs were involved in the provision of minority-language education and second-language instruction. This concept had not, however, been included in the official wording of the BEP objectives, and Quebec vigorously denied that the program was intended to provide for additional costs. For the federal government, however, this was an important qualifier that justified its use of the spending power.[96]

For Ottawa, shifting towards a funding model based on new development would have made the additional costs easy to identify: they would stem directly from programs being introduced. However, when this plan was abandoned, a new model for determining additional costs had to be developed. By early 1981 the federal government defined these costs as costs that would not exist if minority-language education and second-language instruction were not provided; the costs could result from economies of scale, special grants, and additional structures. The federal government was prepared to be flexible in its interpretation of what costs could be accepted under this rubric, but it did demand that the provinces accept this concept. Otherwise, it would be unable to justify its involvement to members of Parliament and the general public.[97]

Gaining provincial acceptance of the additional costs premise proved difficult. Most notably in Quebec, English-language education had been provided for so long that the provincial government did not believe that the costs involved were additional ones; they were considered part and parcel of providing education to its citizens. Other provinces, such as New Brunswick and Manitoba, had no problem with the concept of additional costs and were able to cost out the different programs that the federal funds were spent on.[98] The compromise reached on this issue once again hinged on the specific wording of the protocol agreement; the provinces agreed to accept wording that said that the federal contributions "related" to the additional costs entailed by these programs, a term that did not imply so strongly that the funds were "used" for this purpose.[99]

The issue of additional costs was tightly linked to another hot-button issue for the federal government: accountability. A direct relationship between the federal OLEP funds and additional costs in the provinces would have entailed a rigid reporting structure of how the provinces spent the OLEP monies. Indeed, the federal government did want much greater accountability from the provinces, since accountability had been sparse, particularly with Quebec and the Maritime provinces. The federal government was under great pressure from MPs, citizens, and lobby groups across the country to demonstrate how the OLEP funding was being spent, and it was not able to provide concrete answers.[100] In many cases it seemed as if the money was being poured into a black hole, particularly in Quebec, the recipient of half the OLEP funds.

A wide gulf separated the provinces from each other on the issue of accountability. New Brunswick, desperate for additional funding for its official-languages programs, was willing to completely open its books to the federal government, seeing this as the only way to defend the OLEP's integrity and protect it from arbitrary shifts in federal policy.[101] Manitoba, which had the most rigorous system of accountability in the country, buttressed by a granting formula that required accountability from the school boards receiving the grants, was also completely open to the federal requests.[102] Ontario, which had been moving in the direction of a similar accounting and grants procedure, also conceded that a measure of accountability was in the national interest.[103] Other provinces were less amenable. Alberta, which could have provided reports on how the money was being spent, long having had transparent accounting practices, opposed the federal demands as jurisdictional interference and an attempt to impose its own priorities on the provinces.[104] Quebec was violently opposed to more accountability, since it even challenged the federal assertion that there were additional costs to be accounted for! Together with Saskatchewan, these governments wanted accountability restricted to the simple statistical reporting used for previous agreements.

To solve the accountability conundrum, many third parties weighed in with suggestions. The Canadian Home and School and Parent-Teacher Federation (CHSPTF) argued for strict accountability from the provincial governments to end what it termed "misappropriation" of the OLEP grants.[105] Canadian Parents for French argued that the provinces and boards should at least be accountable to the general public, if not directly to the federal government.[106] They suggested that a year-end statement should be furnished by each province to the federal government about how the federal grants were used and that provinces should make greater efforts to cost their programs. CMEC officials proposed a joint provincial cost study to demonstrate to the federal government the types of costs involved in the OLEP programs and further suggested that the federal government should be involved in crafting the study to give it more legitimacy.[107] This proposal was rejected by Quebec, as well as by other provinces wary of the federal government questioning their expenditures.

A major gulf continued to separate Quebec, which opposed any additional accountability, from New Brunswick, which was willing to provide full accountability, with the other provinces scattered between. A breakthrough on this issue would not be possible until the structure of the protocol was determined, which provided for varying degrees of accountability among the provinces. This compromise solution will be clarified below in the analysis of the structure of the protocol agreement, with its two-option approach to the OLEP.

Visibility. Not only did the federal government want to be able to account for how the provinces were using its money, it also wanted to receive credit for its expenditures. Ottawa saw its programs as an important means of promoting national unity and wanted the public to be aware of its efforts in this respect. Moreover, the Canadian government did not want the provinces to take all the credit for the new developments in official-languages education.

To a certain extent, the federal government had been able to circumvent provincial reluctance to provide visibility through its funding of the Official Language Minority Groups Program. The various French Canadian and Acadian associations routinely publicized the important role being played by the federal government in funding minority-language education and decried the lack of a comparable provincial commitment. Canadian Parents for French went even further, providing great detail about the OLEP in its newsletter and press releases. As Secretary of State officials noted when considering funding applications from the CPF, a "non-governmental body of concerned parents constitutes an effective means of promoting the realization of federal language policies, and of pointing out to the community at large what the federal government is doing for second-language instruction throughout the country."[108] Organisations such as the CPF could also be counted on to pressure the provinces to give credit to the federal government for their contributions.

This indirect campaign for visibility could only go so far, however. Ottawa wanted more credit particularly for the formula payments, where visibility was at its worst. There was initially some resistance to this demand, particularly from Quebec, which was loath to publicize Ottawa's contributions to education.[109] However, the federal government won out on this issue, since it was unwilling to make contributions for which it did not receive acknowledgment. The CMEC reached a consensus that visibility should be provided through an annual CMEC publication on the provinces' provision of minority-language education and second-language instruction, joint press releases with the federal government, and an annual issue of its newsletter devoted to the OLEP.[110] Overall, the debate over visibility was resolved without undue difficulty, and the federal government was able to gain public recognition of the role it was playing in official-languages education, further solidifying its claim to a role in this sector.

Evaluation. One might suspect that evaluating the success of the Bilingualism in Education Program would have been a major aspect of the negotiations leading up to a renewal of the program. Education experts and the commissioner of official languages had cast doubts on the pedagogical merits of the twenty-minute-per-day second-language programs that the BEP funded, even suggesting that they created more hostility to the second language, at the expense of contributing to actual learning.

The federal government had initially requested a role in evaluation as part of its 1977 reforms package, and it received some limited provincial support, primarily from New Brunswick and Manitoba.[111] However, over the course of the negotiations, the provinces formed a common front opposing any federal role in evaluation. Even the more moderate provinces, such as Manitoba and Ontario, while accepting that regular evaluations should be conducted, believed that they should be strictly a provincial matter and focussed on how well the programs were meeting provincial priorities, not federal objectives.[112] The provinces were unwilling to make any major concessions on this issue. Pedagogical evaluation was, they argued, firmly within provincial jurisdiction.

Using its own limited data, the federal government did try to conduct an evaluation of the effectiveness of the BEP based on the 1970–79 period, but the results were inconclusive. The investigators argued that progress in minority-language education and second-language instruction had probably been accelerated by the BEP and that the funds certainly had given the official-language minorities more clout in their demands. However, it was difficult to tie the federal program directly to other positive developments in the provinces, such as the legal recognition of minority-language education in Nova Scotia and Prince Edward Island.[113] Thus, the federal evaluation was unable to produce a causal link between the BEP and improved language learning in the provinces or provincial policy changes in this field.

Despite the provincial refusal to allow the federal government a role in evaluation, Ottawa proceeded to sign a new agreement. The provinces agreed to share any evaluations they undertook with the federal government, but conducting these evaluations was not required by the OLEP agreements, except in the case of special projects. This failure to insist on evaluating the OLEP's contribution to effective language learning points to its highly politicized nature. While the federal government would obviously have been pleased to find out if Canadian language-education programs were top notch, this was not its top priority. Rather, given the jurisdictional restrictions inherent in Canadian federalism, the Trudeau government's main emphasis had to be on ensuring that the OLEP was leading to greater opportunities for official-languages education and that the federal government would be seen to contribute to this. Whether or not the programs were in fact pedagogically sound was left to the provinces to determine.

Protocol Administration: A Role for the CMEC? When it formed in 1967, the CMEC was an association of the provincial ministries of education forged for the purpose of sharing information and coordinating joint efforts in education. The organisation played a very minor role in the BEP at the outset and became actively involved in issues of official languages only in the aftermath of the election of the PQ and the St Andrews conference. In subsequent years, the CMEC secretariat wrote the provincial report on minority-language education, and its biannual meetings provided the forum for interprovincial discussions on the OLEP negotiations. Beginning in October 1979, a task force of representatives from Nova Scotia, Quebec, Ontario, and New Brunswick, supported by the staff of the CMEC secretariat, was responsible for compiling provincial responses to federal proposals and preparing draft provincial responses for comment.

While the CMEC secretariat had assumed an expanding role in the OLEP, its future status in this respect was uncertain. Manitoba expressed support for having the master agreement of the OLEP negotiated and developed by the CMEC. Quebec and other provinces also liked using the CMEC as a common front for the provinces in negotiations with Ottawa.[114] Some organisations, such as the CPF, wanted the CMEC secretariat to become a more independent organisation that could recommend funding arrangements and program implementation independently of political machinations.[115]

It was this last type of proposal that worried the provinces. Alberta, while supporting the CMEC's role as a funnel for provincial messages to the federal government and a forum for discussions, did not want it meddling in provincial modalities of providing minority-language education or interfering in funding arrangements.[116] Quebec too, while considering the CMEC a useful forum for discussions, did not want to lose sovereignty over education to this organisation any more than it wanted to lose it to the federal government.[117] There were thus limits to how far the provinces were willing to extend interprovincial cooperation regarding official languages in education. However, Quebec recognized that the CMEC had to remain functional and, after a brief absence from meetings in the aftermath of the 1982 constitutional talks, decided to return as a fully participating member of this forum in September 1983, in order to prove that the provinces could work together on issues in the national interest and thus prevent the federal government from justifying increased interventions.[118] Given these considerations, the CMEC retained the increased prominence it had assumed in the late 1970s as a forum for discussion and as a formulator of proposals. Ultimately though, any decision on the OLEP negotiated through the CMEC had to be acceptable to all ten provinces, which retained the final say on all decisions.

Protocol Structure. While the first two BEP agreements were relatively straightforward, with fixed payment levels applicable to all provinces, this arrangement had not proven satisfactory to the federal government, since it deprived Ottawa of the ability to target funding where it was most needed. Provinces with ambitious development plans also wanted to alter the program in a way that would allow them to make greater progress. As early as 1977 the CMEC had indicated the need for increased flexibility to better meet individual provincial circumstances.[119] Accomplishing this in such a way as to preserve provincial harmony would prove to be difficult.

In 1979, Manitoba proposed that the CMEC negotiate a master agreement covering the basic principles and arrangements of a new OLEP agreement and then allow provinces to sign bilateral agreements with the federal government that permitted greater flexibility.[120] When the ministers of education gathered at the negotiating table in the spring of 1980, there was a certain degree of pessimism about whether this proposal would be feasible. Alberta, noting Quebec's desire to withdraw from the OLEP, doubted that agreement even on basic principles would be possible.[121]

Despite this pessimism, attempts were made to explore this avenue. Ontario's officials liked the idea of a negotiated plan but noted that it would put provinces in competition with each other for federal dollars, placing the federal government in a very strong position.[122] New Brunswick was very keen on this option, believing that it was in a strong position to negotiate for additional funds, although it stressed that there should be a guaranteed minimum payment for each province and an escalator to cover inflation.[123] But Quebec was opposed to the idea of bilateral agreements, since they could weaken the common front and thus Quebec's defence of the status quo. However, its officials recognized that other provinces were keen on this option and that some concessions would have to be made.[124] In this vein, the CMEC attempted to develop a master agreement that would cover all the provinces and that would include objectives, types of payments, and criteria for funding distribution. Its proposal was presented for discussion in April 1981.[125]

The April proposal was problematic. It was quite similar to the agreements of the 1970s and thus did not meet the needs of New Brunswick, which was willing to be much more accountable to the federal government in exchange for a drastically different program structure.[126] To break the deadlock and satisfy advocates of both interstate and intrastate federalism, Ontario proposed a two-option approach for a new protocol that would have an entitlement option and a negotiation option. The entitlement option would function largely as the BEP had in the past, although the formula payments would be based on a weighted national average (WNA) per-student cost. This would permit redistribution of funds from provinces with higher costs (Ontario, Quebec) and more-developed programs to those with lower per-student costs and greater need for the programs. The entitlement option would require minimal accountability based on statistical data from the provinces and would incorporate a three-year minimum payment floor.

Provinces choosing the negotiation option would be able to enter into bilateral agreements with the federal government, presumably with the aim of getting additional funding, and would negotiate issues such as evaluation and accountability independently.[127] Any province opting for this choice would retain the right to switch back to the entitlement option. This option met the demands of New Brunswick, which was the main force pushing for more freedom to negotiate with the federal government and whose Cabinet had approved independent negotiations with the secretary of state in the event of a CMEC failure to reach consensus.[128] The CMEC secretariat formally adopted this format as a basis for discussions in September of 1981 and presented it to the ministers of education.[129]

Reaction to the two-option proposal varied across the country. British Columbia had serious reservations and doubted that the federal government would accept the proposal without first knowing the details of the negotiated plans. Alberta indicated that it would accept the proposal only if additional funds for the negotiated plans came from a separate funding pool, a sentiment echoed in Saskatchewan. Manitoba was generally favourable, although it wanted additional detail on the nonformula funds, which were very important in that province. Ontario and New Brunswick both expressed support for the two-option plan. Quebec, however, was opposed to its WNA component, which it believed went against the fundamental principle that no province should receive less money under the proposed accords. Prince Edward Island noted that with the new constitutional proposals moving forward, it was absolutely critical that a deal be struck to ensure funding for minority-language education, while Newfoundland expressed no opinion.[130] The objections to the two-option approach could be addressed with further negotiations, however, and the plan was not abandoned. The following January, New Brunswick, assuming that the plan would prove fruitful, began discussions with the federal government for a negotiated agreement.

Coming to Agreement

A great deal of finesse was required to resolve internal disputes among the provinces and then develop proposals that would be acceptable to the federal government. Most of these issues were negotiated by a CMEC task force of ministers and officials that was formed in October 1979 by representatives from Nova Scotia, New Brunswick, Quebec,

Ontario, and New Brunswick, supported by the staff of the CMEC secretariat. Quebec described this task force as the provinces' attempt to reassert their right to set the rules of the game, rather than merely respond to federal proposals.[131] While there are clearly indications from this process that interstate federalism was still having an impact on the OLEP, the final agreement indicates that the Canadian government's strategy of reasserting intrastate federalism had also been successful. By October 1981 most of the key pieces of the final agreement had been tentatively reached. However, some important issues remained to be resolved, necessitating trade-offs among the provinces and the federal government.

Shortly after the two-option approach was proposed at the CMEC, the nine English-speaking provincial premiers came to an agreement with the federal government on the patriation of the Constitution. In November 1981, Quebec, angered by this turn of affairs, pulled its representation from all interprovincial meetings, including the CMEC.[132] The CMEC responded by striking a special committee to work on the protocol agreement, a committee co-chaired by Education Ministers Charles Gallagher of New Brunswick and David King of Alberta, with officials from Manitoba and Ontario.[133] Quebec was consulted informally at first and then partially returned to the CMEC, with special authorization to work on the OLEP negotiations, assuming a position on the committee in April 1982. Although New Brunswick was part of this committee, its representatives nevertheless proceeded with independent negotiations with the federal government to come to a mutually agreeable solution.[134]

Negotiations from January to March 1982 centred on three outstanding issues among the provinces. The issue of additional costs continued to be problematic for Alberta and Quebec but was resolved by using the term "relate" in the proposed CMEC protocol of March 1982 and by the understanding that provinces choosing the entitlement option, or Basic Program Option as it came to be known, could determine for themselves what type of information would be provided to satisfy the federal need for accountability. The four funding categories proposed by the federal government were accepted by the provinces, provided that the Negotiation Option was not locked into these categories and that the categories remained flexible. The other critical issue for Quebec was the weighted national average, which had the potential to cost the province significantly. This issue was resolved within the CMEC by means of a floor. No province would receive less money during any year of the next agreement that was less than it had received during the interim agreement preceding the signing of a new protocol, or during the 1981–82 year.[135] With these issues resolved internally, the CMEC presented its two-option proposal to Secretary of State Gerald Regan and the federal government in March 1982.[136]

The federal government was slow to respond to the provincial proposal, being preoccupied with arrangements for the formal signing of the Constitution Act, 1982, on 17 April 1982. A tentative agreement was reached with Regan's officials in July, but by September there had still been no official response, because of a series of delays in the federal Cabinet.[137] Then in September, Regan was replaced by Serge Joyal, the fifth person to occupy the position of secretary of state in four years, further delaying the approval process. With still no response in early January 1983, Quebec began to be concerned that the reference year for the basic-payment floor would be pushed forward: a possibility that would cost the province even more money as its enrolments in English-language programs continued to slide.[138] Serge Joyal, discussing the proposed protocol with CMEC president David King later that month, indicated a general acceptance of the protocol, although he wanted the 1982–83 year used as the base reference point, not 1981–82. This change was not, however, communicated to the other provinces. In March 1983, Joyal issued a press release indicating that a protocol agreement had been reached and that it included two changes made by his officials: the 1982–83 year was to be used as the base year and the agreement was for three years, not five.[139]

Joyal's announcement turned out to be premature. Quebec was unwilling to accept the change in the base year, which would have cost the province $15 million over the three years of the agreement. Quebec's response necessitated a return to the bargaining table, with Quebec proposing that an average of the 1981–82 and 1982–83 figures be used for all three years and the federal government starting from an acceptance of the average for the first year of the agreement. Quebec argued that it was uniquely penalized by the change, and it wanted compensation for what it would otherwise lose.[140] Discussions dragged on through the summer, but by September 1983 Quebec was inclined to accept Joyal's proposal, which would cost the province only $10 million over the three years. As Quebec's officials noted, pushing off the protocol by one year had already cost the province $12 million, since the increased funding levels had not yet kicked in. Pushing the start date further into the future could potentially move the base year forward yet again, resulting in additional lost revenues.[141] By this point, Quebec had also moderated its stance regarding the CMEC significantly. Education Minister Camille Laurin returned to full participation. Only a truly viable CMEC, he argued, could act as an effective counterweight to Ottawa. Otherwise, the federal government would have ample excuses to intervene on any educational issues of national importance.[142]

After months of delays, the provinces accepted the compromise proposed by Serge Joyal. The Official Languages in Education Program protocol agreement was accepted on 20 December 1983. Ottawa would spend $600 million over the next three years.[143] It was now up to the provinces to determine which option they would choose and to negotiate their arrangements with the Canadian government.

Federal-Provincial Agreements

The choices made by the provinces demonstrate the extent to which the development of official languages in education still differed across the country in the early 1980s. They also indicate how government policies and the demands of official-language-minority communities had shaped the approaches of the provinces to their education programs. Moreover, these choices show how the advocates of interstate and intrastate federalism had reached a workable compromise, one that permitted the co-existence of both versions.

In total, seven provinces opted for the basic-program option and three for the negotiation option: Saskatchewan, Manitoba, and New Brunswick. Alberta signed its bilateral agreement with the federal government on 23 July 1984. The separate reporting of immersion and minority-language education, which Alberta had previously lumped together, clearly showed the gap between the province's commitment to the two programs. Of the infrastructure payments, $165,000 was committed to minority-language education, and $1,725,429 to immersion, a division that highlights the parental interest in immersion in the province.[144]

Ontario had waffled between the negotiation and the basic-program options. Given its size and demographic composition, it stood to break even on practically every plan that had been proposed over the previous four years, and its accountability procedures would allow it to easily meet the federal requirements under a negotiated option.[145] In the end, Ontario chose the simpler route of the basic-program option, signing an agreement with the federal government on 6 June 1984 that would grant it $16.7 million for minority-language education, $4.7 million for French immersion and $10.3 million for French second-language courses, as well as additional funding for special projects such as TVOntario programming, computer-learning materials, curriculum development, and grants for expanded FSL programs.[146]

Further east, the Canada-Nova Scotia Agreement on Official Languages in Education was signed on 2 April 1984. The bulk of its basic contribution was earmarked for FSL programs, at $1,130,271, with $656,220 earmarked for Acadian education. The agreement also covered a number of locally initiated special projects, primarily completion or development of Acadian, French-immersion, or core French programs in individual schools or boards.[147]

Quebec also chose the basic-program option. The language used in its agreement is noteworthy; whereas other agreements make references to the "official languages in education," Quebec's agreement was entitled the *Canada-Quebec Agreement for Minority-Language Education and Second-Language Instruction*.[148] The agreement itself had some important differences from the agreements with other provinces. The basic contributions were for each FTE in English-language educational programs, including French immersion, as well as for each FTE in English second-language instructional programs. The long-standing demand from the QFHSA and the PSBGM for FSL funding was not, however, realized. Quebec was permitted, as other provinces were, to determine how it justified the basic contributions. Unlike other provinces, Quebec did not break its costs down by grants to school boards and central administrative costs. Rather, the province presented a hypothetical cost model that assumed the replacement of the existing system with a unilingual French-language system, with no allowances for confessional school boards or English-language universities or CEGEPs. The province did not enter into many special projects, other than an intensive French program for nonfrancophones to facilitate their entry into French schools and adult-education courses in French as a second language.

While New Brunswick had been the primary agitator for a negotiation option, it was not the only province to choose this route. Although the additional funds made available for provinces choosing this route were limited, Manitoba's officials believed that they would be in a good position to claim a sizeable share of this money, given the high visibility of the BEF, the Collège universitaire de St-Boniface (CUSB), and Manitoba's significant grants to French-language education. Moreover, the word on the grapevine was that Ottawa's officials were well disposed to be generous, given the creativity and initiative that Manitoba had shown in this sector. There were indications that Ottawa was most interested in focusing on minority-language education opportunities in the wake of the Charter, and thus Manitoba focused its proposals in this sector, including further development in MLE at the elementary and secondary levels and new programs for the CUSB.[149]

The agreement signed on 28 May 1984 did significantly increase funding to Manitoba's French-education programs. On top of the basic contribution to Manitoba, which rose from $3,461,000 in 1983–84 to $4,004,000 in 1985–86, the federal government committed an additional $203,000 towards the administrative costs of the BEF.[150]

Moreover, the province received an additional $657,342 for 1983–84 for special projects, including such initiatives as cultural resource-staff people, computer courses, financial assistance for the Collège communautaire St-Boniface, regional education counsellors, and program development at the BEF. Overall, these funds raised Ottawa's contributions to special projects in Manitoba from the normal rate of 50 percent to the level of 60.8 percent.[151]

As mentioned, New Brunswick had been the major advocate of the negotiation option, and it did choose it. The New Brunswick agreement, signed on 30 March 1984, included contributions for both English and French second-language instruction programs. The New Brunswick approach to the new agreements was not broken down in an itemized fashion, as Manitoba's had been. Rather, New Brunswick argued that its costs at both the school board and the Department of Education level were systemically higher than those in other provinces. Under the agreement, New Brunswick received a minimum basic contribution of $17,969,000 for 1983–84, set to rise to $18,631,000 by 1985–86: an increase that was little more in actual dollars than Manitoba's, out of a total contribution that was four times as much. In addition, the province received an increased contribution towards its special projects.[152] Overall, though, New Brunswick did not find the negotiation option as profitable as it had hoped. Only an additional $5 million per year was earmarked for the negotiated plans, which meant that the additional benefits that the province had hoped would flow from this option never materialized, and the province had to contend with significant federal intervention in exchange for the minimal additional funds.[153]

The CMEC fulfilled its obligations under the protocol agreement, producing an annual report on the provinces' use of the additional funds received under the OLEP.[154] Statistics Canada also produced routine reports on the enrolment figures in the various programs, providing a benchmark for comparison of the programs, an example of which can be seen in table 5.2.

One cannot help but be struck by the phenomenal growth of immersion programs over the course of the first fifteen years of the OLEP. Enrolment in these programs had come to outstrip enrolment in the minority-language education programs by ever-increasing margins in many provinces (for example, in Alberta, where French immersion enrolment was sixteen times that of the MLE enrolment) and was continuing to grow at a rapid pace. As table 5.2 shows, significant challenges still remained in many provinces, particularly Alberta, Manitoba, and Nova Scotia, in convincing parents to send their children to minority-language education programs and in cajoling the

Table 5.2
Enrolment in Immersion and Minority-Language Education Programs, 1984–85

Province	ML Population Aged 5–19	Percentage of 5–19 Population	Total Enrolment in ML Education	French-Immersion Enrolment
Alberta	10,050	1.8	1,033	16,637
Manitoba	9,950	3.9	5,838	9,004
Ontario	102,640	4.9	92,025	19,810
Quebec	172,365	14.8	127,603	15,216
New Brunswick	63,640	33.0	47,755	11,009
Nova Scotia	6,070	2.7	4,760	604

Source: Council of Ministers of Education Canada, *Report on French and English Language Education*.

provinces into providing these programs, a task that would be facilitated by section 23 of the Charter. While the CMEC did have an important role to play in accountability and while it had been so crucial in the development of the protocol agreement, the bilateral agreements were negotiated separately, indicating the limits of the coordinated provincial approach to negotiations with Ottawa and the associated interstate version of federalism. Indeed, in the negotiated agreements intrastate federalism was predominant, since provinces hoping for additional federal dollars had to couch their proposals in terms of Ottawa's priorities and had to submit to extensive federal accountability provisions.

CONCLUSION

With the conclusion of the 1983 protocol agreements and the subsequent retirement of Pierre Elliot Trudeau from politics, the chapter in the history of English-French relations in Canada that had begun with the B & B Commission drew to a close. Although it would take several more years before French Canadian and Acadian minorities won school-management rights, major strides had been made between 1963 and 1984 to ensure the future survival of these communities. Between the funding arrangements of the OLEP (and the OLMG) and the constitutional protection of minority-language education afforded under the Charter, the rapid assimilation of French Canadian and Acadian communities had been slowed dramatically. Moreover, the Canadian government, which before the 1960s had treated French Canada with benign neglect, had transformed itself into a vigorous defender of the rights of both of Canada's official-language populations. With the defeat of the 1980 referendum on sovereignty-association, the separatist threat to Canadian unity, although not completely eliminated, had been contained for the time being.

The 1983 OLEP protocol agreements had important ramifications for the state of Canadian federalism. Neither the federal vision of the OLEP as an operation of intrastate federalism nor the provincial preference for interstate federalism had emerged as the clear victor through these negotiations. The federal government's attempts to secure a clear role in evaluation and to fund only developmental programs were largely circumvented or vetoed by the provinces, which defended their jurisdiction over education to the hilt. Moreover, the limits of intrastate federalism were made clear by the realization that Ottawa's official-language programs required the participation and consent of Quebec, the only majority francophone province. Quebec had the power to scuttle such initiatives as the Official Language Monitors Program, and without its involvement, the OLEP would lack a certain legitimacy.

However, more than a decade of federal funding for bilingual programs in education, coupled with active lobbying by federally funded organisations, had fostered high public expectations that the official-languages programs would continue. The provinces were thus largely caught in the position of being unable to cancel them. Moreover, the provinces depended on the federal funds to continue providing minority-language education and second-language instruction and were obliged by the Charter to furnish the former service. The provinces could not risk a complete federal withdrawal from this sector and conceded that Ottawa did have a role to play in promoting Canada's official languages and in creating a national language policy.

The interstate federalism advocated by provinces such as Alberta and Quebec relied significantly on their ability to maintain a common provincial front. As this negotiation process clearly demonstrated, several provinces did not have the financial luxury of being able to turn down Ottawa's offer of increased funds, or they were ideologically averse to the stance adopted by the majority of the provinces. Thus, there were serious limits to the provinces' ability to dictate official-language policy. Moreover, the provinces that opted for the negotiation option allowed the federal government an increased role in shaping their education programs and their policies were at least partly shaped by a desire to conform to federal objectives in minority-language education.

The protocol agreement and the bilateral subagreements also demonstrate the efficacy of the strategies adopted by a number of the lobby groups. While the aggressive stance adopted by the Fédération des francophones hors-Québec did not succeed in winning it a consultative role in the OLEP or the immediate establishment of school-management rights, it could count some impressive victories. Its lobby for accountability succeeded in obtaining the separate reporting and funding of minority-language education and French immersion. Moreover, it was minority-language education rights, not second-language or immersion rights, that were protected under the Charter.

Canadian Parents for French had cause to be pleased, as well. The original BEP agreements made no mention of French immersion at all, and immersion had largely been funded on an ad hoc basis throughout the first few agreements. Under the 1983 protocol, immersion was specifically named and funded at the same level as minority-language education. It had also gained a great deal of credibility and attention at both the provincial and federal levels. By not tying itself too closely to either level of government, the CPF had played a key role in bringing about the new multiyear agreements. It had acted as an intermediary between the two levels of government, conveying information to the federal government on how the provinces were spending the OLEP grants and calling on the provinces to be more accountable, while also lobbying the federal government to retain maintenance funding, raise the total amount of funding available to the program, and ease off on some of its accountability demands.[155]

The CPF was more warmly received by the provinces, and ultimately, it was successful in getting invited to a meeting with four CMEC ministers in June 1981, where it raised a number of its concerns.[156] In many ways, the CPF was less threatening than the FFHQ to the CMEC, since it was generally not demanding rights for its constituents (although it had pushed for a right to choice in language of education and had supported francophone associations at the provincial level). In public it took a much less confrontational approach to the CMEC, acting more as a mediator than as an adversary.[157]

A number of the provincial minority-language groups had reason to be satisfied as well. Their respective provincial governments had signed on to the Charter and had not backed out of the OLEP. Moreover, in the English-speaking provinces, the state of both language rights and language education was much improved over the pre-OLEP days. The same could not be said for the anglophone associations of Quebec. Appeasing the Quebec government had taken precedence over addressing the concerns of the QFHSA and the PSBGM. The basic-program option protected Quebec's right to minimal accountability, and there was no promise of additional funding to the English-language school boards. Moreover, Quebec did not enter into any significant special projects of benefit to its English-speaking minority.

The battles between the federal and provincial governments and concomitant jockeying for position were almost exclusively limited to administrative and jurisdictional elements of the OLEP: finance, accountability, visibility, and objectives. In this process, the pedagogical worthiness of the program and its success in meeting the stated objectives were rarely considered. Although education specialists had criticized the twenty-minute-per-day French second-language programs – the minimum threshold required for the federal grants – as too low to produce effective learning,[158] these concerns were largely overlooked in the negotiation process. As a result, official-language programs in education were not always designed with current pedagogical theory in mind.

While one may conjecture that federal contributions to these programs were likely motivated more by political reasons (among them the need for a nation-wide program including all the provinces) than educational ones (such as funding the best possible types of language programs), the impact of the BEP/OLEP on official languages in education cannot be dismissed. The types of disputes that the provinces, the federal government, and community organisations were engaged in by the early 1980s demonstrated that the necessity and validity of providing these services was no longer in question, a situation that had not been the case in the late 1960s. If one had to choose the primary accomplishment of the BEP/OLEP, it would be that it had promoted its target programs – minority-language education and second-language instruction – to a status whereby they were no longer questioned by political authorities and were increasingly considered to be part and parcel of the educational options available to Canadian children. This was a major discourse shift and one that had important ramifications for the construction of Canadian identity.

CHAPTER SIX

A New Equilibrium: Official-Languages Discourse and Canadian National Identity

The conclusion of the 1983 protocol agreement augured well for the long-term viability of the Official Languages in Education Program. Twenty years later, Heritage Minister Sheila Copps announced an extension of OLEP funding through to 2007–8, the fourth such extension since the protocol was signed. Evaluations of the OLEP undertaken since 1983 have generally been favourable, and its longevity speaks to its success. Yet, some aspects remain problematic, and the issues of control and accountability, which dogged the program in its initial years, continue to create conflict. However, a brief overview of the evolution of the OLEP over the past two decades demonstrates that it has had significant impacts, not only on language learning but on the structure of Canadian federalism and on Canadians' attitudes towards their official languages.

POLITICAL AND CONSTITUTIONAL DEVELOPMENTS SINCE 1983

After taking his famed walk in the snow on 28 February 1984, Pierre Elliott Trudeau announced his retirement from federal politics, after sixteen years as prime minister. The ensuing Liberal leadership convention brought John Turner a victory over Justice Minister Jean Chrétien. But after sixteen years of Liberal government, in the election that followed Canada opted for change, electing the Progressive Conservative Party of Brian Mulroney in a landslide victory. Shortly after the election, Mulroney began to take steps to make the newly patriated Constitution acceptable to Quebec. Working together with Robert Bourassa, who returned as premier in 1985, Mulroney's team crafted the Meech Lake Accord, which was signed by the ten provincial premiers in 1987. Over the next three years, the provincial legislatures debated the accord in an effort to achieve ratification by 1990.

Like Joe Clark before him, Mulroney assumed leadership in a Canada that generally accepted the language-policy course charted by the Trudeau government. His government stayed the course on official languages, revising the Official Languages Act in 1988, with some significant ramifications for the OLEP. Up to 1988, Ottawa's involvement in the OLEP had lacked specific legislative authority. Instead, it relied on the federal spending power, coupled with vague interpretations of the Official Languages Act, 1969, which gave the federal government a role in promoting the two official languages.

The Treasury Board's 1988 revision of the Official Languages Act finally gave the OLEP – and the OLMG – statutory authority, through additions to part 7 of the act.[1] The pertinent new sections read as follows:

Section 41. The Government of Canada is committed to enhancing the vitality of the English and French linguistic minority communities in Canada and to supporting their development and to fostering the full recognition and use of English and French in Canadian society.

Section 42. The Secretary of State, in consultation with other Ministers, is to promote a coordinated approach to the implementation by federal institutions of these commitments.

Section 43. Statutory authority is provided to the Secretary of State for programs aimed at: enhancing the vitality of the English and French linguistic minority communities in Canada and supporting their development; encouraging and supporting the learning and appreciation of English and French; encouraging and assisting the provinces to support the development of English and French linguistic minorities generally and in particular to offer provincial and municipal service in both official languages, and give English and French linguistic minorities opportunities to be educated in their own language; encouraging and assisting the provinces to give Canadians opportunities to learn both official languages; encouraging private and voluntary organisations to provide services in both official languages; encouraging and assisting organisations to project Canada's bilingual character in the country and abroad. The Act allows the Secretary of State to consult the public in the development of policies and the review of programs relating to the advancement and use of the official languages in Canadian society.[2]

With these revisions, the Official Languages in Education Program was conferred with an official status in federal legislation that had been lacking throughout the years of its early development, and the Secretary of State was given a mandate to implement official-language programs. The balance between interstate and intrastate federalism that was established with the 1983 protocol agreements was also preserved. For intrastate advocates, section 43 officially sanctions federal intervention in language-education programs and in the support of minority-language communities; for interstate advocates, section 42 requires that this action be coordinated with provincial ministers.

While amending the Official Languages Act proceeded smoothly, the Meech Lake Accord did not. Although Mulroney's government survived the 1988 election, a number of the provincial governments that had signed the accord did not. Their successors did not ratify the accord, which died in June 1990. The death of Meech, which had been vigorously attacked by former prime minister Trudeau, triggered yet another round of constitutional deliberations. In an effort to stave off another referendum on Quebec's independence – which looked ever more likely after the Bloc Québécois formed in Parliament – Constitutional Affairs Minister Joe Clark cobbled together the Charlottetown Accord. This attempt to win over the Quebec government also ended in failure, as the accord was solidly rejected by Canadians in the 1992 referendum. In the aftermath of the rejection of both Meech and Charlottetown, Canadians decimated Mulroney's Conservative government in the 1993 elections, opting for the Liberal party of Jean Chrétien. Quebecers voted heavily for the Bloc in that election, and then elected a provincial government led by the Parti Québécois under Jacques Parizeau in 1994. The PQ moved swiftly to hold another referendum on sovereignty-association. The campaign was closely fought and was only narrowly won by the "No" forces. But, with the referendum defeated, a period of moderate constitutional stability settled in once again.

Despite the constitutional turmoil of the 1980s and 1990s, both the Mulroney and the Chrétien governments held to the course on the official-language policies established under Trudeau. As the Charter of Rights and Freedoms began to take effect, it would have been difficult for them to do otherwise, given how entrenched these policies were becoming. The Supreme Court took a broad view of the minority-language rights contained in section 23 and in a landmark decision in the *Mahé* case ruled that the Charter provided for minority-language school governance.[3] Further decisions by Canadian courts took a similarly broad view of minority-language education rights, which committed provincial education ministries across the country to expand their provision of these programs.

A New Equilibrium   171

THE EVOLUTION OF THE OLEP AGREEMENTS

While turmoil reigned in Canadian constitutional life, the Official Languages in Education Program continued its steady pace of development. The three-year protocol agreement reached on 20 December 1983 was renewed for an additional two years on 17 September 1985, and its funding was increased by an additional 3 percent.[4] The first protocol agreement proved to be effective in channelling federal dollars towards the provinces in most need of development. Quebec's share of the funding dropped substantially – from 57 percent in 1980–81 to 41 percent in 1985–86, while other provinces posted modest increases (see appendix E for figures).[5] Moreover, with funding levels rebounding from the 1978 cuts, enrolment in both elementary and secondary second-language courses began to climb in the early 1980s.[6]

A second five-year protocol agreement was signed on 17 November 1988 on behalf of the Canadian government by representatives from the secretary of state and by the Council of Ministers of Education, Canada (CMEC), on behalf of the provinces. This renewal, the first since the passage of the Official Languages Act 1988, introduced some new features into the OLEP. Ottawa and the provinces agreed upon key strategic priorities to guide the program's future development, including increasing minority-language education services in accordance with section 23 of the Charter, increasing French-language education services at the postsecondary level, expanding teacher-training programs, expanding French-immersion programs and expanding and further developing regular second-language programs.[7] The parties further agreed to hold annual meetings regarding these priorities and to consult groups within their jurisdiction about how best to implement the programs. The governments also agreed to undertake a joint evaluation of the protocol agreements. Given the difficulties surrounding evaluation of the BEP/OLEP in the late 1970s and early 1980s, this was a positive step forward. Many of these new developments stemmed from recommendations of the first formal evaluation of the OLEP, undertaken in 1987 by education specialist professor Stacy Churchill of OISE, in association with the consulting firm Peat Marwick.[8]

Funding levels continued to climb under the 1988 protocol agreement, exceeding the 1977–78 high-water mark in 1989–90 and reaching over $246 million by 1992–93. There was high demand for these funds, as provinces steadily expanded their minority-language education systems, a process accelerated by the *Mahé* decision. Quebec's share of OLEP funding continued to drop and stood at 34 percent in 1989–90.[9] Yet despite this progress, the bulk of funding continued to fall under the protocol's infrastructure component, which paid for ongoing programs, rather than for development of new initiatives. The evaluations recommended that Ottawa try to free up more money for new development, which was bound to be needed as provinces coped with the expansion of their minority-language education systems and the still-popular French-immersion programs.[10]

After a decade of budget increases and generally positive evaluations, the floor fell out from under the OLEP. Three years lapsed before a new protocol agreement was signed, in 1996. Its budget was slashed by 36.6 percent.[11] The 1993–98 agreement is widely viewed as part of the dark days of the OLEP, funding dropped to its lowest level since 1975, with devastating impacts on second-language learning in Canada. In the wake of the *Mahé* decision, the provinces had to concentrate their resources on minority-language education. Second-language programs were cut, and immersion enrolments plateaued.[12] Even more alarming for language advocates, the reported rate of personal bilingualism among young anglophones fell from 16.3 percent to 12.9 percent.[13] Canadian Parents for French, the Canadian Association of Second-Language Teachers, and francophone associations lashed out at the federal cutbacks, which threatened the long-term viability of Canadian language education.

The third protocol agreement proved to be only a temporary setback, as the 1998 round of agreements gradually restored funding to the program. The 1993 and 1998 agreements also incorporated new provisions to facilitate the development of interprovincial initiatives for official languages in education. Nothing substantial has yet to come of these provisions, but the participants were optimistic about the potential they held for new ventures. The 1998 protocol also included new action plans for the provinces with performance indicators and expected results. Significant kinks had to be worked out of these plans, which were in a pilot phase, but they held the prospect of better accountability for the program.

At the outset of the new century, the Canadian government held the OLEP in high regard and set a course of action to redouble its efforts in official languages. In the spring of 2003, Intergovernmental Affairs Minister Stéphane Dion relaunched the federal government's official language strategy, committing Ottawa firmly to the OLEP. Over $381 million in additional funding was committed to official languages programming over five years.[14] Of particular importance was the government's push to increase personal bilingualism, aiming to double the level of individual bilingualism in Canadians aged fifteen to nineteen, an ambitious goal, since the vast majority of bilingual Canadians are francophones and this objective would require huge increases in the bilingual anglophone population. The Official Languages in Education Program would be the centrepiece of this redoubled effort, which has a target date of 2013.

MINORITY- AND SECOND-LANGUAGE EDUCATION SINCE 1983

The programs funded under the auspices of the OLEP became more firmly entrenched in the Canadian educational landscape over the course of the 1980s and 1990s. There were, however, some variations in the pedagogical success of these initiatives. On the whole, the development of minority-language education was a broad success. As mentioned earlier, a series of court challenges funded by the federal government helped official-language minority communities win the right to manage their own schools. The courts' interpretation of the "where numbers warrant" clause proved to be quite broad, which forced the provinces to establish French-language schools for very small populations.

As the courts gradually defined the provincial governments' obligations to provide minority-language education, the concept of children "ayant droit" to these programs emerged: children who had grown up speaking English in assimilated households but who had the constitutional right to an education in French.[15] Thus, heading into the 1990s, minority-language schools faced the challenge of refrancisation: how to cope with a mixed clientele of students with a wide range of French-language capacities. For the long-term survival of francophone-minority communities to be viable, they would need to recapture the children who had been lost to the majority community. Debates over how to address this issue are ongoing.

Since 1969, a decisive majority of Canadians had come to both accept and support the federal government's intervention to help the minority-language communities survive. Polls taken throughout the 1980s and 1990s demonstrated strong support for the right of minority-language communities to educate their children in their mother tongue. Moreover, they supported the use of federal funds for this objective. While approval of this initiative was extremely high among the minority-language communities – usually around 80 to 90 percent – it was also very strong in the majority-language populations, ranging from 70 to 80 percent.[16] In a strong indication of shifting Canadian attitudes, younger Canadians tended to express stronger levels of support than their parents. While opinions against bilingualism have persisted in a significant proportion of the population, particularly among supporters of the Reform/Alliance/Conservative Party, they remain the opinions of a minority of voters. Indeed, statements made by Conservative official-languages critic Scott Reid during the 2004 election campaign implying that his party might reduce bilingual services led to widespread criticism in the media and cost Reid his portfolio.

While minority-language education became ever more firmly entrenched and the programs became more elaborate and sophisticated, second-language instruction has travelled a bumpier road over the past two decades. Throughout the 1970s, educational experts had argued that the state of core French was a disaster. The standard twenty-minute-per-day programs that were followed in most provinces, they argued, were not only failing to promote individual bilingualism but also creating hostility among students towards language learning in general. Yet no efforts were taken by Ottawa to cajole the provinces into changing their programs or to cut off funding to clearly ineffective programs.

There were some encouraging signs for second-language instruction in the mid-1980s. The Canadian Association of Second Language Teachers produced a study of core French in the late 1980s that pointed out the weaknesses of these programs. In response, several provinces, including Ontario, Alberta, and Prince Edward Island, moved to implement the new National Core French Program, which increased the amount of time allocated to core French.[17] But, unlike the provision of minority-language education, the provision of second-language instruction was not mandated under the Constitution. Thus, in the early 1990s, when provinces were forced to expand their minority-language education programs at the same time as OLEP funding was slashed, FSL courses were among the first to feel the funding crunch. Schools in provinces such as Alberta and Manitoba cut their core French offerings, and enrolments in these programs dropped. Bilingualism among young anglophones also fell during this decade. By the time of the 2003 program review, analysts questioned whether core French was contributing to the federal government's objectives. They further noted that there was still no national tool to measure second-language proficiency in students and that provincial requirements for second-language learning continued to vary widely – from New Brunswick, where it was compulsory for grades 1 to 10, to Alberta, where the programs were completely optional.[18]

Despite these problems, there were some successes to report regarding second-language learning. A majority of Canadians continued to support the federal government's efforts to promote it, ranging between 50 and 70 percent of majority-language speakers. French immersion also continued to be solidly supported. While enrolment in the programs plateaued in the early 1990s, it continued to be stable despite funding cuts that prevented further expansion. Moreover, many cities, from Kelowna to Halifax, continued to experience a level of demand that exceeded class space for the programs. French immersion was widely acknowledged to be the best method of promoting individual bilingualism, and Canadian programs continued to be held up as an international model. The federal government did recognize the weakness of second-language education in the country and made improving it a priority in its 2003 action plan. Minister Dion called for reinvestment in second-language learning, aiming to double the percentage of fifteen- to nineteen-year-olds who had a working knowledge of their second-language, up to 50 percent.[19]

As official-language programs became embedded in the fabric of Canadian educational policies and public attitudes towards language learning, so too did the federal role in language education become more fully entrenched. As might be expected, skirmishes about provincial accountability to the federal government and provincial complaints about the complexity of the accounting process continued. The structure of the OLEP protocol also became increasingly rigid, with both parties unwilling to alter it substantially, for fear of opening a Pandora's box for federal-provincial relations. Nevertheless, the federal government was able to continue to advance its view that official languages were best dealt with through intrastate federalism and continued to work with its allies at the community level to maintain pressure on the provinces.

Questions of consultation with community groups were particularly contentious during the 1980s and 1990s. The Canadian government, which revamped the Official Minority Languages Group Program into the Promotion of Official Languages Program, continued to fund key activities of official-language minority associations. It also continued to seek the input of these communities on the direction that the OLEP should take. For the provinces, this was an ongoing concern. Provincial representatives noted to program evaluators that they feared that "mixed messages" might be transmitted through federal meetings with community groups.[20] Viewing the protocol as a strictly federal-provincial matter, they did not like having it discussed with third parties. If any consultation was to occur, they argued, it should be at the provincial level with groups interested in educational matters. Despite these concerns, the federal government continued its consultations. Its client groups were quite pleased with the willingness of Canadian Heritage (which took over the OLEP in 1993) to consult with them and indeed considered one of the federal government's most important roles to be its leadership in the realm of official languages on their behalf.[21] The target groups of the OLEP were the most likely to raise complaints about provincial accountability and were also the most supportive of a stronger federal role in education.

By the mid-1990s, the federal government's role in official languages had become quite firmly entrenched. The provinces were willing to bend their jurisdictional objections in this sector and routinely commented on how these funds had made significant progress possible.[22] The program also gradually began to take on more of an intrastate character as the decades progressed. In later revisions of the protocol, strategic priorities and action plans began to appear, revisions negotiated by the federal government with the provinces, demonstrating increased collaboration. The provinces also generally accepted the need to redistribute OLEP funding to programs and regions that needed it most, rather than insisting quite so firmly on a province-by-province approach (although some conflict over distribution of funds did occur). Moreover, while they had not been implemented by the early years of the new century, the OLEP did include provisions for the development of interprovincial collaborative ventures in official languages.[23] By this time, the provinces were also quite satisfied with the program as a model of effective federal-provincial collaboration. All parties expected federal funding to official languages in education to continue to flow and believed that the OLEP provided a key method for preserving the vitality of the official-language minority communities. By 2003 the OLEP had become firmly embedded in the fabric of federal-provincial relations. It would have taken substantial effort to weed out federal involvement in language education, and none of the provinces seemed particularly inclined to do so.

CONCLUSION

The early years of the Official Languages in Education Program played a very significant role in transforming the language landscape of Canadian society. Not all provinces implemented the agreements in the same way or with the same speed and commitment, yet none backed out of them, and all have stayed involved with the program to the present day. The program has had significant impacts on the balance between interstate and intrastate federalism in Canada, the contours of the embedded state, and the strategies employed by lobby groups in their quest for official-languages education. As we look at these impacts, it is also possible to reflect on how successful the Trudeau-era language policies were in accomplishing the goals of preventing the disappearance of official-language minority communities, halting the rise of separatist

A New Equilibrium 177

aspirations in Quebec, and refashioning Canadian identity so that Canadians would accept the necessity of an officially bilingual country with government services in English and French.

Canadian Federalism and the OLEP

When the Royal Commission on Bilingualism and Biculturalism conducted its studies, Canadian federalism was in flux. Ottawa's postwar cooperative federalism faced a vigorous challenge from the interstate federalism promoted by Ontario and Quebec. Born into this shifting political climate, the Bilingualism in Education Program faced an uphill battle as the federal government was attempting intrastate action in yet another area of provincial jurisdiction: language education. The Trudeau government argued that questions of minority-language education rights and of language policy as a whole were of national importance. Thus, they were better suited to solutions rooted in intrastate federalism, whereby the federal government would fashion national policies and use its spending power to persuade provincial governments to establish and administer these new policies. The provinces, although eager for an influx of federal government cash, were not enthusiastic about the prospect of Ottawa meddling in primary and secondary education, and they took steps to limit the Canadian government's claim to an active role in this sector. The informality of the initial BEP agreement of 1970 is testament to this provincial effort, with its minimal provisions for accountability and evaluation and nebulous definitions of jurisdiction.

The initial agreements of 1970 were but the starting point for the long struggle between the provinces and the federal government over whose vision of Canadian federalism would prevail in this sector. The provinces pushed an interstate model, whereby the federal government and the provinces would meet as equals to discuss arrangements that would strictly respect provincial jurisdiction. Once Ottawa's efforts to increase its control over the BEP became apparent in the mid-1970s, the provinces adopted a two-pronged strategy. The first was to increase the role of the Council of Ministers of Education, Canada, which became the visible face of the common front of the provinces. Throughout the negotiation phase from 1977 to 1983, the CMEC provided the forum for interprovincial discussions. Its secretariat drafted texts for the provinces to consider and served as the intermediary between provincial ministries of education and the federal government. In this manner, the provinces pushed for an interstate arrangement in which the CMEC and the federal government would meet as equals in a one-to-one relationship, rather than permitting the federal government to play a game of divide and conquer with the provinces.

The second prong of the provincial approach was to design a made-in-the-provinces solution to the minority-language education question. Through the St Andrews and Montreal declarations of 1977 and 1978, the provinces attempted to define how the expansion of minority-language education rights would proceed. They committed themselves to the "best efforts" approach, whereby each province would take the steps that it considered appropriate to develop these programs, rather than allowing the federal government to dictate the schedule. These declarations were coupled with an unequivocal declaration of support for the principle that, where feasible, children of the minority-language community had the right to receive an education in their mother tongue.

The provincial effort to advance interstate federalism and curtail the Canadian government's attempt to expand its sphere of influence was somewhat successful. The provinces successfully blocked Ottawa's attempts to gain a federal role in program evaluation and to steer the OLEP completely towards the development of new programs. Moreover, the protocol agreements clearly stated the provincial supremacy in matters of education.

However, the Trudeau government scored a number of important victories that kept interstate and intrastate federalism in balance. Like the provinces, Ottawa also had a two-pronged strategy for developing the official-languages regime that it wanted. The OLEP was part of the financial/administrative strategy. After thirteen years of receiving federal grants for their official-languages programs in education, the provinces were not in a strong position to withdraw from the OLEP, which had embedded itself in provincial education policies. Many provinces, particularly in the Maritimes and on the Prairies, did not have the financial capacity to cope with a complete cessation of federal payments, while the others simply did not relish the prospect of losing these substantial grants. Thus, they made concessions to the federal demands. While not conceding a federal role in education per se, the provinces did acknowledge the federal government's role in crafting a national language policy, and they acknowledged that educational programs were part of this role. They therefore conceded that the federal government could legitimately fund education programs as part of its efforts in language policy. Moreover, provinces that chose the Negotiation Option, with its increased funding levels and more substantial developmental thrust, were exposed to a greater degree of federal intrusion in education, ranging from the setting of priorities to the structure of evaluations. Over subsequent decades, the Negotiation Option would prove not to be as lucrative as had been hoped, and provinces such as New Brunswick would revert to the Basic Program. The Negotiation Option was nevertheless a federal victory in terms of securing an increased presence for Ottawa in provincial education programs from which it could promote its agenda of minority-language education rights. Moreover, as the OLEP developed through the 1980s and 1990s, the federal government increasingly played a role in setting the program's strategic priorities and carried out evaluations of its structure.

The second part of Ottawa's strategy was its constitutional gambit, to add clout to federal institutions that would defend minority-language rights. Using the provinces' own declarations from St Andrews and Montreal as leverage, Ottawa moved from 1977 to 1982 to enshrine minority-language education rights in the constitution. With these rights protected by the Charter, and enforceable by the Supreme Court, a federal institution, Ottawa now had a legal stick at its disposal to protect its official-languages policy should the carrot approach of financial aid fail. The Charter proved to be a very effective mechanism for enforcing minority-language education rights, although it did little for second-language instruction in Canada.

A Changed Discourse on Official Languages

The Canadian government's programs to promote two official languages have been the object of widespread criticism in the thirty-odd years of their existence. On the national unity front, they have been criticized for failing to stem the tide of Quebec separatism and for failing to foster substantial growth in the size of official-language minority communities elsewhere in the country.[24] The OLEP in particular has been attacked for failing to produce a nation of fluently bilingual citizens. These criticisms have been levied since the late 1970s and continue to the present day. On the surface, they may seem well-founded. However, a more thorough analysis shows that they are in some cases premature, that in some instances they point the finger of blame at the wrong target, that in others they evaluate the federal efforts using a very narrow band of criteria, and that in still other cases they are oblivious to some very tangible benefits. While the OLEP did not provide a cure-all for the language conflicts in Canadian society, it did nevertheless produce substantial changes in government policy at both the national and provincial levels, as well as shifts in Canadian identity politics.

A decade of federal funding of official-language programs in education had a dramatic impact on the demographic trends of the official-language minority communities and increased both the quality and the availability of minority-language education in the country. While assimilation trends in the English-majority provinces were not reversed, they slowed significantly in this period. Moreover, the new education programs and official-language minority group funding threw a life preserver to these communities that allowed them to regroup and plan their future strategies.

Between 1967 and 1982 most provincial governments took concrete steps to increase their French-language program offerings, either by recognizing these programs in the appropriate legislation, as was done in Alberta and Nova Scotia, or by making them obligatory where sufficient demand existed, as in Manitoba, Ontario, and New Brunswick. Federal funding for the programs played a major role in overcoming provincial reluctance to accept and expand them, which, in turn, made possible a shift in the discourse on minority-language education.

By 1977 the provincial premiers were no longer questioning whether minority-language education should be provided but were instead debating the modalities of providing it. In this respect, the OLEP laid the groundwork for section 23 of the Canadian Charter of Rights and Freedoms, which guaranteed access to minority-language education to members of the official-language minority community, where numbers warranted. The OLEP also gave additional clout to the demands of French Canadian and Acadian community associations for French-language education, since they could point to the financial resources available from Ottawa. This progress has continued since the passage of the Charter, as minority-language communities have won the right to school governance and French-language postsecondary institutions outside Quebec have continued to grow.[25] Thus, the impact of the OLEP on access to minority-language education is undeniable.

The success of the OLEP in attaining its second objective, second-language acquisition, has been hotly contested. Many have pointed out that secondary school enrolments in FSL fell throughout the 1970s and that students following the core second-language program largely failed to reach a basic level of French comprehension. While enrolments in core second-language programs did decline, the decline can more properly be attributed to changing university entry requirements and a move towards fewer mandatory courses in secondary school. Furthermore, while the basic twenty-minute-per-day programs funded by the OLEP generally did not produce fluency in the second language, the OLEP was never intended to make all Canadians fluently bilingual. It did attain its objective of providing vastly increased opportunities for interested children to learn the second official language. Moreover, with the OLEP's sliding funding scale, provincial education departments were given a strong incentive to develop more intense FSL programs, including French immersion. While the results of core French programs have been disappointing to date, the immersion programs are widely considered to have been quite effective.

French-immersion programs spread rapidly throughout the provinces over the 1970s, offering children the opportunity to become fluent in their second language. Studies of English-speaking children in the French-immersion programs demonstrated that they displayed a more favourable disposition to French Canadian culture and expanded rights for official-language-minority communities than control groups.[26] The long-term impacts of this generation of immersion children on national unity and public policy are only beginning to be felt now, but one suspects that these "children of Trudeau"[27] are likely to be well-disposed to expanding and continuing a strong official-languages policy for Canada and to building bridges between the two official-language groups. What is clear is that since 1984, official-language programs in education have proven to be an enduring phenomenon. French-immersion continues to thrive, and French minority-language education rights continue to expand across the country. Moreover, the country has not been faced with any major or sustained effort to repeal the Official Languages Act (indeed, the Act was revised and expanded in 1988) or to cancel the OLEP. In these respects, the efforts of the federal government with respect to official bilingualism should not be considered to have failed.

The OLEP clearly altered Canadian discourse about bilingualism and official languages. Language programs that were hotly contested in the 1960s were generally accepted by the 1980s. Through the carrot approach of funding minority-language education and second-language instruction, the federal government helped to make these programs commonplace, part-and-parcel of Canadian education, and official bilingualism became part of the Canadian national identity and the Canadian Constitution. Even if Canadian schoolchildren did not become fluent in their second language, they grew up with direct experience of a country with two official languages. For children of the official-language-minority communities, the change was even more dramatic. By the time of the protocol agreements of 1983–84, most of these children had increased access to education in their own language, and their right to this education was enshrined in the Charter, which provided the support needed for further expansion of classes, schools, and school boards. Thus, they were no longer obliged to assimilate to the majority language by default.

Social Action and the Embedded State

Minority- and second-language education programs would not have evolved as they did under the Official Languages in Education Program without the concerted action of a network of key politicians, civil servants, and lobby groups at both the national and provincial levels. This network played a very important role in driving the OLEP forward, crafting provincial education policy, and maintaining dialogue between the Canadian government and the provinces. It was through the actions of these individuals and organisations that other factors that might have inhibited the development of the OLEP – including demographics, financial constraints, and ideological opposition – were overcome to allow the programs to flourish.

The embedded state helped to develop the commitment of the provinces to the OLEP on two levels: first, within the government itself and second, through the action of lobby groups. As we have seen, language policy throughout this period was shaped by key individuals within both the federal and provincial governments, including civil servants, deputy ministers, Cabinet ministers, and even premiers and the prime minister. The personal ideologies of these individuals led them to stress certain priorities over others: French immersion was pushed very strongly by Raymond Hébert in Manitoba, for example, while Ontario's Premier Davis was more concerned with FSL programs and Terence Donahoe's priority for Nova Scotia was Acadian education. In all cases, however, it was the commitment of these individuals to various aspects of the OLEP that kept these programs moving forward, despite opposition from various sources, often including other members of their own governments. As new initiatives were introduced in their departments, bureaucracies grew up to defend them and work to maintain them in the future. The client groups served by these programs would also work to ensure that these new initiatives were not discontinued.

Sympathetic governments and bureaucracies could also facilitate the positive reception of the demands of lobby groups, whose strategies were particularly important in the success that they achieved. Most of the lobby groups who took an interest in the OLEP achieved notable victories (with the exception of the Quebec anglophone groups), and several common elements contributed to their success. In most cases, they were at their most successful when they were able to demonstrate the broad-based benefits of official-languages programs in education. This tactic was used most notably by the CPF, which touted the functional benefits of individual bilingualism for employment opportunities. It was also used by a number of provincial francophone associations, including ACFA, the SFM, and FANE, which were reaching out to their English-speaking governments.

Avoiding the appearance of being too overtly attached to one level of government was also a key tactic for these lobby groups. Although many were funded by the federal government and were often most sympathetic to its objectives, associations such as the CPF, ACFA, the SANB, and even the FFHQ made sure to criticize both levels of government, so as to protect a position of independence. The CPF went furthest in this respect, offering its services as an intermediary between Ottawa and the provincial governments.

In some provinces, such as New Brunswick and Ontario, the French minority population was strong enough, both in size and in community coherency, that lobby groups representing these communities (ACFO, the AEFO, the SNA, the SANB, and so on) were able to take strong, aggressive positions vis-à-vis their provincial governments and succeed in winning concessions. In other provinces, where the minority population was less significant, lobby groups tended to adopt a more conciliatory approach to their governments, a strategy that won small, incremental gains. An intriguing aspect of the francophone lobbying strategy in respect to education rights was the "good cop/bad cop" routine that these groups employed in the provinces. The FFHQ, which was basically a national umbrella organisation of the provincial associations, engaged in many hostile attacks on both the provincial and the federal governments and regularly released polemics filled with invective. At the national level, this strategy was fairly safe: the Trudeau government supported minority-language education rights and was unlikely to change this position. At the provincial level, however, the confrontational stance of the FFHQ, which kept minority-language education rights in the press and the public eye, made the proposals being advanced by moderate organisations such as ACFA, the SFM, and FANE seem much more reasonable in the eyes of the provincial governments, which then adopted the moderate proposals. It was through this strategy, in combination with the other tactics described above, that the social-action groups and other facets of the embedded state were able to protect and promote the OLEP so effectively.

Bilingual Today, United Tomorrow?
OLEP and Canadian National Unity

Political scientist Kenneth McRoberts, in his recent work *Misconceiving Canada: The Struggle for National Unity*, is extremely critical of the Trudeau government's efforts to address Quebec nationalism and its policies of bilingualism and multiculturalism. His criticism, which has been supported by a number of other academics, is rooted in the belief that the federal government should have concentrated its efforts on promoting the French language and culture in the province of Quebec, rather than on promoting a vision of national bilingualism and multiculturalism in English-speaking Canada that was fundamentally unacceptable in francophone Quebec. The Official Languages in Education Program is thus considered by McRoberts and his supporters as ultimately a failure.

A closer examination of the program reveals, however, that another interpretation is more accurate. The vision of Canada promoted by McRoberts is rooted in a French Quebec–English Canada duality that rejects any chance for the survival for French Canadian and Acadian minorities outside Quebec or for cooperation between Canada's English- and French-speaking communities. His argument that a federal policy promoting French in Quebec would lead to a peaceful coexistence in Canada is wishful thinking and conjecture. Indeed, had the Trudeau government followed this policy, abandoning any hope of cooperation and communication between Canada's two official-language communities, it would likely have alienated Western Canada and reinforced the case for Quebec separatism. Ties between the two main language groups would have been increasingly severed, and the minority communities in each province would have been allowed to disappear. Moreover, as the Quebec government's actions in the field of language policy during the 1970s amply prove, the province was well equipped within the confines of Canadian federalism to promote the French language within its own borders.

The outcomes of the OLEP, which aimed to promote a pan-Canadian, English-French conception of duality, suggest that McRoberts' fatalistic vision does not describe the inevitable outcome of a Canadian language policy. Over the course of the OLEP's development, the French Canadian and Acadian minorities that had been in dire straits – facing high assimilation rates, an isolationist Quebec, and a dearth of French-language government services – were given the supports needed to ensure that they would have the time and funds to regroup. At the same time, the federal language policy successfully encouraged the provinces to expand their minority-language education services. This financial aid in turn laid the groundwork that made possible section 23 of the Charter of Rights and Freedoms, a provision that has since led to major victories in French minority-language education rights. While the progress made in revitalising these communities has not been overly rapid, substantial gains have been made, and these communities have not completely died out, as many were predicting thirty-odd years ago.

Second-language instructional programs also received a major boost from the OLEP-funded programs. True, francophones do not feel as much at home in Calgary as in Rimouski, nor do anglophones feel as comfortable in Chicoutimi as in Toronto. Nor are all Canadians fluently bilingual. But to criticize the OLEP on this basis would be to have idealistic and unrealistic expectations of what type of change could be effected given the demographic composition of Canada. OLEP funding did keep FSL programs active, and it did lead to the expansion of provincial course offerings. The cultural components of these programs exposed children to their country's other official-language communities and fostered an awareness of the larger reality in Canada beyond their provincial borders. More successful still were the French-immersion programs, which grew from pilot projects in a few provinces to a thriving nation-wide initiative. The full impact of the second-language programs on Canadian unity is still difficult to measure. However, one may conjecture that a Canada that fosters the ability of its citizens to communicate in both official languages stands a greater chance of fostering national unity than one where bilingualism is the burden of discontented francophones who were forced to assimilate to the English language.

The question of the ultimate success of the Official Languages in Education Program must to a certain extent remain open. Too often, educational initiatives are judged on the basis of short-term results, before programs have had time to mature and their full impacts are visible. Canada is now beginning to feel the impact of the OLEP's political socialization efforts, as the children who were educated in its programs are reaching voting age and positions of influence. At a minimum, they demonstrate even greater support for official bilingualism than their parents. The full ramifications of the OLEP on Canadian identity will continue to evolve over the next few decades. The OLEP has clearly proven to be a durable initiative, however, and the programs it sponsored – minority-language education, French immersion, and second-language instruction – have become institutionalized and continue to grow and develop today, a good indication of the continued support in Canadian society for the vision that underlies them. Moreover, despite tensions in Canadian federalism, cooperation between the Canadian and provincial governments based on a mutual recognition of jurisdictions over education and language policy has continued to be possible as the OLEP regularly passes through successive renewals. There is thus reason to believe that the ongoing objective of continually renewing and reinforcing Canadian national unity, a clear goal of the Official Languages in Education Program, was enhanced by this imaginative, if somewhat complicated, program.

APPENDIX

Federal Funding of the Official Languages in Education Program

The following tables provide more detailed information on the federal government's expenditures on the Official Languages in Education Program. Tables A1, A2, and A3 provide information on the federal government's contributions to the OLEP's three largest components: minority-language education, second-language instruction, and special projects. Tables A4 and A5 provide the total amounts that the federal government spent each year on the OLEP, broken down by province.

Table A1
Federal Contributions under the Elementary- and Secondary-Level Minority-Official-Language Education Formula, 1970/71–1982/83 ($)

Year	Alberta	Manitoba	Ontario	Quebec	New Brunswick	Nova Scotia	Total (Canada)
1970–71	131,983	236,057	7,127,873	21,299,852	2,816,979	344,598	32,032,439
1971–72	178,634	356,309	11,315,267	23,798,306	4,057,212	324,787	40,121,015
1972–73	175,658	392,549	9,849,543	19,827,598	3,678,871	341,593	34,373,026
1973–74	131,757	304,147	10,733,459	31,823,646	3,939,255	250,987	47,293,235
1974–75	216,155	553,002	10,500,853	25,217,298	3,201,210	381,353	40,227,293
1975–76	316,347	710,465	15,376,659	27,831,084	3,516,344	486,145	48,524,203
1976–77	405,311	869,240	16,909,655	43,078,698	8,384,478	638,301	70,728,553
1977–78	578,520	1,026,317	18,951,122	75,956,277	7,524,897	720,934	105,348,635
1978–79	827,965	1,349,114	22,986,005	56,842,171	7,232,687	740,218	90,850,581
1979–80	972,972	1,050,531	17,355,593	42,500,136	6,145,643	481,817	69,353,132
1980–81	1,135,555	1,224,583	17,456,552	41,809,837	6,829,546	495,958	70,005,517
1981–82	1,434,200	1,412,049	17,931,724	37,637,042	8,209,420	539,954	68,514,703
1982–83	2,139,921	1,961,004	24,297,934	32,182,941	8,153,534	664,337	71,180,534
Total	8,644,938	11,445,367	200,792,239	479,804,886	73,690,076	6,410,982	788,552,866

Source: Canada, Secretary of State, Language Programmes Directorate, Education Support Programmes Branch, *Federal-Provincial Programmes for the Official Languages in Education – Supplementary Tables 1970–71 to 1982–83* (1983), 14–16.

Table A2
Federal Contributions under the Elementary- and Secondary-Level Second-Official-Language Instruction Formula, 1970/71–1982/83 ($)

Year	Alberta	Manitoba	Ontario	Quebec	New Brunswick	Nova Scotia	Total (Canada)
1970–71	579,653	354,959	3,061,979	5,635,954	218,585	310,223	11,605,987
1971–72	680,007	465,742	4,674,307	6,644,155	320,759	349,733	14,634,191
1972–73	587,196	408,601	3,971,881	5,860,970	289,475	347,621	12,793,682
1973–74	410,827	288,114	4,229,429	8,731,620	291,886	296,889	15,500,170
1974–75	625,501	444,972	3,722,576	7,560,566	253,447	458,441	14,536,471
1975–76	756,655	573,768	5,871,482	9,351,686	284,951	564,029	19,623,447
1976–77	832,021	736,535	7,022,852	14,777,074	648,798	705,653	27,252,506
1977–78	936,368	708,888	8,743,949	20,908,996	550,560	783,747	35,415,387
1978–79	990,264	733,856	11,284,890	16,842,912	560,727	791,923	33,792,644
1979–80	926,642	558,068	8,755,844	17,250,650	498,650	590,182	30,829,223
1980–81	911,962	588,768	8,967,322	14,891,215	528,315	630,489	29,200,164
1981–82	1,042,821	663,396	10,048,499	13,886,989	618,035	709,052	29,537,331
1982–83	1,181,661	805,078	10,044,326	12,807,653	628,976	891,435	28,975,201
Total	10,452,468	7,330,745	90,399,336	155,150,440	5,693,073	7,429,417	303,696,404

Source: Canada, Secretary of State, Language Programmes Directorate, Education Support Programmes Branch, *Federal-Provincial Programmes for the Official Languages in Education – Supplementary Tables, 1970–71 to 1982–83* (1983), 26–8.

Table A3
Federal Contributions under the Special Projects Program, 1970/71–1982/83 ($)

Year	Alberta	Manitoba	Ontario	Quebec	New Brunswick	Nova Scotia	Total (Canada)
1970–71	–	–	–	–	–	–	–
1971–72	–	–	–	–	–	–	–
1972–73	–	–	–	–	21,755	–	169,566
1973–74	49,770	2,130	2,101,000	459,012	197,478	7,035	2,844,991
1974–75	112,015	221,695	2,191,004	714,994	520,058	178,110	4,747,767
1975–76	72,190	554,739	1,562,282	1,310,241	98,297	215,917	5,307,943
1976–77	1,413,187	846,919	1,880,786	2,319,876	1,636,981	503,561	10,192,956
1977–78	815,299	1,037,691	2,913,544	3,227,761	1,078,346	765,346	12,616,167
1978–79	904,645	1,221,670	3,860,319	1,928,817	1,606,425	1,220,339	14,311,975
1979–80	795,853	1,199,213	3,488,783	2,693,416	1,963,051	844,764	13,890,324
1980–81	642,484	1,248,862	3,413,900	2,368,704	1,875,029	832,928	13,830,240
1981–82	578,528	1,413,425	3,737,076	1,580,625	2,294,525	988,968	14,766,604
1982–83	598,089	1,751,168	4,055,481	3,151,200	3,187,502	1,101,491	18,185,995
Total	5,982,060	9,497,512	29,204,175	19,754,646	14,479,467	6,659,070	110,864,528

Source: Canada, Secretary of State, Language Programmes Directorate, Education Support Programmes Branch, *Federal-Provincial Programmes for the Official Languages in Education – Supplementary Tables, 1970–71 to 1982–83* (1983), 32–5.

Table A4
Federal Contributions under All Official Languages in Education Programs, 1970/71–1982/83 ($)

Year	Alberta	Manitoba	Ontario	Quebec	New Brunswick	Nova Scotia	Total (Canada)
1970–71	872,375	806,357	12,271,065	30,294,019	3,275,176	3,725,176	50,508,933
1971–72	1,163,938	1,188,315	21,830,903	40,760,496	6,740,472	905,915	74,608,290
1972–73	1,214,058	1,260,411	18,734,768	37,053,653	5,900,481	1,018,528	67,582,775
1973–74	1,095,168	2,152,659	22,941,084	52,905,402	6,710,314	892,369	90,014,674
1974–75	1,552,712	1,896,368	22,656,080	51,762,076	6,736,885	1,561,542	90,853,838
1975–76	2,026,428	2,585,920	31,281,350	59,844,603	6,615,365	1,893,664	111,494,307
1976–77	3,623,248	3,471,576	34,904,630	95,196,839	14,623,572	2,560,308	162,809,470
1977–78	3,458,942	4,019,494	40,510,808	145,910,086	13,901,113	3,042,762	222,519,772
1978–79	3,979,490	4,663,165	49,236,126	120,256,215	14,382,901	3,655,310	209,783,349
1979–80	3,795,291	3,898,142	39,051,321	101,165,160	12,643,926	2,605,993	175,377,468
1980–81	4,084,923	4,221,372	38,956,557	95,357,972	13,130,402	2,797,137	171,781,519
1981–82	4,541,756	4,709,203	41,512,055	89,494,315	15,402,414	3,084,332	173,524,664
1982–83	5,666,952	5,836,609	48,583,894	80,622,125	16,193,312	3,650,416	176,276,619
Total	37,076,281	40,709,591	422,470,641	1,000,622,966	136,346,333	28,401,891	1,777,135,678

Source: Canada, Secretary of State, Language Programmes Directorate, Education Support Programmes Branch, *Federal-Provincial Programmes for the Official Languages in Education – Supplementary Tables, 1970–71 to 1982–83* (1983), 64–8.

Table A5
Federal Contributions under All Official Languages in Education Programs, 1983/84–2001/2 ($)

Year	Alberta	Manitoba	Ontario	Quebec	New Brunswick	Nova Scotia	Total (Canada)
1983–84	5,290,684	5,935,934	47,546,157	81,892,192	21,386,576	4,122,151	178,062,419
1984–85	6,128,499	6,126,872	49,568,212	81,738,755	22,435,778	4,152,889	184,886,220
1985–86	6,818,416	6,621,630	51,860,325	81,238,864	25,454,128	4,082,770	193,102,297
1986–87	7,456,021	7,449,789	56,213,324	78,952,328	26,350,915	4,401,923	200,956,799
1987–88	8,059,097	7,789,404	55,915,421	76,636,890	26,446,915	4,392,152	200,240,459
1988–89	9,300,481	8,686,270	60,142,299	77,525,033	27,659,396	4,642,317	220,059,950
1989–90	10,237,508	8,872,069	66,130,555	76,859,133	29,910,113	5,622,869	225,336,025
1990–91	10,063,017	10,028,473	68,058,875	77,761,042	25,769,434	8,716,214	233,664,523
1991–92	10,645,431	10,439,699	69,816,577	82,737,467	27,518,724	7,709,135	243,196,655
1992–93	12,129,483	9,970,568	76,007,245	82,418,629	26,185,468	6,992,354	246,334,046
1993–94	10,538,254	8,771,811	70,729,253	72,113,257	23,575,253	7,893,978	220,544,203
1994–95	13,010,739	11,110,367	73,090,739	67,590,976	25,373,284	7,968,301	229,133,485
1995–96	13,814,861	10,279,104	55,307,418	53,918,332	20,648,318	8,529,671	196,065,559
1996–97	15,097,789	10,745,245	47,265,697	50,058,954	17,262,478	7,372,745	174,327,908
1997–98	11,018,609	9,192,184	46,820,724	49,845,807	16,200,698	7,350,544	174,820,765
1998–99	9,308,488	8,054,533	55,100,061	42,469,629	13,497,721	5,817,497	159,644,256
1999–2000	13,662,598	11,835,737	67,232,068	51,528,384	17,304,441	6,977,167	194,440,979
2000–1	10,758,000	11,540,300	69,204,700	51,090,016	17,304,000	6,885,000	193,701,851
2001–2	8,541,000	11,565,300	77,253,336	50,833,000	18,742,045	5,406,500	200,878,072

Source: Canada, Secretary of State, Official Languages in Education, Descriptive and Financial Summary, Minority Language Education and Second Language Instruction, Federal-Provincial/Territorial Agreements, 1983–84 to 1987–88 and 1988–89 to 1992–93 (1989, 1994). Additional statistics furnished by Canadian Heritage.

Note: Figures for 1993–2002 include specific grants for minority-language-school management in the English-majority provinces. Figures do not include the Summer Language Bursary Program or the Official Language Monitors Program.

Notes

INTRODUCTION

1 Laforest, *Trudeau and the End of a Canadian Dream*, 73.
2 McRoberts, *Misconceiving Canada*; Dion, *Pour une véritable politique linguistique*.
3 Laurendeau, *Journal tenu pendant la Commission royale*, 339–45.
4 M. Martel, *Le deuil d'un pays imaginé*; Gervais, *Des gens de résolution*.
5 For example, on the question whether francophone minority communities are redefining themselves in terms of province-based identities, Gaétan Gervais argues that the adoption of a new Franco-Ontarian identity, as opposed to a French Canadian one, is largely limited to academics and members of the artistic community, while most others continue to use the two terms interchangeably. Gervais, *Des gens de résolution*, 211.
6 Archives of Ontario (AO), RG2-200, Council on French-Language Schools, Acc. 17121, Box 2, File: Fed/Prov – Bilinguisme 1972, Secretary of State News Release; "Federal-Provincial Program on Bilingualism in Education Agreement Reached with Provinces concerning Financial Assistance," 9 September 1970.
7 Cairns, "From Interstate to Intrastate Federalism?" 15–22; Smiley and Watts, *Intrastate Federalism*; Skogstad, "Federalism and Agricultural Policy," 189–90.
8 Stevenson, *Unfulfilled Union*, 221–3.
9 Ibid., 223–9.
10 Bakvis and Chandler, "The Future of Federalism," 306–18.
11 Interested readers may wish to consult related works by Alan Cairns, Theda Skocpol, and Eric Nordlinger. For example, see Nordlinger, *On the Autonomy of the Democratic State*.

12 Pal, *Interests of State*.
13 Cairns, "The Embedded State," 53–86. Cairns, "Canadian Administrative State," 62–97.
14 Joy, *Languages in Conflict*.
15 Kenneth McRoberts' *Misconceiving Canada* is typical of the literature criticizing the Trudeau-era policies, as discussed above. More positive assessments can be found in Aunger, "Language Legislation"; Pal, *Interests of State*.
16 M. Martel, *Le Deuil d'un pays imaginé*; Behiels, *Canada's Francophone Minority Communities*.
17 The literature on French Canadian community development has been quite productive in this regard. In particular, see the works by Danielle Juteau-Lee, Gaétan Gervais, David Welch, Angéline Martel, Joseph-Yvon Thériault, Jean Daigle, and Raymond Hébert in the bibliography.
18 My approach to studying the impact of lobby groups is a modified form of the social-movement-theory approach employed by Linda Cardinal in her study of Franco-Ontarian politics in the 1980s and 1990s. Cardinal, *Chroniques d'une vie politique mouvementée*; see also Smith, *Lesbian and Gay Rights*.
19 Stevenson, *Community Besieged*; Levine, *The Reconquest of Montreal*; Rudin, *The Forgotten Quebeckers*.
20 Other disciplines, including education, have paid somewhat more attention to this topic. See Makroploulos, "French Immersion Developments in Canada."

CHAPTER ONE

1 Choquette, *Language and Religion*, 57.
2 Ibid., 45–81.
3 Marie-France Kingsley argues that the attempt to eliminate French-language schooling in Ontario in fact served to politicize the collective identity of the Franco-Ontarians, by giving them a cause to rally around. Kingsley, "Le rôle de l'ACFO," xi.
4 Bordeleau, Bernard, and Cazabon, "L'éducation en Ontario français," 444.
5 "Historique de l'enseignement en français," 8–9.
6 Johnson and McKee-Allain, "La société et l'identité," 221–2. Even in 1991, the percentage of individuals in the francophone counties of New Brunswick over the age of fifteen without a grade 9 education was 24.4, compared to 19.5 in New Brunswick as a whole, and 13.9 in Canada.
7 Rawlyk and Hafter, *Acadian Education*, 41.
8 Archives du Centre Acadienne, Université Ste-Anne (ACA), MG8 Fonds Fédération Acadienne de la Nouvelle-Écosse (FANE), vol. 16, B.4, fiche

21b: L'école acadienne et la loi 65, Alexander J. Boudreau, *Education for Acadians in Nova Scotia*, October 1969.
9 Official Language Act, S.M. 1890, c.14.
10 Crunican, *Priests and Politicians*, 7–8; An Act Respecting the Department of Education, S.M. 1890, c.37; An Act Respecting Public Schools, S.M. 1890, c.38.
11 Brown and Cook, *Canada 1896–1921*, 259.
12 Leblanc, "L'enseignement français au Manitoba," 37–8.
13 Hébert, "Historique de la législation scolaire au Manitoba," 11.
14 Allaire, "Le rapport à l'autre," 172.
15 Alberta, *Affirming Francophone Education*, 7.
16 Gill, "Language Policy," 19–20.
17 Behiels, *Quebec and the Question of Immigration*; Vigod, *Quebec before Duplessis*, 156–9.
18 Little, "Watching the Frontier Disappear," 371.
19 Rudin, *The Forgotten Quebeckers*; Stevenson, *Community Beseiged*.
20 Waddell, "State, Language and Society," 78.
21 Levine, *The Reconquest of Montreal*.
22 Smith, "Invasion, Succession and Conflict," 1–83; Macdonald, "In Search of a Language Policy," 220.
23 Taddeo and Taras, *Le débat linguistique au Québec*, 92–4.
24 An excellent discussion of the different political ideologies that were vying for influence in Quebec can be found in Behiels, *Prelude to Quebec's Quiet Revolution*. On the development of the neonationalist school of Quebec history, see Lamarre, *Le devenir de la nation québécoise*.
25 Stanley, *Louis Robichaud*, 156.
26 Richard, "Prelude to a Second Acadian Renaissance."
27 Belliveau, "Chronique d'une affirmation collective."
28 Bureau, *Mêlez-vous de vos affaires*, 25.
29 CP, S1 – Fonds SFM, 89/745/605 – Education, Lionel Orlikow, Manitoba; *(French in Limbo) Need for Policy Direction*, 30 July 1978.
30 Rawlyk, *Acadian Education*, 38–43.
31 Martel, *Le deuil d'un pays imaginé*, 34.
32 Royal Commission on Bilingualism and Biculturalism (RCBB), *Report*, book 1, *The Official Languages*, 174–5.
33 Nova Scotia Archives and Records Management (NSARM), RG100, Office of the Premier, vol. 103, file: Confederation of Tomorrow – Proceedings, Background Paper on the Role of the English and French Languages in Canada, 16 Nov. 1967.
34 NA, RG47-10 Privy Council Office, Federal-Provincial Relations Office, Federal-Provincial Constitutional Conferences, 1969–1971, vol. 83, file: The Ontario Position on the Spending Power, 4–5.

35 NA, RG2, series A-5-a Privy Council Office, vol. 6323, Cabinet Conclusions of July 18 1967 Meeting, 7–8.
36 Aunger, "Les communautés francophones de l'Ouest," 285. Figures are based on French mother-tongue figures. As we shall see, the figures for those of French origin are substantially higher in some provinces.
37 Aunger, "Les communautés francophones de l'Ouest," 285; Gilbert, "Les espaces de la francophonie ontarienne," 65; Statistics Canada, *Seventh Census of Canada, 1931*, vol. 2, table 58, 811.
38 Roy, "Settlement and Population Growth," 178.
39 Castonguay, "The Decline of French," 93.
40 Viaud, "La géographie du peuplement francophone," 85. Johnson and McKee-Allain "La société et l'identité," 215.
41 A. Martel, *Rights, Schools and Communities*.
42 M. Martel, *Le Deuil d'un pays imaginé*.
43 Savas, "L'impact des politiques d'aide du Secrétariat," 11–54; Allaire, "De l'église à l'état," 229–45.
44 Ouellet, "L'historiographie francophone," 126; Welch, "Social Construction"; Juteau-Lee, "The Franco-Ontarian Collectivity."
45 Welch, "Social Construction," 206.
46 This issue was raised almost annually in the *Annual Report of the Commissioner of Official Languages* during the years when Keith Spicer occupied this office, from 1970 to 1976. For example, Commissioner of Official Languages, *1972/73 Annual Report*, 45; *1973/74 Annual Report*, 30.
47 Welch, "Social Construction," 206.
48 Interviews with Alain Landry and Jane Dobell, formerly senior civil servants in the Department of the Secretary of State.

CHAPTER TWO

1 NA, RG33, series 80, Royal Commission on Bilingualism and Biculturalism (RCBB). This theme occurs repeatedly. For example, see vol. 41, file 730-153, Mémoires, Nouveau-Brunswick, Société nationale des acadiens (1964), 26–9.
2 Royal Commission on Bilingualism and Biculturalism (RCBB), *Report*, book 1, *Official Languages*, 86.
3 Ibid.
4 Ibid., 138–9.
5 Ibid., 158.
6 RCBB, *Report*, book 2, *Education*, 3.
7 RCBB, *Official Languages*, 126.
8 NA, RG33, series 80, RCBB, vol. 221, binder: Meetings 51–4, Minutes of Meeting no. 51, 2–4 February 1967, 41.
9 Ibid., 41 and 46.

Notes to pages 40–6

10 RCBB, *Education*, 20.
11 NA, RG33, series 80, RCBB, vol. 221, binder: Meetings 39–44, Minutes of Meeting no. 43, 18–20 May 1966, 7-8.
12 Ibid., binder: Meetings 45–50, Minutes of Meeting no. 46, 20–21 July 1966, 18–19.
13 Ibid., binder: Meetings 39–44, Minutes of Meeting no. 43, 18–20 May 1966, 7–8.
14 Ibid., binder: Meetings 55–60, Minutes of Meeting no. 57, 31 May to 2 June 1967, 20–2.
15 RCBB, *Education*, 191–2.
16 Ibid., 206.
17 Ibid., Recommendation no. 31, 230.
18 Bourasssa, "The French Language," 141.
19 McRoberts, *Misconceiving Canada*, 64.
20 RCBB, *Official Languages*, xxxviii–xxxix.
21 Ibid., xxxi–xxxiii.
22 McRoberts, *Misconceiving Canada*, 64–6.
23 RG2, Privy Council Office, series A-5-a, vol. 6338, Cabinet Conclusions, file: 4 Jan.–13 Feb. 1968, Conclusions from the 17 January 1968 Cabinet Meeting, 3.
24 Pal, *Interests of State*, 103.
25 CEA, Fonds 146 Armand-Saintonge, fiche 146.83 Sous-comité sur les langues officielles: Documents, Troisième réunion du sous-comité des langues officielles – compte rendu sommaire des délibérations, 12 May 1969.
26 For example, see Trudeau, "A Constitutional Declaration of Rights," 54–5; Interview with Senator Pierre De Bané.
27 Interviews with Sen. De Bané and Sen. Jean-Robert Gauthier.
28 Provincial Archives of Alberta (PAA), 88.88, Advanced Education – Program Support Branch, box 8, file: Federal-Provincial Task Force on Bilingualism in Education, Statement of Secretary of State Gérard Pelletier in the House of Commons, 6 November 1969.
29 CEA, Fonds 146 Armand-Saintonge, fiche 146.81, Sous-comité sur les langues officielles, Aide-mémoire sur les formes possibles d'aide fédérale aux provinces, 7 February 1968.
30 Ibid., fiche 146.79, Comité ministériel des langues officielles, Suggestions sur le programme de coopération fédéral-provincial concernant le bilinguisme dans le domaine de l'éducation présenté par la délégation fédérale, 15 April 1970.
31 Macdonald, "In Search of a Language Policy," 228.
32 Archives nationales du Québec (ANQ), E42 Ministère des Affaires intergouvernementales (MAIG) 1993–08-002/5, file: Commission Laurendeau-Dunton, Quebec's response to volume 2 of the RCBB report – education, October 1969.

33 Archives of Ontario (AO), RG77-3, Correspondence of the Executive Secretary to the Office of the Government Coordinator on Bilingualism, TR 83-1201, T. box 8, file: Constitutional Conferences on Official Languages, Secretariat Report on the Proceedings of the 3rd Meeting of the Ministerial Committee on Official Languages, 8 June 1970.
34 *Constitutional Conference Proceedings, Second Meeting, 10–12 February 1969*, 224.
35 Ibid.
36 Quoted in Quebec Federation of Home and School Association – News Archives, *QFHSA News*, vol. 10(3), November 1972.
37 PANB, RS 416 Louis Robichaud, 1967, file 109: Conference of Tomorrow 1967, Opening Statement of Louis Robichaud at the Confederation of Tomorrow Conference, 25 November 1967 and Final Statement of Premier Robichaud at the Conference, 1 December 1967.
38 PANB, RS 416, Louis Robichaud, 1968, file 145: Committee of Officers on the Constitution, Letter from P. Trudeau to L. Robichaud, 12 November 1968.
39 *Constitutional Conference Proceedings, Second Meeting, 10–12 February 1969*, 55.
40 PANB, RS 416 Louis Robichaud, 1969, file 131: Committee of Officials on the Constitution, Letter from Maxwell Cohen to Louis Robichaud re: Constitutional Conference, 24 February 1969. Observations by Maxwell Cohen, 1 October 1969.
41 Ibid., Committee of Officials on the Constitution, Statement of L. Robichaud, 6 November 1969.
42 CEA, Fonds 146 Armand-Saintonge, fiche 146.86 Langues officielles au Nouveau-Brunswick – Domaine de l'éducation, Memorandum from Pierre Vachon to Education Officials, 14 April 1970.
43 Stanley, *Louis Robichaud*, 180.
44 *Constitutional Conference Proceedings, First Meeting, 5–7 February 1968*, 25–7.
45 PAA, 76.422, Federal and Intergovernmental Affairs, box 4, file: Constitutional Conference, Subcommittee on Official Languages, 1969–71, Letter from W. Davis to G. Pelletier, 21 October 1969.
46 AO, RG77-3, Correspondence of the Executive Secretary to the Office of the Government Coordinator on Bilingualism, TR83-1201, T. box 11, file: education 1969–71, Memo from Charles Beer, Federal-Provincial Affairs Secretariat, to E.D. Greathed, Director, FPAS, 25 June 1969.
47 AO, RG77-3, Correspondence of the Executive Secretary to the Office of the Government Coordinator on Bilingualism, TR 83-1201, T. box 11, file: Education 1969–71, Proposal from Dept. of Treasury and Economics to Obtain Federal Assistance regarding the Provision of French Language Education in Ontario, to Cabinet Committee on Policy Development, 25 September 1969.

Notes to pages 51–5   199

48 PAA, 76.422, Federal and Intergovernmental Affairs, box 4, file: Constitutional Conference, Subcommittee on Official Languages, 1969–71, Letter from W. Davis to G. Pelletier, 21 October 1969.
49 Interview with Raymond Théberge, past president of the SFM.
50 Hébert, "Historique de la législation scolaire," 11.
51 Silla, *École bilingue ou unilingue*, 46.
52 PAA, 76.422, Federal and Intergovernmental Affairs, box 3, file: Constitutional Conference, Subcommittee on Official Languages 1969–71, Memorandum of Telephone Conversation between J.J. Frawley and Premier Manning, 4 June 1968.
53 NA, RG47-10, Privy Council Office, Federal-Provincial Relations Office, Federal-Provincial Constitutional Conferences, 1969–1971, box 82, file: Verbatim Reports 10–12 February 1969, 171.
54 PAA, 76.422, Federal and Intergovernmental Affairs, box 4, file: Constitutional Conference, Subcommittee on Official Languages, 1969–71, A Position Proposal on French Instruction, prepared by P. Lamoureux and R. Rees, Alberta Education, January 1969.
55 Ibid., *Edmonton Journal*, "Bilingual Aid Called Blackmail," by Ben Tierney, 15 November 1969.
56 PAA, 80.226, ACFA provinciale, box 15, file: Commission Worth de planification en éducation, 1969–70, Brief Presented by the French-Canadian Association to the Commission on Educational Planning, January 1970.
57 Nova Scotia Archives and Records Management (NSARM), RG100, Office of the Premier, vol. 103, file: Confederation of Tomorrow – Submissions, Statement of Minister of Education Gérard Doucet, November 1967.
58 CEA, fonds 146 Armand-Saintonge, fiche 146.90, Langues officielles au Nouveau-Brunswick – Le bilinguisme hors de la province du Nouveau-Brunswick, Preliminary Proposal Experiment in Bilingual Education Nova Scotia, 1968.
59 NSARM, RG100, Office of the Premier, vol. 110, file 9: Federal Provincial Constitutional Conference – Committee on Official Languages, Confidential Report to the Minister of Education on the Activities of the Subcommittee on Official Languages, 4 July 1968.
60 Ibid., vol. 109, file 3: Federal-Provincial Constitutional Conference, Feb. 10–12, 1969, Memo from H. Stevens, Director, Federal-Provincial Fiscal Relations, Dept. of Finance and Economics, to John MacDonald, Deputy Attorney General, and Innis MacLeod, Clerk of the Privy Council, re: Federal-Provincial Conference, 29 January 1969.
61 Ibid., vol. 110, file 9: Federal Provincial Constitutional Conference – Committee on Official Languages, Confidential Report to the Minister of Education on the Activities of the Subcommittee on Official Languages, 4 July 1968.
62 Ibid., vol. 109, file 6: Federal-Provincial Constitutional Conference, Dec. 18–20 1969, Nova Scotia Position on Official Languages in Education, December 1969.

63 PANB, RS 416 Louis Robichaud, 1969, file 131: Committee of Officials on the Constitution, Letter from G. Pelletier to L. Robichaud re: BEP, 17 December 1969.
64 *Constitutional Conference Proceedings, Third Meeting, 8–10 December 1969*, 233.
65 AO, RG77-3, Correspondence of the Executive Secretary to the Office of the Government Coordinator on Bilingualism, TR 83-1201, T. box 8, file: Constitutional Conferences on Official Languages, Secretariat Report on the Proceedings of the 3rd Meeting of the Ministerial Committee on Official Languages, 8 June 1970.
66 CEA, Fonds 146 Armand-Saintonge, fiche 146.86, Langues officielles au Nouveau-Brunswick – Domaine de l'éducation, Memo from Pierre Vachon to Premier Robichaud, 15 May 1970.
67 PAA, 76.422, FIGA, box 4, file: Constitutional Conference, Subcommittee on Official Languages, 1969–71, Letter from G. Pelletier to W. Davis, 4 November 1969.
68 *Constitutional Conference Proceedings, Third Meeting, 8–10 December 1969*, 229–34.
69 AO, RG2-200, Council on French-Language Schools, acc. 17121, box 2, file: Fed/Prov – Bilinguisme 1972, Secretary of State News Release, "Federal-Provincial Program on Bilingualism in Education Agreement Reached with Provinces concerning Financial Assistance," 9 September 1970.
70 Interviews with A. Landry, Normand Martin, former New Brunswick Deputy Minister of Education and past civil servant with the Secretary of State Department, and Georges Tsai, former Director-General of the Language Programs Branch, Secretary of State.
71 "Ottawa Grants $50 million Aid for Bilingualism in Schools," *Globe & Mail*, 10 September 1970, 1; "9% pour l'enseignement de la minorité, 5% pour la langue seconde – Modalités de l'accord au sujet des langues officielles," *Le Droit*, 10 September 1970, 1.
72 "Bilingual Plan Gives $12 Million to Quebec," *Montreal Star*, 10 September 1970, 28; "La langue seconde: Québec recevra $24 millions en 70," *Le Devoir*, 10 September 1970, 1.
73 "9% pour l'enseignement de la minorité, 5% pour la langue seconde – Modalités de l'accord au sujet des langues officielles," *Le Droit*, 10 September 1970, 1; "L'entente fédérale-provinciale sur le bilinguisme vient d'aboutir," *L'Évangéline*, 10 September 1970, 1.
74 "Quebec Gets Half Bilingual Grants," *Edmonton Journal*, 10 September 1970, 19; "Alberta Gains $1 Million Culture Grant – Half Bilingual Bonanza Goes to Quebec," *Calgary Herald*, 10 September 1970, 59.
75 "Ottawa Will Pay 5% to Teach a Second Official Language," *Toronto Star*, 10 September 1970, 80.

76 "Ottawa versera en 1970 $24 millions au Québec – Pour défrayer le coût de l'enseignement d'une langue seconde," *La Presse*, 10 September 1970, 1; "La langue seconde: Québec recevra $24 millions en 70," *Le Devoir*, 10 September 1970, 1.
77 *Constitutional Conference Proceedings, Third Meeting, 8–10 December 1969*, 229–36.

CHAPTER THREE

1 Pal, *Interests of State*.
2 Hryniuk, *20 Years of Multiculturalism*, 3.
3 AO, RG2-200, Council on French-Language Schools, acc. 17121, box 2, file: Fed/Prov – Bilinguisme 1972, Secretary of State News Release, "Federal-Provincial Programme on Bilingualism in Education – Further Arrangements concerning Financial Assistance," 20 January 1972.
4 Interview with Boyd Pelley, Council of Ministers of Education Canada Secretariat.
5 PAA, 88.88, Advanced Education – Program Support Branch, box 5, file: Regina Conference April 1973, Federal-Provincial Programme of Cooperation for Bilingualism in Education at the Pre-university Levels: A Working Summary of the Provincial Reports, 1973.
6 AO, RG2-200, Council on French-Language Schools, acc. 18915, box 3, file: Conférence à Halifax – Bilinguisme 1974, Memo from Douglas Spry to H. K. Fisher, ADM of Education, 28 January 1974.
7 AO, RG2-200, Council on French-Language Schools, acc. 17986, box 4, file: Conférence à Regina – Bilinguisme 1973, L'aide fédérale à l'enseignement des langues officielles, 18 December 1972.
8 Despite the road that we have yet to travel, there is still reason to be thrilled that communications have been reestablished and to rightly feel a certain pride in the progress accomplished to date (my translation). AO, RG2-200, Council on French-Language Schools, acc. 18915, box 3, file: Conférence à Halifax – Bilinguisme 1974, Notes d'un discours par l'hon. Hugh Faulkner prononcé à la conférence à Halifax, 21 January 1974.
9 PAA, 88.88, Advanced Education – Program Support Branch, box 3, file: Halifax Conference 1974, Summary: Federal-Provincial Conference on BEP, Halifax, 24 January 1974.
10 Interviews with Sen. J-R Gauthier and Sen. P. De Bané.
11 AO, RG2-200, Council on French-Language Schools, acc. 18915, box 3, file: Conférence à Halifax – Bilinguisme 1974, Notes d'un discours par l'hon. Hugh Faulkner, 21 January 1974.
12 PAA, 89,159, Education – Information Services, box 3, file: Federal Assistance to French Instruction in Alberta 1975, Secretary of State News Release. Renewal of Federal-Provincial Programme on Bilingualism in

Education – Agreement Reached with Provinces concerning the Continuance of Financial Assistance, 27 March 1974.
13 CRCCF, Fonds AEFO, Canadian Teachers Federation, C11-6/4/5, Canadian Teachers Federation Conference Report – Development of Bilingualism in Education, 23 January 1976.
14 "Quebec MP Criticizes Bilingualism Extension," *Globe & Mail*, 28 March 1974, 1; "Matte: Ottawa subventionne une minorité nantie et dominante," *Le Droit*, 28 March 1974, 11.
15 PAA, 89.159, Education – Information Services, box 4, file: Federal Assistance to French Instruction in Alberta, January 1971.
16 Interview with Adrien Bussière, formerly of Alberta Education.
17 PANB, RS 924 Education – Deputy Minister Armand Saintonge, box 2-11-6-2, file: Secrétariat d'État, Federal-Provincial Programme of Cooperation for the Development of Bilingualism in Education at the Pre-university Levels; Alberta Report, May 1973.
18 PAA, 85.360, ACFA, box 20, file: Dossier éducation et dossier constitutionel ACFA 1950, 1971–75, ACFA Brief to the Edmonton Separate School Board, January 1971.
19 Nogue, "Parent Expectations with Respect to Bilingual Schools."
20 PAA, 85.360, ACFA, box 1, file: Réunions et autres documents – Bureau de l'éducation – ACFA 1974–77, Brief from ACFA to Premier Peter Lougheed, 24 July 1974.
21 PAA, 85.360, ACFA, box 20, file: Dossier éducation et dossier constitutionnel ACFA 1950, 1971–75, ACFA Brief to the Edmonton Separate School Board, January 1971.
22 Alberta, Commission on Educational Planning, *A Future of Choices*, 188–9, 304.
23 PAA, 89.159, Education – Information Services, box 4, file: Federal Assistance to French Instruction in Alberta 1975, Letter from J.E. Reid, Director of Student Evaluation and Data Processing Services, to Secretary-Treasurers re: BEP Funding, 20 November 1975. The same letter, with modified dates, appears each year.
24 PAA, 80.226, ACFA provinciale, box 63, file: FFHQ 1975–78, Letter from Hubert Gauthier, FFHQ, to Julian Koziak, Minister of Education, re: BEP, 9 November 1976.
25 PAA, 85.360, ACFA, box 20, file: Dossier éducation et dossier constitutionnel ACFA 1950, 1971–75, The Federal-Provincial Program of Cooperation for Bilingualism in Education – Alberta, 1976.
26 My translation: manifestent un peu de lassitude. Les luttes incessantes les ont affaiblis. Alain Nogue and Roger Motut, "Situation Actuelle," *Revue de l'Association canadienne d'éducation de langue française* 6(2) (1976): 45.

27 PAA, 85.360, ACFA, box 1, file: Réunions et autres documents – Bureau de l'éducation – ACFA 1974–77, Reaction of ACFA to the Report of the Commission on education planning, n.d.
28 PAA, 85.360, ACFA, box 1, file: Réunions et autres documents – Bureau de l'éducation – ACFA 1978 (1), Statement by Peter Lougheed and Education Minister Julian Koziak re: Minority Language Instruction, 24 February 1978.
29 PAA, 85.360, ACFA, box 21, file: Dossier éducation et dossier constitutionnel ACFA 1976–77, ACFA Plan of Action, January 1977.
30 Interviews with Raymond Hébert and Raymond Théberge, former president of the SFM.
31 Centre du patrimoine (CP), S1 – SFM, 44/7 Education, Brief Submitted to the Minister of Education, Saul Miller, by the SFM, February 1971.
32 Ibid., 45/1 Bilinguisme, Distribution of Federal Grants re: B & B Program in Education, January 1971.
33 Ibid., Minority-Language Catch-up Programs, 1972.
34 Ibid., 23/12 Bilinguisme, Excerpt from Provincial Reports on Federal-Provincial Program of Bilingualism in Education, Tabled in House of Commons – Manitoba, 12 June 1973.
35 Ibid., 23/12 Bilinguisme, Excerpt from Provincial Reports on Federal-Provincial Program of Bilingualism in Education, Tabled in House of Commons – Manitoba, 12 June 1973. Interviews with Raymond Théberge and Gérard Gagnon, former animateur with the BEF, 16 May 2002.
36 Hébert, "Historique de la législation scolaire," 12.
37 PAM, E15 BEF – Committee Files, GR601, box 3: Special Projects, French Education in Manitoba, 1972–73, Synthesis Report Prepared by Olivier Tremblay, 27 June 1973.
38 CP, S1 – SFM, 23/12 Bilinguisme, Excerpt from Provincial Reports on Federal-Provincial Program of Bilingualism in Education, Tabled in House of Commons – Manitoba, 12 June 1973.
39 PAM, E14 BEF, GR 587, box 28, Memos reçus Avril 1974 – Sept. 1976, Memo from Lionel Orlikow to Ben Hanuschak, Minister of Education, re: Establishment of the BEF, 17 June 1974.
40 CP, S1 – fonds SFM, 31/3 Bureau de l'éducation française, BEF Cadre de travail 1974–79, Deuxième Version, by Olivier Tremblay, 12 August 1974.
41 Hébert et al., *Rendement académique et langue d'enseignement chez les élèves Franco-Manitobains.*
42 CRCCF, Fonds FFHQ, Dossiers d'information – enseignement du français au Canada, 1961–82, C84/92/5, Législation provinciale sur les langues officielles du Canada, January 1977.
43 PAM, E14 BEF, GR 1384, box 19, file 74.5.2 Entente fédérale-provinciale pour le bilinguisme en éducation, Use of Federal Monies for the Promotion of Bilingualism in Manitoba, 16 May 1975.

44 PAM, E14 BEF, GR 1384, box 16, file 71.5 News Service – Communiqués, News Release – New French Language Grant System Is Set, 7 May 1976.
45 Interview with Gérard Gagnon, former animator with the BEF.
46 Interview with R. Hébert.
47 PAM, E14 BEF, GR 1384, box 16, file 71.5 News Service – Communiqués, News Release – Federal-Provincial Aid for French Instruction Expanded and New Manitoba Projects to be Jointly-Funded, 24 September 1976.
48 Commissioner of Official Languages Library, file: Manitoba – Education, Manitoba Education, Bureau de l'Éducation Française, Pour un Réseau d'Écoles Françaises au Manitoba, November 1975.
49 Interview with R. Hébert.
50 This was typical of the Davis government's approach to French-language government services in sectors other than education, including health care. See Hayday, "Pas de problème."
51 QFHSA, Canadian Home and School and Parent-Teacher Federation Reports, 1971–72, Bilingualism Liaison with Other PTA Associations in Canada, Annual Report.
52 Ontario, *Report of the Ministerial Commission on French Language Secondary Education*; Ontario, *Franco-Ontarian Elementary and Secondary Education*; Interview with Jane Dobell.
53 Stanley McDowell, "Pelletier Warns Provinces on Grants for Bilingualism," *Globe & Mail*, 1972.
54 AO, RG77-1, Correspondence of the Government Coordinator of French Language Services, TR 84-467, T. box 29, file: Summary of the Main Points and Recommendations of the Report of the Ministerial Commission on French-language Secondary Education, March 1972.
55 Centre de recherche en civilisation canadienne-française (CRCCF), Fonds ACFO, Langues officielles, 1968–78, C2/478/5, Norman Webster, "French Language Education: For Anglophone Bigots, the Going Is Tough," *Globe & Mail*, 12 January 1973.
56 Pierre Allard, "$4 millions auraient disparu entre le Fédéral et les conseils scolaires," *Le Droit*, 19 April 1973, 1.
57 CRCCF, Fonds ACFO, Bilinguisme en Ontario, 1970–77, C2/477/8, Union des parents et de contribuables francophones, section Carleton, "Le scandale des programmes ontariens de bilinguisme en éducation," 1 May 1974. The standard allotment of time for FSL programs was one-fifteenth of an average school day; i.e., a student who took only the FSL class would receive one-fifteenth of the amount of French instuctional time received by a student in the minority-language stream.
58 AO, RG2-200, Council on French-Language Schools, acc. 17986, box 4, file: Federal-Provincial General 1973, Letter from Thomas Wells to Omer Deslauriers re: *Le Droit* article, 1 June 1973.

59 AO, RG2-200, Council on French-Language Schools, acc. 17121, box 2, file: Fed/Prov – Projets de rattrapage 1972, Letter from Thomas Wells, Minister of Education, to Gerard Pelletier, 28 September 1972.
60 AO, RG2-200, Council for Franco-Ontarian Education, acc. 20180, box 4, file: General 1976, Letter from G.H. Waldrum to Peter Roberts, 16 December 1975.
61 AO, RG2-200, Council on French-Language Schools, acc. 20123, box 4, file: Federal-Provincial – Secretariat d'État 1975, Memo from André Chénier to Dr D.W. Ko, 7 July 1975.
62 CEA, Fonds 41 SNA, fiche 41-17-15 Correspondance, Letter from Hector Cormier, secrétaire administratif of SNA, to Lorne McGuigan, Minister of Education, 23 September 1971.
63 Ibid., fiche 41-18-2 Correspondance, Letter from Hector Cormier to Keith Spicer, Commisioner of Official Languages, 29 February 1972; "Octrois fédéraux pour les langues officielles – La province accusée de détournement de fonds," *Évangéline*, 3 March 1972, 1.
64 Interviews with Armand Saintonge, former Deputy Minister of Education of New Brunswick, and Harvey Malmberg, former Deputy Minister of Education of New Brunswick.
65 CEA, Fonds 41 SNA, fiche 41-17-15 Correspondance, Letter from Hector Cormier, secrétaire administratif of SNA, to Premier Hatfield, 23 August 1971.
66 A bilingual school system is a utopian dream and an instrument of assimilation. Whether knowingly or not, it will create a generation of young people who are neither anglophones nor francophones. Bravo, say some well-intentioned people, finally we will have Canadians. But will we not, rather, be creating monsters who no longer have a connection with their heritage, in the broader sense of the term (my translation). "Un problème épineux," *Évangéline*, 26 May 1972, 6.
67 PANB, RS 924, Education – Deputy Minister Armand Saintonge, box 2-1-5-5, file: Langues Secondes, Propositions pour un plan de rénovation de l'enseignement des langues au Nouveau-Brunswick, March 1974.
68 Interviews with H. Malmberg and A. Saintonge.
69 CEA, Fonds 42 SANB, fiche 42-4-16 Mémoires, Présentation de la SANB au premier ministre du N.-B. M. Richard Hatfield touchant à l'éducation, les langues officielles, l'économie et la santé, 30 March 1976; Thériault, "L'Acadie politique et la politique en Acadie," 34–47.
70 My translation: "Les francophones ne veulent pas répéter l'erreur de beaucoup d'anglophones en se bornant à apprendre une seule langue. Ils voient la nécessité et la valeur du bilinguisme mais ne veulent pas pour autant se noyer dans les écoles d'assimilation." "Qui veut des écoles bilingues," *Évangéline*, 20 January 1976, 6.

71 Archives du centre acadien, Université Ste-Anne (ACA), MG8 Fonds Fédération acadienne de la Nouvelle-Écosse (FANE), vol. 16, B. 3, fiche 20: École française de Halifax.

72 My translation. Ibid., fiche 16a: Foyer Écoles, Communiqué de presse. "Nous voulons des étudiants bilingues," n.d.

73 Ibid.: Foyer Écoles, Statement of the Committee on Acadian Education, n.d.

74 Ibid., B. 7, fiche 51: Correspondance – Allan E. Sullivan, Ministre de l'Éducation, Letter from Paul Gaudet to Allan Sullivan re: Meeting with Dept. of Education Officials re: Acadian Education, 2 March 1973.

75 Ibid., fiche 46: Education – Rapports et réunions divers, Minutes of Meeting of Representatives of Acadian Community with Department of Education Officials, 11 April 1973.

76 PANB, RS 924 Education – Deputy Minister Armand Saintonge, box 2-11-6-2, file: Secrétariat d'État, Federal-Provincial Programme of Cooperation for the Development of Bilingualism in Education at the Pre-University Levels, Nova Scotia Report, May 1973.

77 ACA, MG8 Fonds FANE, vol. 16, B. 7, fiche 44: Mémoire présenté à la commission royale sur l'éducation, Mémoire présenté à la commission royale d'enquête sur l'éducation, les services publiques et les relations provinciales-municipales, par la Fédération francophone de la NE, December 1971.

78 Nova Scotia, *Royal Commission on Education, Public Services and Provincial-Municipal Relations Report* (1974), vol. 3, Education, chapter 53, Second Language, 15–17.

79 Fédération des francophones hors-Québec (FFHQ), *Les Héritiers du Lord Durham*, vol. 2, *La Fédération Acadienne de la Nouvelle-Écosse*, 73.

80 "Besoins en matière d'enseignement en français," *Revue de l'Association canadienne d'éducation de langue française 6(3) (1976)*: 36–7.

81 "L'enseignement en français et la Nouvelle-Écosse," *Évangéline*, 9 July 1974, 6.

82 NSED, Kings County Amalgamated School Board and Department of Education – Province of Nova Scotia Cooperative Educational Survey (1977), 203.

83 FFHQ, *Les Héritiers du Lord Durham*, vol. 2, *La Fédération Acadienne de la Nouvelle-Écosse*, 90–1.

84 My translation: Le Québec veut tout simplement plus d'argent à ce titre et que les subventions fédérales à cet effet continuent d'être les plus inconditionelles possible. ANQ, E42 Ministère des affaires intergouvernementales (MAIG) 1993-08-002/21, file: Bilinguisme en éducation au niveau pré-universitaire, Memo from Joseph Turi, MAIG to Arthur Tremblay, 24 May 1972.

85 QFHSA, Quebec Federation of Home and School Association Files, QFHSA resolutions regarding the use of federal grants, 1973.

86 QFHSA, Quebec Federation of Home and School Associations – News Archives, *QFHSA News*, vol. 11 (4), March 1974.
87 Private Files of Mrs Winifred Potter. Letter from Winifred Potter, to Heward Graftey, MP, Brome-Missisqoui, re: 21 June 1973 question in House of Commons, 9 July 1973.
88 ANQ, E42 MAIG 1993–08-002/21, file: Bilinguisme en éducation au niveau pré-universitaire, Reunion fédérale-provinciale de fonctionnaires sur le bilinguisme – Regina 3 et 4 avril 73, 9 April 1973.
89 Commission of Inquiry on the Position of the French Language and on Language Rights in Quebec, *Report of the Commission of Inquiry on the Position of the French Language and on Language Rights in Quebec*, book 1, *The Language of Work*, 148–92.
90 "Francisation" refers to a process whereby business would move their principle language of operations to French.
91 Coleman, "From Bill 22 to Bill 101," 467.
92 W. Potter files, Letter from E.A. Landry, Federal-Provincial Relations, Language Programs Branch, Secretary of State, to Winifred Potter, 16 July 1974.
93 W. Potter files, Letter from E.A. Landry to Winifred Potter, 12 November 1974.
94 QFHSA, Canadian Home and School and Parent-Teacher Federation Reports, 1974–75, Annual Report of the Bilingualism Committee.
95 QFHSA, Quebec Federation of Home and School Association Files, Notes from meeting between QFHSA, PSBGM and Claude Beauregard, Department of Education, re: Bilingual Grants from Ottawa, 23 May 1975.
96 QFHSA, Quebec Federation of Home and School Association – News Archives, *QFHSA News*, vol. 12 (4), March 1975; QFHSA Files, QFHSA Resolutions 76/10 and 76/12 regarding use of federal grants for minority language schools, 1976; QFHSA Files, Brief from the QFHSA to the Quebec Minister of Education re: the use being made by the Government of Quebec of the formula payments received by Quebec under the terms of the federal-provincial programme for the development of bilingualism in education, 19 April 1976.
97 Protestant School Board of Greater Montreal Archives (PSBGM), box 12, June 23, 1976, Board Meeting Minutes, Letter from Hugh Faulkner to Marcel Fox, Director General of PSBGM, 7 June 1976.
98 Ibid., August 12, 1976, Board Meeting Minutes, Letter from Marcel Fox, Director General of PSBGM, to Jean Bienvenue, Minister of Education, announcing resolution in support of QFHSA position on bilingualism grants (Resolution of 29 June 1976), 14 July 1976.
99 Ibid., June 23, 1976, Board Meeting Minutes, Letter from William Munroe, Deputy Director General of the PSBGM to Marcel Fox re: QFHSA Brief, 18 June 1976.

100 W. Potter files, Letter from Ian Watson, MP, to Hugh Faulkner, 14 June 1977; Letter from Ian Watson to Hugh Faulkner, 27 November 1974.
101 QFHSA, Quebec Federation of Home and School Associations – News Archives, QFHSA News, vol. 12 (4), March 1975.
102 ANQ, E42 Ministère des affaires intergouvernementales (MAIG) 1994-03-001/69, file: Entente Fédérale-Provinciale sur le bilinguisme en éducation, avant 1981, Letters between Elizabeth O'Connell, President of QFHSA and Hugh Faulkner, Secretary of State, re: BEP Objectives, 10 February 1975.
103 Ibid., file: Entente Fédérale-Provinciale sur le bilinguisme en éducation, avant 1981, Rapport Sommaire sur la rencontre sur le bilinguisme en éducation entre le MEQ et le Secrétariat d'État, 29 September 1975.
104 QFHSA, Quebec Federation of Home and School Association Files, Notes from meeting between QFHSA, PSBGM, and Claude Beauregard, Department of Education, re: Bilingual Grants from Ottawa, 23 May 1975.
105 ANQ, E42 MAIG 1993-08-002/21, file: Bilinguisme en éducation au niveau pré-universitaire, Notes from meeting between François Cloutier, Minister of Education, and Hugh Faulkner, Secretary of State, 28 November 1974.
106 ANQ, E42 MAIG 1994-03-001/101, file: Conférence sur le bilinguisme en éducation, Victoria, Dossier présenté au CCFI lors de la 3e conférence sur le bilinguisme en éducation et dans l'administration publique tenue à Victoria, 3 March 1975.
107 ANQ, E42 MAIG 1994-03-001/69, file: Entente Fédérale-Provinciale sur le bilinguisme en éducation, avant 1981, Letter from Claude Beauregard, ADM MEQ, to D.G. Hamilton, Department of the Secretary of State re: BEP conference, 14 August 1975.
108 The FFHQ was renamed the Fédération des communautés francophones et acadiennes du Canada (FCFAC) in 1991. This change resulted from pressure from some of its member groups, particularly the SANB, which wanted the organisation's name to reflect the fact that it was composed of francophone and Acadian minority communities.
109 PANB, RS 417 Richard Hatfield, box 13-5-6-3, file: 2803-1, Public Schools – French Language – General 1977, Minority Language Schooling in Canada – Summary of Status in Each Province, 1977.
110 "French Education Funds Misdirected, Says Organisation," Edmonton Journal, 8 November 1976, 13.
111 FFHQ, Les Héritiers du Lord Durham (1976).
112 CRCCF, Fonds AEFO, Canadian Teachers Federation, C11-6/4/5, Canadian Teachers Federation Conference Report – Development of Bilingualism in Education, 23 January 1976.
113 Rideout, Policy Changes of the Ten Canadian Provinces.
114 QFHSA, Canadian Home and School and Parent-Teacher Federation Reports, 1975–76 Annual Report of the Bilingualism Committee.

115 Interview with J. Dobell; PAA, 80.328, Education, Curriculum Branch, box 1, file: Federal-Provincial Conference on BEP Quebec May 1976, Letter from Peter Roberts to Departments of Education re: BEP, January 1976.
116 CRCCF, Fonds ACFO, FFHQ 1976–81, C2/463/3, Transcript from Parliamentary Committee on Broadcasting, Films and Assistance to the Arts, 27 April 1976.
117 AO, RG2-200, Council for Franco-Ontarian Education, acc. 20180, box 4, file: Federal-Provincial – Conférence sur le bilinguisme en éducation 9 – 11 mai Quebec 1976, Minutes from the Federal-Provincial conference on Bilingualism in Education, 11 May 1976.
118 Interviews with J. Dobell, A. Landry, G. Gagnon.
119 RG2-200, Council for Franco-Ontarian Education, acc. 20180, box 4, file: General 1976, Minutes from Meeting with Secretary of State, 7 April 1976.
120 Swain, *Bilingual schooling*; Lambert and Tucker, *Bilingual Education of Children*.

CHAPTER FOUR

1 D'Anglejan, "Language Planning in Quebec," 41.
2 William Johnson, "Lévesque Plays Bouncy Overture on the premiers," *Globe and Mail*, 25 July 1977, 7.
3 Government of Quebec, *Charter of the French Language* (1977).
4 Archives of Ontario (AO), RG58-9-1, Ministry of Intergovernmental Affairs, TR83-1499, box 52, file: SD 7g – Bilingualism – Quebec Language Policy, Letter from Premier Lévesque to Premier Davis, 21 July 1977.
5 AO, RG58-9-1, Ministry of Intergovernmental Affairs, TR83-1499, box 19, file: Fed. Lang. 4.2.4, Briefing Notes re: Quebec's Proposal on Reciprocal Minority Language Education Rights, 1 August 1977.
6 AO, RG58-9-1, Ministry of Intergovernmental Affairs, TR83-1499, box 52, file: SD 7g – Bilingualism – Quebec Language Policy, Letter from Premier Davis to Premier Lévesque, 21 July 1977.
7 Provincial Archives of New Brunswick (PANB), RS 417 Richard Hatfield, box 16-14-9-1, file 2320-2 Minority Language 1978, Letter from Premier Hatfield to Alex Morris, QFHSA, 13 March 1978.
8 AO, RG58-9-1, Ministry of Intergovernmental Affairs, TR83-1499, box 19, file: Fed. Lang. 4.2.4, Briefing Notes re: Quebec's Proposal on Reciprocal Minority Language Education Rights, 1 August 1977.
9 PANB, RS 417 Richard Hatfield, box 13-5-6-3, file: 2803-1 Public Schools – French Language – General 1977, Letter from Premier Hatfield to anglophone Premiers, 5 August 1977.
10 Jeffrey Simpson and William Johnson, "Lévesque Loses Last Hope for Schooling Agreements," *Globe and Mail*, 19 August 1977, 2.

11 William Johnson, Robert Williamson and Jeffrey Simpson, "Leaders Pledge School Rights, but No Pacts," *Globe and Mail*, 20 August 1977, 1.
12 MacMillan, *The Practice of Language Rights*, 78–82.
13 Archives Nationales du Québec (ANQ), E42 Ministère des Affaires intergouvernementales 1994–03-001/82, file: Conseil des ministres de l'éducation 1975–79, Letter from Jacques-Yvan Morin to Premier Lévesque, 23 January 1978.
14 ANQ, E42 MAIG 1994–03-001/82, file: Conseil des ministres de l'éducation 1975–79, Memo from Florent Gagné, MAIG, 13 January 1977.
15 ANQ, E42 MAIG 1994–03-001/82, file: Conseil des ministres de l'éducation 1975–79, Letter from Jacques-Yvan Morin to Claude Morin re: CMEC meeting, 9 September 1977.
16 Council of Ministers of Education Canada, *State of Minority Language Education*.
17 Provincial Archives of Alberta (PAA), 85.360, ACFA, box 22, file: Dossier éducation et dossier constitutionnel ACFA 1981, Statement of Policy and Legislation for Providing Instruction in Languages Other than English in Alberta, January 1981.
18 William Johnson, "Premiers Agree on Language Rights, but ...," *Globe and Mail*, 24 February 1978, 1.
19 ANQ, E42 MAIG 1994–03-001/69, file: Entente fédérale-provinciale sur le bilinguisme en éducation, avant 1981, Letter from Claude Morin, Ministre des affaires intergouvernementales, to Jacques-Yvan Morin, Ministre de l'éducation, 24 July 1978.
20 National Archives of Canada (NA), RG6, Secretary of State, file 4020–180/9, Bilingualism in Education – Alberta, Excerpt from "A National Understanding" re: Federal Position on Language Education, 1979, 70.
21 Pierre Elliot Trudeau, "PM's Letter on Language to Premier Lévesque," *Globe and Mail*, 10 September 1977, 56.
22 Peter Miller, "Task Force Naïve to Entrust Language Rights to Provinces, PM Says," *Globe and Mail*, 27 January 1979, 13.
23 AO, RG77-1, Correspondence of the Government Co-ordinator of FLS, TR 84-467, temporary box 26, file: Secretariat d'État, Notes for Opening Remarks by the Undersecretary of State to the Federal-Provincial Conference on Bilingualism in Education, 2 May 1977.
24 NA, RG122 Commissioner of Official Languages (COL), acc. 1997–98/632, box 18, file 1140-1-1: Official Languages – General, Language Rights – Education – Second Language, Keith Spicer "A Bilingual New Deal" (1976).
25 For examples, see Commissioner of Official Languages, *1970/71 Annual Report*, 95; Commissioner of Official Languages, *1973/74 Annual Report*, 27.

Notes to pages 107–10   211

26 AO, RG2-200, Council for Franco-Ontarian Education, acc. 22309, box 5, file: Federal-Provincial – General 1977, Statement by the Secretary of State on Bilingualism in Education at the CMEC Meeting in Quebec City, 13 January 1977.

27 AO, RG2-200, Council for Franco-Ontarian Education, acc. 22309, box 5, file: Federal-Provincial – General 1977, Statement by the Secretary of State on Bilingualism in Education at the CMEC Meeting in Quebec City, 13 January 1977.

28 AO, RG77-1, Correspondence of the Government Coordinator of FLS, TR 84-467, temporary box 26, file: Secretariat d'Etat, Notes for Opening Remarks by the Undersecretary of State to the Federal-Provincial Conference on Bilingualism in Education, 2 May 1977.

29 AO, RG2-200, Council for Franco-Ontarian Education, acc. 22309, box 5, file: Divers – Conférence de Banff, 2 et 3 mai 1977, Report Prepared by Secretary of State on the Federal-Provincial Conference on Bilingualism in Education – Banff, 3 May 1977.

30 Canadian Heritage Library (PCH), SOS. Lang. 1978 (6), Secretary of State. Discussion Paper. Negotiation of New Federal-Provincial Agreements for Bilingualism in Education, 11 December 1978.

31 AO, RG2-200, Council on Franco-Ontarian Education, acc. 23267, box 5, file: Federal-Provincial – Reconduite de l'entente 1979, Highlights of the Discussion Held by the CMEC at Its Meeting with Hon. John Roberts, 11 December 1978.

32 Provincial Archives of Manitoba (PAM), E14 Bureau de l'éducation française (BEF), GR 1384, box 19, file 74.5.2, Entente fédérale-provinciale pour le bilinguisme en éducation, Secretary of State Press Release, 25 January 1979.

33 Sylvia Stead, "Ministers Fear Cutback for bilingualism," *Globe and Mail*, 14 January 1977, 9.

34 PAM, E14 BEF, GR 1384, box 18, file 74.5.1 Comité consultatif, Minutes of the CMEC Ad Hoc Meeting of the Deputy Ministers of the Executive Committee Minutes, 30 August 1977.

35 ANQ, E42 MAIG 1994–03-001/69, file: Entente fédérale-provinciale sur le bilinguisme en éducation, avant 1981, Rationale Document for Renewal of the BEP, 1977.

36 AO, RG2-200, Council for Franco-Ontarian Education, acc. 22309, box 5, file: Divers – Conférence de Banff, 2 et 3 mai 1977, Report Prepared by Secretary of State on the Federal-Provincial Conference on Bilingualism in Education – Banff, 3 May 1977.

37 PAM, E14 BEF, GR 1384, box 18, file 74.5.1 Comité consultatif, Minutes of the CMEC Ad Hoc Meeting of the Deputy Ministers of the Executive Committee, 30 August 1977.

38 Paule des Rivières, "Les coupures fédérales compromettent le programme d'enseignement des langues," *Le Devoir*, 27 September 1978, 7.
39 PAA, 85.360, ACFA, box 28, file: Divers documents – Canadian Parents for French (Alberta Branch) 1977–79, Canadian Parents for French Newsletter, no. 1, June 1977.
40 PAA, 85.360, ACFA, box 28, file: Divers documents – Canadian Parents for French (Alberta Branch) 1977–79, Canadian Parents for French Newsletter no. 1, June 1977.
41 PAM, E14 BEF, GR 1384, box 24, file 83: Canadian Parents for French, Jurisdiction in Language Issues. Notes for a speech by Georges Tsai to the CPF Annual Conference, Calgary, 12 October 1978.
42 PAA, 85.360, ACFA, box 28, file: Divers documents – Canadian Parents for French (Alberta Branch) 1977–79, CPF Newsletter no. 6, March 1979, 1.
43 My translation. AO, RG2-200, Council for Franco-Ontarian Education, acc. 22309, box 5, file: Federal-Provincial – CMEC – Éducation dans la langue de la minorité 1977, FFHQ Communiqué de presse; "Les Gouvernements jouent avec l'éducation des minorités," 16 November 1977.
44 CRCCF, Fonds ACFO, FFHQ 1976–78, C2/463/10, FFHQ Communiqué de Presse: "De l'action s.v.p.," 17 February 1978.
45 AO, RG2-200, Council on Franco-Ontarian Education, acc. 21765, box 6, file: Federal-Provincial – Reconduite de l'entente 1978, FFHQ Communiqué de presse – "Premiers concernés, derniers consultés," 28 September 1978.
46 Archives du centre acadien (ACA), MG8 Fonds Fédération acadienne de la Nouvelle-Écosse (FANE), vol. 16, B. 9, fiche 66b: Documents gouvernement – éducation, Letter from Bette Stephenson, CMEC Chair, to Paul Comeau, President of FFHQ, 20 November 1978.
47 My translation: tous nouveaux arrangements … sont nécessairement fonction pour le Québec de son évolution politique et que de ce fait, de tels arrangements devraient être considérés comme provisoires. ANQ, E42 MAIG 1994-03-001/69, file: Entente fédérale-provinciale sur le bilinguisme en éducation, avant 1981, Dossier Presented to the Comité de coordination des relations intergouvernementales preparé par le ministère de l'Éducation et le ministère des Affaires intergouvernementales, 13 April 1977.
48 Ibid.
49 ANQ, E42 MAIG 1994-03-001/69, file: Entente fédérale-provinciale sur le bilinguisme en éducation, avant 1981, Internal Ministry of Intergovernmental Affairs Document concerning Bilingualism in Education Program Objectives and the Renewal, 13 April 1977.
50 PAA, 86.231 Department of Education, Curriculum Branch, box 1, file 210: New Agreement (77-05-17 – 77-10-26), Notes for Comments on the Discussion Paper Prepared by the CMEC re: Negotiation of a New Agreement on Bilingualism in Education, 26 July 1977.

51 ANQ, E42 MAIG 1994-03-001/69, file: Entente fédérale-provinciale sur le bilinguisme en éducation, avant 1981, Étude sur la dualité du reseau public d'enseignement au Québec, 2 January 1979.
52 PAM, E14 BEF, Central Records, TR 1384, box 19, file 74.5.2: Entente fédérale-provinciale pour le bilinguisme en éducation, Position Paper of the Protestant School Board of Greater Montreal re: BEP, and Letter to John Roberts, 29 September 1977.
53 PAA, 83.258 Department of Advanced Education, box 1, file: CMEC Discussion Paper on Bilingualism in Education, Statement of the Quebec Department of Education regarding the Statement of the Secretary of State on Bilingualism in Education, 25 April 1977.
54 ANQ, E42 MAIG 1994-03-001/69, file: Entente fédérale-provinciale sur le bilinguisme en éducation, avant 1981, Memo from Florent Gagné, MAIG, to Pierre LeFrançois, 21 December 1977.
55 Quebec Federation of Home and School Association Files (QFHSA), Brief from the QFHSA to the Secretary of State re: Funding of Federal-Provincial Programmes for Bilingualism in Education after the End of the Present Programme, March 1979, 25 April 1977; Protestant School Board of Greater Montreal Files (PSBGM), box 13, January 25, 1978, Board Meeting Minutes, Brief Presented by the PSBGM to the Task Force on Canadian Unity, 18 January 1978.
56 PSBGM, box 14, November 22, 1978, Board Meeting Minutes, Report from Joan Dougherty, PSBGM, on Meeting of the Council of Quebec Minorities, 13 November 1978. The Council of Quebec Minorities, the first province-wide association of nonfrancophone groups in the province, was the forerunner of Alliance Quebec, which emerged from this group in 1982.
57 PAA, 83.258, Advanced Education, box 1, file: CMEC Discussion Paper on Bilingualism in Education, Letter from H. Koselar, D.M. of Education and E.K. Hawkesworth to Lucien Perras re: Alberta's Position on the BEP, 17 May 1977.
58 "Alberta's Best Efforts to Total $2.5 Million," *Calgary Herald*, 27 February 1978, B1.
59 PAA, 85.202, Advanced Education – Program Planning, box 1, file: Bilingualism General, Memo from P. Lamoureux to E.K. Hawkesworth, 13 December 1978.
60 PAA, 83.258, Advanced Education, box 5, file: Bilingualism 1977, Notes on the Meeting on Federal-Provincial Bilingual Agreement, 16 February 1977. Briefing Material for the Federal-Provincial Conference on BEP, Banff, 1 May 1977.
61 Oakland Ross, "A French Toehold in the Foothills," *Globe and Mail*, 9 February 1977, 8; Oakland Ross, "French Spreads, Costs Climb," *The Globe and Mail*, 10 February 1977, 8; Interview with Alain Nogue, former Education Coordinator of ACFA.

62 Interiews with Adrien Bussière, formerly of Alberta Education, and A. Nogue.
63 Interview with A. Nogue.
64 PAA, 96.640, ACFA, box 7, file 200, Brief Presented by ACFA to Julian Koziak, 11 January 1979.
65 PAA, 85.360, ACFA, box 1, file: Réunions et autres documents – Bureau de l'éducation – ACFA 1978 (1), Mémoire présenté par ACFA à J. Koziak, 19 January 1978.
66 PAA, 85.360, ACFA, box 1, file: Réunions et autres documents – Bureau de l'éducation – ACFA 1974–77, Brief from ACFA to Premier Peter Lougheed, January 1977.
67 PAA, 85.360, ACFA, box 1, file: Réunions et autres documents – Bureau de l'éducation – ACFA 1978 (1), News Release; Déclaration d'ACFA au sujet des nouvelles initiatives du gouvernement albertain concernant l'instruction dans la langue de la minorité, 8 March 1978.
68 "Lougheed, Koziak Outline Policy: Minority Language Instruction in Alberta," *Calgary Herald*, 2 March 1978, A7.
69 PAA, 96.640, ACFA, box 7, file 200, Brief Presented by ACFA to Julian Koziak re: The Availability of and the Accessibility to Instruction in the French Language in Alberta, 11 January 1979.
70 Manitoba Education, *1977 Annual Report of the Manitoba Department of Education*.
71 Centre du patrimoine (CP), S1 – Fonds Société franco-manitobaine (SFM), 38/5 Education, Entente Québec-Manitoba en matière d'éducation, 25 January 1977.
72 Ibid., Statement of Elaboration on Languages of Instruction under the Public Schools Act section 258, 13 April 1977.
73 Robert Jankiewicz, "French-Only School Called Separatism," *Winnipeg Free Press*, 15 April 1977, 1.
74 Peter Hadekel, "Lyon Raps PM on Bilingualism," *Winnipeg Free Press*, 5 November 1977, 1.
75 CP, S1 – Fonds SFM, 89/747/619 Éducation recherches 1978–79, Study of proposed Bill 22 (Manitoba), January 1979.
76 Blay, *L'Article 23*, 343; Hébert, "The Manitoba French-Language Crisis."
77 CP, S1 – Fonds SFM, 56/14 Bureau de l'éducation française (BEF), Situation scolaire au Manitoba 1977.
78 Ibid., 38/5 Éducation, Manitoba Policy on French Education, 20 January 1977.
79 Ibid., 89/745/606 – Education, Canadian Parents for French Manitoba Policy statement, January 1979; 89/747/619 Education recherches 1978–79; Association des commissaires d'écoles de langue française du Manitoba position relative aux propositions du BEF concernant la révision de la section 258, January 1979.
80 PAA, 85.202, Advanced Education – Program Planning, box 4, file: Federal-Provincial Agreement 1979, Manitoba Proposal for Renewal of the BEP, January 1979.

81 PAA, 83.258, Advanced Education, box 1, file: CMEC Discussion Paper on B in E, Letter from Ian Turnbull, Minister of Education, to Lucien Perras re: BEP Agreement, 22 April 1977; CP, S1 – Fonds SFM, 38/5 Education, Memo from Raymond Hébert to Lionel Orlikow, 26 August 1977.
82 PAM, E14 BEF, GR 1384, box 19, file 74.5.2, Entente fédérale-provinciale pour le bilinguisme en éducation, Memo from Raymond Hébert to David M. Sanders, ADM for Dept. of Municipal and Urban Affairs re: Charter of Rights and Negotiations on the BEP, 2 February 1979.
83 "Francophones Cash Misdirected," *Toronto Star*, 16 April 1977, A12.
84 CRCCF, Fonds AEFO, Régie et finances, subventions 1977–80, C50/60/8, French Language Instructional Units under Part XI of the Education Act – Planning Guide, 1978.
85 AO, RG77-1, Correspondence of the Government Coordinator of FLS, TR 84-467, temporary box 31, file: Ministère de l'Éducation 1978 et 1979, French as a First Language Initiatives Undertaken by the Ontario Ministry of Education, 1978.
86 CRCCF, Fonds AEFO, Régie et finances, subventions 1977–80, C50/60/8, The Year in Review – Some Learnings, Prepared by Harry Fisher, Ministry of Education, 21 September 1978.
87 AO, RG2-200, Council for Franco-Ontarian Education, acc. 22309, box 5, file: Federal-Provincial – Reconduite de l'entente fédérale-provinciale 1977, Letter from Remy Beauregard, ACFO, to Thomas Wells, John Roberts, and Jacques-Yvan Morin, 12 December 1977.
88 Gérin, *D'un obstacle à l'autre*, 47–8. The Conseil scolaire would finally be inaugurated in 1988.
89 Churchill, *Les coûts d'enseignement dans les écoles et classes de langue française*. This research was later supported by Churchill, Frenette, and Quazi, *Éducation et besoins des Franco-Ontariens*.
90 AO, RG77-1, Government Coordinator of FLS, TR 84-467, temporary box 38, file: Bureau du Premier ministre 2, Letter from Premier Davis to Hélène de Celles regarding Decision of Government Not to Go Further with Its Bilingualism Programs, 17 July 1978.
91 AO, RG77-1, Government Coordinator of FLS, TR 84-467, temporary box 38, file: Bureau du Premier ministre 2, Memo from Ulrich Ferdinand to Mary Louise Gaby, 30 March 1979.
92 AO, RG2-200, Council for Franco-Ontarian Education, acc. 22309, box 5, file: Federal-Provincial – CMEC – Éducation dans la langue de la minorité 1977, Memo from J.W. Giroux to Thomas Wells, 21 September 1977.
93 AO, RG2-200, Council on Franco-Ontarian Education, acc. 21765, box 6, file: Federal-Provincial – Reconduite de l'entente 1978, Memo from G.H. Waldrum to Bette Stephenson, 1 September 1978.
94 AO, RG2-200, Council on Franco-Ontarian Education, acc. 21765, box 6, file: Federal-Provincial – Reconduite de l'entente 1978, Letter from Bette Stephenson to Jacques-Yvan Morin, 11 October 1978.

95 PANB, RS 306, Department of Education – Administration Records, file D1 – Conference on French Immersion, January 27 '77, Policy Statement on Immersion Classes, 6 January 1977.
96 PANB, RS 417, Richard Hatfield, box 13-5-6-3, file: 2803-3 French School Districts and Boards – French 1977, Remarks of Leon Laforest, AEFNB, at a Meeting with Premier Hatfield and Charles Gallagher, 18 March 1977.
97 Cormier and Michaud, *Richard Hatfield*, 134–7.
98 PCH, SOS. Lang. 1979 (3), *Governance, Practices and Costs of Bilingual Education – The World of Reality: Case Studies of Bilingual Education in Manitoba, New Brunswick and Ontario*, directed by Lionel Orlikow, January 1979.
99 PANB, RS 417, Richard Hatfield, box 16-14-9-4, file: 2803-1, Public Schools – Language 1978, Brief from the NBTA to the Ministry of Education on Second Language Instruction, 20 December 1978.
100 Ibid., file 2803-2 Public Schools – Immersion 1978, Petition Cards Opposed to French Schools and Bilingualism, 6 March 1978.
101 AO, RG77-3, Correspondence of the Executive Secretary to the Office of the Government Coordinator on Bilingualism, TR 83-1201, temporary box 3, file: Province of New Brunswick, Statement Given by the Government of New Brunswick at the Opening of the Federal-Provincial Conference on Bilingualism in Education – Banff, 2 May 1977.
102 PANB, RS 417, Richard Hatfield, box 12-12-3-3, file: 2322-1, New Brunswick Official Language Act 1979, Memo from P. Malmberg to Premier Hatfield and Charles Gallagher re: Implications of Federal Moves in Renegotiation of Official Languages Agreement, 31 January 1979.
103 PAA, 83.258, Advanced Education, box 1, file: CMEC Discussion Paper on B in E, Letter from C. Moir to L. Perras, 2 June 1977.
104 ACA, MG8 Fonds FANE, vol. 16, B. 2, fiche 14a: Rapports divers, Bref historique du système d'éducation et la situation actuelle (en N-É), January 1979.
105 Interviews with Jean-Roland Aucoin, formerly of Nova Scotia Education, and Gérald Boudreau, Université Ste-Anne, Chair of the Fédération des parents acadiens de la Nouvelle-Écosse, formerly Chair of the Clare School Board.
106 ACA, MG8 Fonds FANE, vol. 16, B. 6, fiche 34: Commission scolaire Argyle, Letter from Pat Murphy, Commission Scolaire d'Argyle, to Paul Comeau, ED of FANE, 2 August 1977.
107 Ibid., vol. 16, B. 1, fiche 3: Rapports de l'agent de développement en éducation, Rapport mensuel de l'agent de developpement en éducation – comté de Richmond, 31 October 1977.
108 My translation. Ibid., B. 8, fiche 59b: Enseignement du français divers, Objectifs de la FANE face à l'éducation en français, January 1978.
109 "Funds for French 'Misused,'" *Montreal Star*, 14 September 1977, A18.

110 Lois Burke Fowle, "Loss of Funding Would Be Detrimental – Gaudet," *Halifax Chronicle Herald*, 9 December 1978, 5.
111 PCH, SOS. Lang. 1978 (4), Peter Atkinson, *Study on School Finances and Language Learning in the Canadian Provinces*, 12 July 1978. ACA, MG8 Fonds FANE, vol. 16, B. 4, fiche 21a: L'école acadienne et la loi 65, Rencontre entre la FANE, Premier Smith et George Mitchell, Ministre d'Éducation, re: Éducation acadienne en N-É, 7 October 1977.
112 ACA, MG8 Fonds FANE, vol. 16, B. 7, fiche 46: Education – rapports et réunions divers, Rapport de Jean Comeau de sa rencontre avec le gouvernement, 23 March 1979.
113 Ibid., fiche 57: Correspondance – Terence Donahoe, Ministre de l'Éducation, Letter from FANE to Premier and Minister of Education, 23 March 1979.
114 "Federal Spending on Bilingualism to Fall by a Third," *Globe and Mail*, 20 February 1979, 8.

CHAPTER FIVE

1 National Archives of Canada (NA), RG6, Secretary of State, file 4020–180/7, Bilingualism in Education – Manitoba, Letter from Francis Fox, Secretary of State, to Keith Cosens, Manitoba Minister of Education, 31 March 1980.
2 Provincial Archives of Alberta (PAA), 89.416, Education – Finance and Administration, box 11, file: French Language Instruction, Memo from P. Lamoureux to E.A. Torgunrud, 7 September 1979.
3 PAA, 85.360, ACFA, box 22, file: Dossier éducation et dossier constitutionnel ACFA 1980, Letter from David King, Minister of Education, to Superintendents re: Formula Payments of BEP, 1 May 1980.
4 PAA, 85.360, ACFA, box 22, file: Dossier éducation et dossier constitutionnel ACFA 1981, Language Learning Alternatives in the Schools of Alberta, 5 May 1981.
5 Canadian Heritage Library (PCH), SOS. Lang. 1981(4), *French Language Programmes in Alberta*, Ottawa, Language Programmes Directorate, Education Support Branch, Secretary of State, January 1981.
6 PAA, 85.202, Advanced Education – Program Planning, box 4, file: Federal-Provincial Agreement 1979, Memo from J.P. Meekison, Deputy Minister of Foreign and Intergovernmental Affairs (FIGA) to E.K. Hawkesworth, Deputy Minister of Education, 9 October 1979; PAA, 85.360, ACFA, box 22, file: Dossier éducation et dossier constitutionnel ACFA 1980, ACFA News Release, "Francophones Leave Caucus Committee Meeting with Mixed Feelings," 5 June 1980.
7 PAA, 88.88, Advanced Education – Program Support Branch, box 4, file: Comité d'éducation ACFA, Memo to Leo Bosc, ACFA, from Alain Nogue re: La politique de l'ACFA en matière d'éducation française et la question de l'homogénéité, 25 November 1979.

8 For example, PAA, 85.360, ACFA, box 28, file: Divers documents – Canadian Parents for French (Alberta Branch) 1980–81, Letter from Carole Anderson, CPF, to Peter Lougheed, 27 October 1980.
9 PAA, 85.360, ACFA, box 22, file: Dossier éducation et dossier constitutionnel ACFA 1980, ACFA News Release, "Francophones Leave Caucus Committee Meeting with Mixed Feelings," 5 June 1980.
10 Blay, *L'Article 23*, 345.
11 Hébert, "The Manitoba French-Language Crisis," 61.
12 PAM, E14 BEF, GR 1450, box 16, file: Recouvrement Entente Bilaterale 83/4, Official Languages in Education Agreement – Manitoba, 1 March 1983.
13 Centre du patrimoine (CP), S1 – Fonds SFM, 89/747/635 Organismes: BEF 1980–81, Opérationalisation des recommandations du document, "À la recherche du millard" par la SFM, 1980; 89/747/604 Education générale 1974–79, Brief from the SFM to the Intersessional Committee of the Legislative Assembly of Manitoba for Revision of the Public Schools Act, 22 October 1979.
14 PAM, E14 BEF, GR 1449, box 87, file 128, À la recherche du millard, Letter from Ron Duhamel to R.A. McIntosh, 8 July 1981.
15 CRCCF, Fonds AEFO. Subventions pour l'éducation en langue française 1977–80, C50-7/10/12, Letter from Jacques Aubé, Trustee with Carleton Catholic School Board, to Harry Fisher, Deputy Minister Education, 16 May 1980.
16 CRCCF, Fonds AFCSO, Ministre de l'Éducation Bette Stephenson 1979–82, C11/131/4, Déclaration du docteur Bette Stephenson, ministre de l'Éducation, 5 October 1979. In April 1980, Minister Stephenson agreed to the construction of a French-language secondary school for Penetanguishene, but it was to be composed of portable classrooms, rather than "bricks-and-mortar"; Sylvestre, *Penetang*, 86.
17 CRCCF, Fonds AEFO, Régie et finances, subventions 1977–80, C50/60/8, Nouvelles initiatives pour l'éducation en français en 1980, 29 February 1980.
18 AO, RG77-1, Government Coordinator of FLS, TR 84-467, Temporary Box 17, file: Bureau du Premier ministre 1, Memo from Thomas Wells, Minister of Intergovernmental Affairs to Premier Davis re: French Language Issues, 1 May 1981.
19 Archives nationales du Québec (ANQ), E42 Ministère des Affaires intergouvernementales (MAIG) 1989–11-004/95, file: Relations fédérales et provinciales: Affaires éducatives et culturelles – éducation, Letter from Claude Morin to Jacques-Yvan Morin, 18 October 1979.
20 ANQ, E42 MAIG 1989–11-004/95, file: Relations fédérales et provinciales: Affaires éducatives et culturelles – éducation, Letter from J.-Y. Morin to C. Morin, 28 March 1980.
21 Protestant School Board of Greater Montreal Archives (PSBGM), box 15, May 23, 1979, Board Meeting Minutes, Letter from Marcel Fox, PSBGM,

to John Roberts, Secretary of State, 18 May 1979; NA, RG6, Secretary of State, file 4200-180/5 Bilingualism in Education – Quebec, Letter from Marcel Fox to David MacDonald, 20 July 1979.
22 *Debates of the House of Commons – Official Report (Hansard)*, twenty-first Parliament, first Session, 1979.
23 Commissioner of Official Languages Library (COL), PSBGM; *The Effect of Bill 101 on English Education and the Inherent Inequities in the Language Provisions of the Law*, October 1980.
24 PSBGM, box 18, October 1, 1981 Board Meeting Minutes, Letter from André Rousseau, Quebec Ministry of Education to Marcel Fox, 8 July 1981.
25 Stevenson, *Community Besieged*, 181–2.
26 New Brunswick, *Report of the Committee on the Organization and Boundaries of School Districts in New Brunswick*.
27 Cormier and Michaud, *Richard Hatfield*, 137.
28 PANB, RS 417, Richard Hatfield, box 15-9-3-5, file: 2803-1 Public Schools – Language 1980, Letter from Charles Gallagher, Minister of Education to Francis Fox, 19 November 1980.
29 Ibid., file: 2803-2 Public Schools – Immersion Classes 1980, Letter from Susan Purdy, CPF to Premier Hatfield, 30 June 1980.
30 Edwards, "French Immersion in New Brunswick."
31 PANB, RS 417, Richard Hatfield, box 42-4-7-2, file: 2803-2 Dist. 10 – Chatham 1981, Letter from Daniel Gervais, SANB Grand-Rivière, to Charles Gallagher, 16 September 1981.
32 Ibid., file: 2803-1 Public Schools – Language 1981, Memo from Ross McKean to Premier Hatfield, 26 October 1981.
33 Edwards, "French Immersion in New Brunswick."
34 Archives du centre acadien (ACA), MG8 Fonds Fédération acadienne de la Nouvelle-Écosse (FANE), vol. 16, B. 7, fiche 57: Correspondance – Terence Donahoe, Ministre de l'Éducation, An Interview with the Honorable Terence Donahoe, Minister of Education, on the Occasion of the Cabinet Meeting at Université Ste-Anne, 8 November 1979.
35 Ibid.
36 Gaudet, "Survey of Acadian Attitudes," 112.
37 ACA, MG8 Fonds FANE, vol. 5, B. 3b, fiche 2: Canadian Parents for French, CPF Panel Discussion Memo: "French Education in Nova Scotia: Unresolved Issues," January 1981.
38 Ibid., vol. 16, B. 7, fiche 46: Éducation – rapports et réunions divers, Report by John Levangie, Dept of Education, on Ministerial Response to Recommendations re: Acadian schools, 22 October 1981.
39 Ibid., vol. 16, B. 4, fiche 21b: L'école acadienne et la loi 65, Speech by Terence Donahoe on Bill 65 and the Establishment of Acadian Schools in Nova Scotia, 23 August 1983.
40 Julien, "Chéticamp," 270.

41 Centre des études acadiennes (CEA), Fonds 41 Société nationale de l'Acadie (SNA), fiche 41-43-276, Éducation en N-E – Fédération des parents de la Nouvelle-Écosse, "La Fédération des parents Acadiennes," *Le Courrier*, 9 May 1984, 6.
42 "Government Won't Insist on Language Grant Rules," *Montreal Gazette*, 30 October 1979, 10.
43 PAA, 85.360, ACFA, box 22, file: Dossier éducation et dossier constitutionnel ACFA 1980, letter from Dick Johnston, Minister of Federal and Intergovernmental Affairs to Roger Lalonde, ACFA President, 14 May 1980; Cormier and Michaud, *Richard Hatfield*, 138.
44 ACA, MG8 Fonds FANE, vol. 16, B. 7, fiche 57: Correspondance – Terence Donahoe, Ministre de l'Éducation, An Interview with the Honorable Terence Donahoe, Minister of Education, on the Occasion of the Cabinet Meeting at Université Ste-Anne, 8 November 1979.
45 PAA, 85.360, ACFA, box 22, file: Dossier éducation et dossier constitutionnel ACFA 1980, Letter from Dick Johnston, Minister of FIGA, to Roger Lalonde, ACFA President, 14 May 1980.
46 This was repeated by almost all the individuals interviewed for this book, including Harvey Malmberg, Armand Saintonge, Gerald McCarthy, and Mark Goldenberg. There was a sense that the state of MLE rights might change in light of the Charter, but this did not figure directly in the deliberations surrounding the OLEP, though it may have been in the minds of many participants.
47 Comeault, "L'Affaire Forest," 107.
48 PSBGM, box 17, October 22, 1980, Board Meeting Minutes, Statement by William Davis to the Federal-Provincial Conference of First Ministers on the Constitution, and letter to Joan Dougherty of the PSBGM, 12 September 1980.
49 PSBGM, box 17, October 22, 1980, Board Meeting Minutes, Statement by Richard Hatfield to the Federal-Provincial Conference of First Ministers on the Constitution, 8 September 1980.
50 OCOL, PSBGM Presentation to the Prime Minister, Premiers, and the Senate–House of Commons Committee on the Constitution, 1 October 1980; QFHSA, QFHSA Submission to the Joint Committee of the Senate and the House of Commons on the Proposed Constitution Act 1980, 1 December 1980.
51 PAA, 85.360, ACFA, box 28, file: Divers documents – Canadian Parents for French (Alberta Branch) 1980–81, Brief from the CPF to the CMEC regarding the BEP, January 81.
52 PAA, 85.457, ACFA, box 7, file: Dossier éducation et dossier constitutionnel ACFA 1979–83, Brief from ACFA Presented to the Special Joint Committee on the Proposed Resolution respecting the Constitution, January 1981.
53 A. Martel, *Rights, Schools and Communities*. Since the passage of the Charter, there has been a vigorous debate over whether francophone mi-

nority schools should be aiming to "reclaim" children who have been assimilated but who are of French origin.

54 PANB, RS 632, Education Minister – Speeches, vol. 5 1979–80, Summary Statement by Charles Gallagher to CMEC, 22 September 1980; PANB, RS 417, Richard Hatfield, box 15-9-3-5, file: 2803-1 Public Schools – Language 1980, Bilingualism in Education Position Paper of the Government of New Brunswick, 1 October 1980.
55 AO, RG 58-9-1, Ministry of Intergovernmental Affairs, TR 83-1499, box 19, file: Fed. Lang. 4.2.4, Memo from Edward Greathed to D.W. Stevenson re: Bilingualism in Education Program, 9 December 1980.
56 Interviews with Senator J.-R. Gauthier, and Senator Serge Joyal, former secretary of state.
57 Interview with Gerald McCarthy, former deputy minister of education.
58 Archives of Ontario (AO), RG 58-9-1, Ministry of Intergovernmental Affairs, TR 83-1499, box 50, file: SD-5^e Education – Bilingualism in Education Programs 1, 1974–1980, CMEC BEP Discussion Paper, 1 October 1979.
59 NA, RG 6, Secretary of State, file 4200-1 Bilingualism in Education – General, Letter from David MacDonald to Joe Clark, 19 November 1979.
60 NA, RG 6, Secretary of State, file 4200-1 Bilingualism in Education – General, Letter from Joe Clark to David MacDonald, 4 December 1979. Letter from John Crosbie, Minister of Finance, to David MacDonald, 5 December 1979.
61 NA, RG 6, Secretary of State, file 4200-1, Bilingualism in Education – General, Letter from Sinclair Stevens, President of the Treasury Board, to Joe Clark, 13 December 1979.
62 Julia Turner, "Bilingualism Curbs Don't Reflect Federal Rhetoric," *Globe & Mail,* 24 September 1980, 8.
63 PANB, RS 417, Richard Hatfield, box 47-8-8-4, file 2803-1, Public Schools – Language 1982, Briefing Notes to Cabinet Secretariat on Bilingualism in Education, 26 January 1982.
64 ANQ, E42 MAIG 1994–03-001/17, file: 43rd Meeting of CMEC 1983, Letter from Serge Joyal, Secretary of State to Bette Stephenson, Chair of CMEC, 22 March 1983.
65 Fédération des francophones hors-Québec (FFHQ), *À la recherche du millard.*
66 PAM, E14 BEF, GR 1384, box 19, file 74.5.2, Entente fédérale-prov. pour le bilinguisme en éducation, Position Paper re: Negotiations for a New 5-year Agreement for BEP, Manitoba, January 1979.
67 Ibid., Entente fédérale-prov. pour le bilinguisme en éducation, Memo from Raymond Hébert to David M. Sanders, ADM for Dept. of Municipal and Urban Affairs, 2 February 1979.
68 PANB, RS 417, Richard Hatfield, box 15-9-3-5, file: 2803-1 Public Schools – Language 1980, Bilingualism in Education Position Paper of the Government of New Brunswick, 1 October 1980.

69 PAA, 88.88, Advanced Education – Program Support Branch, box 8, file: Federal-Provincial Task Force on B in E, Memo from J. Hrabi to Boyd Pelley re: A Proposal for Funding the Federal-Provincial Program on Bilingualism in Education, 25 July 1980.
70 PAM, E14 BEF, GR 1384, box 18, file 74.5, CMEC Générale, Minutes of 17 June 1981 Meeting of CMEC Provincial Officials, Toronto, 2 October 1981.
71 PANB, RS 632 Education Minister – Speeches, vol. 5, 1979–80, Statement by Charles Gallagher to CMEC, 22 November 1980.
72 AO, RG2-200, Council on Franco-Ontarian Education, acc. 23267, box 5, file: Federal-Provincial – Reconduite de l'entente 1979, Letter from Jacques Giroux to Gérard Raymond re: CMEC meeting, 17 October 1979.
73 PAA, 88.88, Advanced Education – Program Support Branch, box 8, file: Fed.-Prov. Task Force on B in E, Memo from J. Hrabi to Boyd Pelley, 25 July 1980.
74 ANQ, E42 MAIG 1999–01-001/52, file: Bilinguisme en éducation, Réponses du MEQ au questionnaire relatif au BEP, 26 May 1980.
75 AO, RG2-40, Council of Ministers of Education, Canada (CMEC), acc. 18921, box 2, file: 34th CMEC – October 21/22 1979, Letter from Patricia English, Canadian Teacher's Federation, to Bette Stephenson, CMEC, 10 September 1979.
76 FFHQ, *À la recherche du millard*; CRCCF, Fonds FFHQ, Publications – À la recherche du millard, C84/41/11, FFHQ; "Pour un partage équitable du millard federal," 23 April 1981; AO, RG2-40, CMEC, acc. 22321, box 2, file: Bilingualism (CMEC) (D. Ferguson's file), vol. 3, 1981, "The Federal Education Programs for Official Languages," statement by Miss Jeannine Séguin, president of the FFHQ, 17 September 1981.
77 Interview with Adrien Bussière; Poyen, "Canadian Parents for French," 86; PAM, E14 BEF, GR 1449, box 71, file 74.5.2, Entente, Memo from Raymond Hullen to Ron Duhamel, 15 April 1982.
78 AO, RG2-40 CMEC, acc. 21776, box 1, file: Bilingualism (CMEC) (D. Ferguson's file), vol. 2, 1982, Draft Protocol for Agreements between the Government of Canada and the Provincial Governments for Minority-Language Education and Second-Language Instruction, 31 March 1982.
79 PANB, RS 417, Richard Hatfield, box 47-8-8-4, file 2803-1, Public Schools – Language 1982, Briefing Notes to Cabinet Secretariat on Bilingualism in Education, 26 January 1982.
80 PAM, E14 BEF, GR 1449, box 71, file 74.5.2, Entente, CMEC Memo regarding Protocols for Agreements, 2 June 1982.
81 COL, file: Canadian Teachers' Federation, The Teaching of French as a Second Language – A Position Paper Developed by the CTF Commission on French as a Second Language, 1 November 1981.
82 AO, RG2-40, CMEC, acc. 18921, box 2, file: 34th CMEC – October 21/22, 1979, Memo from Lucien Perras, CMEC to Members of the Council, 28 September 1979.

83 NA, RG6, Secretary of State, file 4020–180/6, vol. 4, Bilingualism in Education – Ontario, Exchange of Correspondence between Janet Poyen, CPF, and Francis Fox, 1 December 1980.
84 PAA, 88.88, Advanced Education – Program Support Branch, box 8, file: Bilingualism 1980-, Letter from J. Hrabi and D. Berghofer, Alberta Education, to Boyd Pelley, CMEC, 19 March 1980; AO, RG58-9-1, Ministry of Intergovernmental Affairs, TR 83-1499, box 50, file: SD-5^e Education – Bilingualism in Education Programs 1, 1974–1980, Working Document from the Federal-Provincial Task Force on the BEP, 5 March 1980.
85 PAA, 88.88, Advanced Education – Program Support Branch, box 8, file: Bilingualism 1980–, Letter from J.-Y. Morin to Francis Fox, and Alberta's Comments on the Letter, 30 April 1980.
86 AO, RG2-40, CMEC, acc. 21776, box 1, file: Bilingualism (CMEC) (D. Ferguson's file), vol. 2, 1982, Draft Protocol for Agreements between the Government of Canada and the Provincial Governments for Minority-Language Education and Second-Language Instruction, 31 March 1982.
87 AO, RG2-40, CMEC, acc. 18921, box 2, file: CMEC – General – Oct.-Dec. 1979, Memorandum of Record – CMEC Meeting with the Secretary of State, Toronto, Oct. 21–22, 1979, 25 October 1979.
88 PAA, 88.88, Advanced Education – Program Support Branch, box 8, file: Bilingualism 1980–, Letter from J.-Y. Morin to Francis Fox, and Alberta's comments on the letter, 30 April 1980.
89 ACA, MG8 Fonds FANE, vol. 5, B. 3b, fiche 2: Canadian Parents for French, "Yalden Says No to Slowdown on Minority Schooling," *Globe & Mail*, 3 December 1980.
90 NA, RG6, Secretary of State, file 4020–180/10, Bilingualism in Education – British Columbia, Letter from Francis Fox to Jacques-Yvan Morin, Quebec Minister of Education, 20 June 1980.
91 PAM, E14 BEF, GR 1449, box 71, file 74.5.2, Entente, CMEC Memo from Lucien Perras, 5 June 1981.
92 PANB, RS 417, Richard Hatfield, box 15-9-3-5, file: 2803-1 Public Schools – Language 1980, Bilingualism in Education Position Paper of the Government of New Brunswick, 1 October 1980.
93 Interview with Normand Martin, former Deputy Minister of Education.
94 AO, RG2-40 CMEC, acc. 18921, box 2, file: 34th CMEC – October 21/22 1979, Memo from Lucien Perras, CMEC, to Members of the Council, 28 September 1979.
95 PAM, E14 BEF, GR 1384, box 18, file 74.5.1 comité consultatif, BEP Notes for April 1981 Meeting of Provincial Officials of CMEC in Toronto, 22 April 1981.
96 Interview with Mark Goldenberg, formerly of the Secretary of State Department, 26 April 2002.
97 AO, RG2-40, CMEC, acc. 22321, box 4, file: Binder SOS/CMEC meeting, Dec. 3/81, Letter from Francis Fox, SOS, to Lynn Verge, CMEC President, re: BEP Negotiations, 30 March 1981.

98 PAM, E14 BEF, GR 1384, box 19, file 74.5.2, Entente fédérale-prov. pour le bilinguisme en éducation, Coûts additionels de l'éducation française au Manitoba, January 1979; PANB, RS 632 Education Minister – Speeches, vol. 5 1979–80, Statement by Charles Gallagher to CMEC, 22 September 1980.

99 PAM, E14 BEF, GR 1449, box 71, file 74.5.2, Entente, Memo from Raymond Hullen to Ron Duhamel re: Protocol for BEP Agreements, 15 April 1982; Interview with B. Pelley.

100 Interview with M. Goldenberg.

101 PANB, RS 417, Richard Hatfield, box 15-9-3-5, file: 2803-1, Public Schools – Language 1980, Bilingualism in Education Position Paper of the Government of New Brunswick, 1 October 1980.

102 PAM, E14 BEF, GR 1384, box 19, file 74.5.2, Entente fédérale-prov. pour le bilinguisme en éducation, Coûts additionels de l'éducation française au Manitoba, January 1979.

103 PAA, 88.88, Advanced Education, box 8, file: Federal-Provincial Task Force on Bilingualism in Education, Questionnaire re: Bilingualism in Education, responses from Ontario, 1 May 1980.

104 Interviews with M. Goldenberg, and Alain Landry, formerly of the Secretary of State Department; PAM, E14 BEF, GR 1449, box 71, file 74.5.2, Entente, Memo from Raymond Hullen to Ron Duhamel, 15 April 1982.

105 QFHSA, Canadian Home and School and Parent-Teacher Federation Files, Canadian Home and School and Parent-Teacher Federation Statement of Policy on Education, January 1981.

106 PAM, E14 BEF, GR 1449, box 81, file 83, CPF, CPF Position regarding Funding for Bilingualism in Education, January 1981.

107 AO, RG2-40, CMEC, acc. 22321, box 4, file: Binder SOS/CMEC Meeting Dec. 3/81, BEP – Report of Provincial Officials to CMEC Executive Committee, 24 June 1981. BEP – Report of Provincial Officials to CMEC Executive Committee – Briefing Notes Item 15, 30 July 1981.

108 NA, RG6, Secretary of State, file 4020–180/6, vol. 1, Bilingualism in Education – Ontario, Memo from Pierre Juneau, Undersecretary of State, to Francis Fox, 14 July 1980.

109 PAA, 88.88, Advanced Education – Program Support Branch, box 8, file: Bilingualism 1980–, Letter from J.-Y. Morin to Francis Fox, and Alberta's comments on the letter, 30 April 1980.

110 AO, RG2-40, CMEC, acc. 22321, box 4, file: Binder SOS/CMEC meeting, Dec. 3/81, BEP – Report of Provincial Officials to CMEC Executive Committee, 24 June 1981.

111 PAM, E14 BEF, GR 1384, box 19, file 74.5.2 Entente fédérale-prov. pour le bilinguisme en éducation, Position Paper re: Negotiations for a New 5-year Agreement for BEP, Manitoba, January 1979. PAA, 88.88 Advanced Education – Program Support Branch, box 8, file: Federal-Provincial Task

Notes to pages 155–7

Force on Bilingualism in Education, Letter from P. Malmberg, Deputy Minister of Education to Lucien Perras, 21 May 1980.
112 AO, RG2-40, CMEC, acc. 18921, box 2, file: 34th CMEC – October 21/22 1979, Memo from Lucien Perras, CMEC, to Members of the Council, 28 September 1979.
113 Canada, *Bilingualism in Education Evaluation Report 1970–1979*.
114 PAM, E14 BEF, GR 1384, box 18, file 74.5.1 comité consultatif, Minutes of the 39th Executive Committee Meeting, CMEC, 6 April 1981.
115 PAA, 85.360, ACFA, box 28, file: Divers documents – Canadian Parents for French (Alberta Branch) 1980–81, Brief from the CPF to the CMEC regarding the BEP, January 1981.
116 PAA, 88.88, Advanced Education – Program Support Branch, box 8, file: Bilingualism 1980–, Letter from J. Hrabi and D. Berghofer, Alberta Education, to Boyd Pelley, CMEC, 19 March 1980.
117 ANQ, E42 MAIG 1994–03-001/17, file: 42e réunion du CMEC, Victoria 24-25 Jan. 83, Mandate of the Quebec Delegation for the Victoria Conference of the CMEC, 23 January 1983.
118 ANQ, E42 MAIG 1994–03-001/17, file: 43rd Meeting of CMEC 1983, Memo from Roger Haeberlé to Jean-Marc Léger re: withdrawal of Quebec from the CMEC, 13 September 1983.
119 NA, RG6, Secretary of State, file 4020–180/10, Bilingualism in Education – British Columbia, Letter from Francis Fox to Jacques-Yvan Morin, Quebec Minister of Education Quebec, 20 June 1980.
120 PAM, E14 BEF, GR 1384, box 19, file 74.5.2, Entente fédérale-prov. pour le bilinguisme en éducation, Position Paper re: Negotiations for a New 5-Year Agreement for BEP, Manitoba, January 1979.
121 PAA, 88.88, Advanced Education – Program Support Branch, box 8, file: Bilingualism 1980–, Alberta's Comments on the CMEC Questionnaire, 1 May 1980.
122 PAA, 88.88, Advanced Education, box 8, file: Federal-Provincial Task Force on Bilingualism in Education, Questionnaire re: Bilingualism in Education, Responses from Ontario, 1 May 1980.
123 PAA, 88.88 Advanced Education – Program Support Branch, box 8, file: Federal-Provincial Task Force on Bilingualism in Education, Letter from P. Malmberg, Deputy Minister of Education to Lucien Perras re: New Brunswick's Response to the April 22nd CMEC Questionnaire, 21 May 1980.
124 ANQ, E42 MAIG 1999–01-001/52, file: Bilinguisme en éducation, Réponses du MEQ au questionnaire relatif au BEP, 26 May 1980.
125 PAM, E14 BEF, GR 1384, box 18, file 74.5.1 comité consultatif, BEP Notes for meeting of provincial officials of CMEC in Toronto, April 1981, 22 April 1981.
126 PAM, E14 BEF, GR 1449, box 71, file 74.5.2, Entente, Discussion Paper on Accountability and Additional Costs Prepared by the CMEC, 12 June 1981.

127 Ibid.
128 PANB, RS 417, Richard Hatfield, box 42-4-7-2, file: 2803-1 Public Schools – Language 1981, Memo from Cabinet Secretary Paul Léger to Premier Hatfield, 16 July 1981.
129 AO, RG2-40, CMEC, acc. 21776, box 1, file: Bilingualism (CMEC) (D. Ferguson's File), vol. 3, 1982, Letter from David Ferguson to Bette Stephenson, 20 April 1982.
130 AO, RG2-40, CMEC, acc. 22321, box 4, file: Binder SOS/CMEC Meeting Dec. 3/81, Bilingualism in Education Protocol for Bilateral Agreements, and Provincial Comments on CMEC Proposal to the Secretary of State, 1 November 1981.
131 ANQ, E42 MAIG 1994–03-001/69, file: Entente fédérale-provinciale sur le bilinguisme en éducation, avant 1981, Letter from Camille Laurin, Minister of Education, to Jacques Parizeau, Minister of Finance, 6 February 1981.
132 ANQ, E42 MAIG 1994–03-001/17, file: 43rd Meeting of CMEC 1983, Memo from Roger Haeberlé to Jean-Marc Léger, 13 September 1983.
133 PAM, E14 BEF, GR 1385, box 1, file: CMEC, Draft Text of the 1981–82 CMEC Annual Report, 6 December 1982.
134 PANB, RS 417, Richard Hatfield, box 47-8-8-4, file 2803-1, Public Schools – Language 1982, Briefing Notes to Cabinet Secretariat on Bilingualism in Education, 26 January 1982.
135 AO, RG2-40, CMEC, acc. 21776, box 1, file: Bilingualism (CMEC) (D. Ferguson's File), vol. 3, 1982, Letter from David Ferguson to Bette Stephenson, 20 April 1982.
136 Ibid. vol. 2, 1982, Draft Protocol for Agreements between the Government of Canada and the Provincial Governments for Minority-Language Education and Second-Language Instruction, 31 March 1982.
137 Ibid., box 2, file: CMEC – 41st Council Meeting, Sept. 27–28 1982, CMEC Communiqué, "Education Ministers Urge Action on Bilingualism Funding," 28 September 1982.
138 ANQ, E42 MAIG 1994–03-001/17, file: 42e réunion du CMEC, Victoria 24–25 Jan. 83, Notes from Quebec Ministry of Education re: Victoria Meeting with Secretary of State and CMEC, 25 January 1983.
139 Ibid., file: 43rd Meeting of CMEC 1983, Letter from Serge Joyal, Secretary of State to Bette Stephenson, Chair of CMEC, 22 March 1983.
140 Ibid., file: 34e reunion du CCSME, Excerpt from aide-mémoire pour M. Jacques Girard et M. Jean-Marc Leger for the 34e reunion du CCSME, 1 August 1983.
141 ANQ, E42 MAIG 1999–01-001/50, file: Dossiers de contention Quebec-Ottawa, 1983, Status of Protocol on BEP, 30 September 1983.
142 ANQ, E42 MAIG 1994–03-001/17, file: 43rd Meeting of CMEC 1983, Memo from Roger Haeberlé to Jean-Marc Léger, 13 September 1983.

143 CP, Fonds SI – SFM, 89/750/672 – Langues officielles dans l'enseignement, Joint press release from Secretary of State and CMEC, "Le president du CMEC et le Sécretaire d'État signent un protocole concernant l'enseignement des langues," 20 December 1983.
144 *Canada-Alberta Agreement on the Official Languages in Education.*
145 AO, RG2-40, CMEC, acc. 21776, box 1, file: Bilingualism (CMEC) (D. Ferguson's File), vol. 3, 1982, Letter from David Ferguson to Bette Stephenson, 20 April 1982.
146 *Canada-Ontario Agreement on the Official Languages in Education.*
147 *Canada–Nova Scotia Agreement on the Official Languages in Education.*
148 *Canada-Quebec Agreement for Minority-Language Education and Second-Language Instruction.*
149 Handwritten note from Ron Duhamel to Maureen Hemphill on PAM, BEF, GR 1449, box 71, file 74.5.2, Entente, Memo from Ron Duhamel to Maureen Hemphill, 17 May 1983.
150 PAM, E15 BEF – Committee Files, GR601, box 3: Special Projects, Letter from Serge Joyal to Maureen Hemphill, 28 March 1984.
151 *Canada-Manitoba Agreement on the Official Languages in Education.*
152 *Canada–New Brunswick Agreement on the Official Languages in Education.*
153 Interview with Normand Martin, 16 May 2002.
154 CMEC, *Report on French and English Language Education.*
155 Pal, *Interests of State*, 170; COL, file: Canadian Parents for French, *Canadian Parents for French Newsletter*, no. 14, July 1981, 1; PAA, 85.360, ACFA, box 28, file: Divers documents – Canadian Parents for French (Alberta Branch), 1977–79, *Canadian Parents for French Newsletter*, no. 7, July 1979, among others.
156 COL, file: Canadian Parents for French, *Canadian Parents for French Newsletter*, no. 14, July 1981, 1.
157 Interview with B. Pelley.
158 As noted earlier, this theme consistently ran through the Commissioner of Official Languages' annual reports. It was also at the root of the Gillin plan, to which New Brunswick moved in the 1970s for its FSL programs, a plan that drastically increased the daily class time allocated to FSL. Robert Gillin was the chair of the Ontario Ministry of Education's Committee on the Teaching of French in the mid–1970s.

CHAPTER SIX

1 McRae, "Official Bilingualism," 77–9.
2 Treasury Board of Canada, *A Comparison between the Official Languages Acts of 1969 and 1988.*
3 *Mahé v. Alberta*, [1990] 1 S.C.R. 342; Behiels, *Canada's Francophone Minority Communities.*

4 Canada, *Summary of Federal-Provincial and Federal-Territorial Agreements for Minority-Language Education and Second-Language Instruction 1983–1984, 1984–1985, 1985–1986*, 6.
5 Peat, *Evaluation*, Exhibit III-18.
6 Ibid., Exhibit III-11.
7 Canada, *Descriptive and Financial Summary: Federal-Provincial/Territorial Agreements 1988–89 to 1992–93*.
8 Peat, *Evaluation*.
9 Pageau, *Official Languages*, 67.
10 Ibid., 19–24.
11 Canadian Parents for French, *Focus on French Second Language Education*, 1.
12 Ibid., 1–5; Makropoulous, "Sociopolitical Analysis of French Immersion," 115.
13 Prairie Research, *Evaluation* (1997).
14 Canada, *The Next Act*, 25–6.
15 A. Martel, *Rights, Schools and Communities*.
16 Prairie Research, *Evaluation* (2003); Peat, *Evaluation*, xv.
17 CPF, *Focus on FSL*, 12.
18 Prairie Research, *Evaluation* (2003).
19 Canada, *The Next Act*, 25–6.
20 J. Phillip Nicholson, *Evaluation of the 1988–89 to 1992–93 Protocol*, 16.
21 Prairie Research, *Evaluation* (1997), 23–6.
22 Peat, *Evaluation*, v-12.
23 Prairie Research, *Evaluation* (1997), 25.
24 For example, Pelletier, "La francophonie canadienne"; Castonguay, *L'assimilation linguistique*; McRoberts, *Misconceiving Canada*; Laforest, *Trudeau and the End of a Canadian Dream*.
25 Behiels, *Canada's Francophone Minority Communities*.
26 This conclusion appeared in a number of studies, including Goldfarb, *Bilingualism in Canada*; Allen and Swain, *Language Issues and Education Policies*.
27 Annau, *Just Watch Me*.

Bibliography

ARCHIVAL SOURCES

Archives du centre acadienne, Université Ste-Anne (ACA)

MG8 Fonds Fédération acadienne de la Nouvelle-Écosse

Archives nationales du Québec (ANQ)

E42 Ministère des Affaires intergouvernementales

Archives of Ontario (AO)

RG2-40 Education, Council of Ministers of Education, Canada
RG2-185 Education, Assistant Deputy Minister, Franco-Ontarian Education, 1981–1983
RG2-200 Education, Council for Franco-Ontarian Education, 1976–1980
RG2-200 Education, Council on French-Language Schools, 1972–1975
RG18-519 Royal Commission on Bilingualism in the Ontario Public Service
RG58-9-1 Ministry of Intergovernmental Affairs
RG77-1 Correspondence of the Government Coordinator of French Language services
RG77-3 Correspondence of the Executive Secretary to the Office of the Government Coordinator on Bilingualism

Archives of the Protestant School Board of Greater Montreal (PSBGM)

Board Meeting Minutes of the Protestant School Board of Greater Montreal

Centre de recherche en civilisation canadienne-française (CRCCF)

C2 Fonds Association canadienne-française de l'Ontario
C6 Fonds La Chasse-Galerie
C11 Fonds Association française des conseils scolaires de l'Ontario
C50 Fonds Association des enseignants franco-ontariens
C84 Fonds Fédération des francophones hors-Québec

Centre des études acadiennes, Université de Moncton (CEA)

Fonds 41 Société nationale de l'Acadie
Fonds 42 Société des Acadiens du Nouveau-Brunswick
Fonds 146 Armand-Saintonge

Centre du patrimoine, St Boniface (CP)

S1 Fonds Société franco-manitobaine

National Archives of Canada (NA)

RG2 Series A-5-a, Privy Council Office
RG6 Secretary of State
RG33 Series 80, Royal Commission on Bilingualism and Biculturalism
RG47-10 Privy Council Office, Federal-Provincial Relations Office, Federal-Provincial Constitutional Conferences 1969–1971
RG122 Commissioner of Official Languages

Nova Scotia Archives and Records Management (NSARM)

RG100 Office of the Premier

Personal Archives of Mrs Winifred Potter

Former editor of the QFHSA News and PSBGM Commissioner

Provincial Archives of Alberta (PAA)

76.422 Federal and Intergovernmental Affairs
80.226 Association canadienne-française de l'Alberta (ACFA) provinciale
80.328 Education – Curriculum Branch
83.258 Department of Advanced Education
85.202 Advanced Education, Program Planning
85.360 ACFA

85.457 ACFA
86.231 Department of Education, Curriculum Branch
88.88 Advanced Education, Program Support Branch
89.159 Education, Information Services
89.416 Education, Finance and Administration
90.479 Education, Finance and Administration
96.640 ACFA

Provincial Archives of Manitoba (PAM)

E13 Education, Bureau de l'éducation française – French Language Program Files
E14 Education, Bureau de l'éducation française – Central Records
E15 Education, Bureau de l'éducation française – Committee Files

Provincial Archives of New Brunswick (PANB)

RS 306 Department of Education – Administration Records
RS 416 Louis Robichaud
RS 417 Richard Hatfield
RS 632 Education Minister – Speeches
RS 924 Education – Deputy Minister Armand Saintonge

Quebec Federation of Home and School Association Files (QFHSA)

Canadian Home and School and Parent-Teacher Federation Reports
QFHSA Board Meeting Resolutions
QFHSA Briefs

INTERVIEWS

Aucoin, Jean-Roland, 13 March 2002
Belliveau, Maurice, 8 May 2002
Boudreau, Gérald, 16 May 2002
Bussière, Adrien, 4 February 2002
De Bané, Sen. Pierre, 13 February 2003
Dobell, Jane, 4 June 2002
Duhamel, Sen. Ronald, 19 March 2002
Gagnon, Gérard, 16 May 2002
Gauthier, Sen. Jean-Robert, 17 February 2003
Goldenberg, Mark, 26 April 2002
Hébert, Raymond, 15 March 2002
Joyal, Sen. Serge, 18 February 2003

Lamoureux, Philip, 12 February 2002
Landry, Alain, 10 April 2002
McCarthy, Gerald, 27 March 2002
Malmberg, Harvey, 7 March 2002
Martin, Normand, 16 May 2002
Nogue, Alain, 15 February 2002
Pelley, Boyd, 9 January 2002
Potter, Winifred, 3 October 2001
Rioux, Marie-Claude, 27 June 2001
Saintonge, Armand, 14 March 2002
Théberge, Raymond, 28 February 2001
Toole, Barry, 14 March 2002
Tsai, Georges, 26 April 2002

NEWSPAPERS AND BULLETINS

Calgary Herald
Canadian Parents for French Newsletter
Le Devoir
Le Droit
Edmonton Journal
L'Évangéline
Fredericton Gleaner
Globe and Mail
Halifax Chronicle-Herald
Montreal Star
Montreal Gazette
Ottawa Citizen
Le Petit Courrier
Revue de l'Association canadienne d'éducation de langue française
QFHSA News
Le Soleil
Toronto Star
Winnipeg Free Press

PUBLISHED PRIMARY DOCUMENTS

Alberta. Commission on Educational Planning. *A Future of Choices – A Choice of Futures: Report of the Commission on Educational Planning*. Edmonton: Queen's Printer 1972.
– Alberta Learning. French Language Services Branch. *Affirming Francophone Education – Foundations and Directions: A Framework for French First Language Education in Alberta*. 2001.

Alliance Quebec. *A Policy for the English-Speaking Community of Quebec.* 30 May 1982.
Andrew, J.V. *Bilingual Today, French Tomorrow: Trudeau's Master Plan and How It Can Be Stopped.* Richmond Hill, ON: BMG Publishing 1977.
Atkinson, Peter. *Study on School Finances and Language Learning in the Canadian Provinces.* 12 July 1978.
Bain, Bruce. "Toward an Integration of Piaget and Vygotsky: Bilingual Consideration." *Linguistics* 160 (September 1975): 5–20.
Canada. *The Canadian Charter of Rights and Freedoms: A Guide for Canadians.* Ottawa: Minister of Supply and Services Canada 1982.
– *Constitutional Conference Proceedings, First Meeting, 5–7 February 1968.* Ottawa: Queen's Printer 1968.
– *Constitutional Conference Proceedings, Second Meeting, 10–12 February 1969.* Ottawa: Queen's Printer 1969.
– *Constitutional Conference Proceedings, Third Meeting, 8–10 December 1969.* Ottawa: Queen's Printer 1970.
– Canadian Heritage. Official Languages Support Programs. *Descriptive and Financial Summary: Federal-Provincial/Territorial Agreements 1988–89 to 1992–93.*
– Dominion Bureau of Statistics. *Seventh Census of Canada, 1931.* Ottawa: King's Printer 1933.
– Office of the Commissioner of Official Languages. *Annual Report of the Commissioner of Official Languages.* Ottawa: Queen's Printer 1970–1984.
– Privy Council Office. *The Next Act: New Momentum for Canada's Linguistic Duality. The Action Plan for Official Languages.* March 2003.
– Secretary of State. *Discussion Paper: Negotiation of New Federal-Provincial Agreements for Bilingualism in Education.* 11 December 1978.
– *Federal-Provincial Programme of Co-operation for Development of Bilingualism in Education: Press Releases and Highlights of Provincial Reports.* June 1973.
– Language Programmes Directorate, Education Support Programmes Branch. *Descriptive and Financial Summary of Federal-Provincial Programmes for the Official Languages in Education.* 1983.
– *Federal-Provincial Programmes for the Official Languages in Education – Supplementary Tables 1970–71 to 1980–81.* 1981.
– *Federal-Provincial Programmes for the Official Languages in Education – Supplementary Tables 1970–71 to 1982–83.* 1983.
– *French Language Programmes in Alberta.* January 1981.
– *French Language Programmes in Manitoba.* January 1981.
– Official Languages in Education. *Descriptive and Financial Summary: Minority-Language Education and Second-Language Instruction, Federal-Provincial/Territorial Agreements, 1983–84 to 1987–88.* 1989.

- Program Evaluation Directorate. *Bilingualism in Education Evaluation Report 1970–1979*. 1 March 1983.
Canada. Treasury Board of Canada. *A Comparison between the Official Languages Acts of 1969 and 1988*. February 1989.
Canada-Alberta Agreement on the Official Languages in Education. 23 July 1984.
Canada-Manitoba Agreement on the Official Languages in Education. 28 March 1984.
Canada-New Brunswick Agreement on the Official Languages in Education. 20 March 1984.
Canada-Nova Scotia Agreement on the Official Languages in Education. 2 April 1984.
Canada-Ontario Agreement on the Official Languages in Education. 6 June 1984.
Canada-Quebec Agreement for Minority-Language Education and Second-Language Instruction. 2 May 1984.
Canadian Parents for French. *Focus on French Second Language Education: A Canadian Parents for French Position Paper on the Renewal of the Official Languages in Education Program and a New Protocol for Agreements*. Ottawa: 1997.
Canadian Teachers' Federation. *The Teaching of French as a Second Language – A Position Paper developed by the CTF Commission on French as a Second Language*. 1 November 1981.
Churchill, Stacy. *Les coûts d'enseignement dans les écoles et classes de langue française*. Toronto: Ministry of Education 1979.
Churchill, Stacy, Normand Frenette, and Saeed Quazi. *Éducation et besoins des Franco-Ontariens – Le diagnostique d'un système d'éducation*, Vol. 1. Toronto: Le Conseil de l'éducation franco-ontarienne, 1985.
Council of Ministers of Education Canada. *Report on French and English Language Education in Minority Settings, and Teaching of English and French as Second Languages*. July 1985.
- *The State of Minority Language Education in the Ten Provinces of Canada*. 1978.
Cummins, James. "Educational Implications of Mother Tongue Maintenance in Minority Language Groups." *Canadian Modern Language Review* 34(3) (February 1978): 395–416.
Cummins, James, and M. Gulutsan. "Bilingual Education and Cognition." *Alberta Journal of Educational Research* 20(3) (September 1974): 259–69.
Fédération des francophones hors-Québec. *Deux poids, deux mesures – Les francophones hors Québec et les anglophones au Québec: Un dossier comparatif*. Ottawa: FFHQ 1978.
- *Les Héritiers du Lord Durham*. 2 vols. Ottawa: FFHQ 1976.

- *À la recherche du millard: Analyse critique des programmes fédéraux de langues officielles dans l'enseignement.* January 1981.
Gaudet, Joseph Charles. "Survey of Acadian Attitudes towards the Implementation of the Official Languages Program in the Acadian Schools of Nova Scotia." MA diss., Dalhousie University, 1980.
Goldfarb Consultants Ltd. *Bilingualism in Canada: A Research Report.* Ottawa: Secretary of State 1976.
Hébert, Raymond, et al., Centre de recherches, Collège universitaire St-Boniface. *Rendement académique et langue d'enseignement chez les élèves francomanitobains.* 1976.
J. Philip Nicholson Policy and Management Consultants. *Evaluation of the 1988– 89 to 1992–93 Protocol for Agreements between the Government of Canada and the Provincial Governments for Minority-Language Education and Second-Language Instruction: Final Report.* Ottawa: Secretary of State 1992.
Joy, Richard. *Languages in Conflict.* Ottawa, R.J. Joy 1967.
Lambert, Wallace, and G. Richard Tucker. *Bilingual Education of Children: The St Lambert experiment.* Rowley: Newbury House Publishers 1972.
Laurendeau, André. *Journal tenu pendant la Commission royale d'enquête sur le bilinguisme et le biculturalisme.* Outremont, QC: VLB Éditeur 1990.
Manitoba. Department of Education. *Annual Report of the Manitoba Department of Education.* 1969–1984.
– Bureau de l'éducation française. *Pour un réseau d'écoles françaises au Manitoba.* November 1975.
New Brunswick. Committee on the Organization and Boundaries of School Districts in New Brunswick. *Report of the Committee on the Organization and Boundaries of School Districts in New Brunswick.* Fredericton, NB: Government of New Brunswick 1979.
– Department of Education. *Report of the Internal Committee on the Teaching of French Second Language in New Brunswick.* March 1979.
Nogue, Alain. "Parent Expectations with respect to Bilingual Schools." MEd diss., University of Alberta, 1973.
Nova Scotia. Commission on Public Education Finance. *Report of the Commission on Public Education Finance (Nova Scotia).* 1982.
– Department of Education. *Kings County Amalgamated School Board and Department of Education – Province of Nova Scotia Cooperative Educational Survey.* 1977.
– *Nova Scotia Department of Education Annual Report.* 1969–1984.
Nova Scotia. *Royal Commission on Education, Public Services and Provincial-Municipal Relations: Report.* 1974.
Orlikow, Lionel, director. *Governance, Practices and Costs of Bilingual Education – The World of Reality: Case Studies of Bilingual Education in Manitoba, New Brunswick and Ontario.* January 1979.

Ontario. Franco-Ontarian Sub-Committee of the Commission on Declining School Enrolments in Ontario. *Franco-Ontarian Elementary and Secondary Education.* Toronto: Ontario Institute for Studies in Education 1978.
- Ministerial Commission on French Language Secondary Education. *Report of the Ministerial Commission on French Language Secondary Education.* Toronto: Queen's Printer 1972.
- Ministerial Committee on French Language Schools in Ontario. *Report of the Committee on French Language Schools in Ontario.* Toronto: The Committee 1968.
- Minister of Education. *Report of the Minister of Education.* Toronto: Queen's Printer 1969–1983.
Pageau, Skuce Vézina. *Official Languages in Education Program: An Evaluation. Final Report.* Ottawa: Secretary of State 1992.
Peat Marwick & Partners and Stacy Churchill. *Evaluation of the Official Languages in Education Program – Final Report.* Ottawa: Program Evaluation Directorate of the Secretary of State 1987.
Prairie Research Associates. *Evaluation of Federal-Provincial Agreements as Mechanisms for Delivery of the Official Languages Support Programs.* Ottawa: Canadian Heritage, 1997.
- *Evaluation of the Official Languages in Education Program.* Ottawa: Canadian Heritage 2003.
Protestant School Board of Greater Montreal. *The Effect of Bill 101 on English Education and the Inherent Inequities in the Language Provisions of the Law.* October 1980.
Quebec. Commission of Inquiry on the Position of the French Language and on Language Rights in Quebec. *Report of the Commission of Inquiry on the Position of the French Language and on Language Rights in Quebec. Book 1, The Language of Work: The Position of French in Work and Consumer Activities of Quebecers.* Quebec: Government of Quebec 1972.
Rawlyk, George, and Ruth Hafter. *Acadian Education in Nova Scotia: An Historical Survey to 1965.* Ottawa: Royal Commission on Bilingualism and Biculturalism 1970.
Rideout, Brock. *Alberta – Minority Official-Language Education and Second Official-Language Teaching: A Study of Education, Finance, and Policy, 1967–1982.* June 1983.
- *Policy Changes of the Ten Canadian Provinces between 1967 and 1976 with respect to Second-Language Learning and Minority-Language Education as Expressed in Acts, Regulations, Directives, Memoranda, and Policy Statements of Provincial Departments and Ministries of Education.* Ottawa: Secretary of State, n.d.
Royal Commission on Bilingualism and Biculturalism. *Report of the Royal Commission on Bilingualism and Biculturalism.* Book 1, *The Official Languages*; book 2, *Education.* Ottawa: Queen's Printer 1967–68.

Silla, Ousmane. *École bilingue ou unilingue pour les franco-albertains.* 1974.
Statistics Canada. *Minority and Second Language Education, Elementary and Secondary Levels, 1978-79.* 1979.
– *Minority and Second Language Education, Elementary and Secondary Levels, 1984-85.* January 1985.
Swain, Merrill, ed. *Bilingual Schooling. Some experiences in Canada and the United States. A report on the Bilingual Education Conference, Toronto, March 11-13, 1971.* Toronto: Ontario Institute for Studies in Education 1972.
Swain, Merrill, and Henri Barik. *Five Years of Primary French Immersion – Annual Reports of the Bilingual Education Project to the Carleton Board of Education and Ottawa Board of Education up to 1975.* Toronto: Ontario Institute for Studies in Education 1976.
Trudeau, Pierre Elliott. "A Constitutional Declaration of Rights." In *Federalism and the French Canadians*, 52-60. Toronto: Macmillan 1968.
– "Why Are They Forcing French Down Our Throats?" Ottawa: Queen's Printer 15 July 1969.

SECONDARY LITERATURE

Alexander, Malcolm, and Brian Galligan, eds. *Comparative Political Studies: Australia and Canada.* Melbourne: Pitman 1992.
Allaire, Gratien. "De l'église à l'état: Le financement des organismes francophones de l'Ouest, 1945-1970." In *L'État et les minorités. Textes du colloque tenu au Collège universitaire de Saint-Boniface les 6 et 7 novembre, 1992*, ed. Jean Lafontant, 229-45. Saint-Boniface: Centre d'études franco-canadiennes de l'Ouest 1993.
– "Le rapport à l'autre: L'évolution de la francophonie de l'Ouest." In *Francophonies minoritaires au Canada: L'état des lieux*, ed. Joseph Yvon Thériault, 163-89. Moncton: Éditions d'Acadie 1999.
Allen, Patrick, and Merrill Swain. *Language Issues and Education Policies.* Willowdale, ON: Pergammon Press 1984.
Annau, Catherine, director. *Just Watch Me: Trudeau and the 70s Generation.* Ottawa: National Film Board of Canada 1999.
Anton, Thomas. *American Federalism and Public Policy: How the System Works.* New York: Random House 1989.
Aunger, Edmund. "Language Legislation and Official Bilingualism: The Uneasy Coexistence of Canada's Language Communities." In *Canada: Confederation to Present*, produced by Bob Hesketh and Chris Hackett. Edmonton: Chinook Multimedia 2001.
– "Les communautés francophones de l'Ouest: la survivance d'une minorité dispersée." In *Francophonies minoritaires au Canada: L'état des lieux*, ed. Joseph Yvon Thériault, 283-304. Moncton: Éditions d'Acadie 1999.

- "Obsèques prématurées: La disparition des minorités francophones et autres illusions nationalistes." *Review of Constitutional Studies* 7 (2002): 120–42.
Bakvis, Herman. "Political Parties, Party Government." In *Parties and Federalism in Australia and Canada*, ed. Campbell Sharman, 1–22. Canberra: Australian National University 1994.
- *Regional Ministers: Power and Influence in the Canadian Cabinet.* Toronto: University of Toronto Press 1991.
Bakvis, Herman and William Chandler. "The Future of Federalism." In *Federalism and the Role of the State*, ed. Herman Bakvis and William Chandler, 306–18. Toronto: University of Toronto Press 1987.
- eds. *Federalism and the Role of the State.* Toronto: University of Toronto Press 1987.
Bastarache, Michel, André Braën, Emmanuel Didier, and Pierre Foucher, eds. *Language Rights in Canada.* Montreal: Les Éditions Yvon Blais 1987.
Bauer, Julien. *Les minorités au Québec.* Boréal 1994.
Behiels, Michael Derek. *Canada's Francophone Minority Communities: Constitutional Renewal and the Winning of School Governance, 1960–2000.* Montreal: McGill-Queen's University Press 2004.
- *Prelude to Quebec's Quiet Revolution: Liberalism versus Neo-Nationalism, 1945–1960.* Montreal: McGill-Queen's University Press 1985.
- *Quebec and the Question of Immigration: From Ethnocentrism to Cultural Pluralism, 1900–1985.* Ottawa: Canadian Historical Association 1991.
Belliveau, Joel. "Chronique d'une affirmation collective: Identité, altérité, et rapport à l'autorité dans le journal Liaisons de l'Université de Moncton, 1958–1967." Paper presented at the Canadian Historical Association Annual Meeting, May 2002.
Bienvenue, Rita M. "French Immersion Programs: New Identities and Recurring Concerns." *Journal of Cultural Geography* 8 (1988): 105–14.
- "Language Policies and Social Divisions in Manitoba." *American Review of Canadian Studies* 19(2) (1989): 187–202.
Blay, Jacqueline. *L'Article 23: Les péripéties législatives et juridiques du fait français au Manitoba, 1870–1986.* Saint-Boniface: Les Éditions du blé 1987.
Bordeleau, Louis-Gabriel, Roger Bernard, and Benoît Cazabon, "L'éducation en Ontario français." In *Francophonies minoritaires au Canada: L'état des lieux*, ed. Joseph Yvon Thériault, 435–74. Moncton: Éditions d'Acadie 1999.
Borins, Sandford F. *The Language of the Skies: The Bilingual Air Traffic Control Conflict in Canada.* Montreal: McGill-Queen's University Press 1983.
Bosher, J.F. *The Gaullist Attack on Canada 1967–1997.* Montreal: McGill-Queen's University Press 1999.
Boucher, Neil. "L'Église, l'état et l'élite du Québec en Acadie néo-écossaise, 1880–1960." In *Les relations entre le Québec et l'Acadie: De la tradition à*

la modernité, ed. Fernand Harvey and Gérard Beaulieu, 73–94. Québec: Les Presses de l'Université Laval 2000.

Boudreault, Françoise. "La francophonie ontarienne au passé, au présent et au futur: un bilan sociologique." In *La francophonie ontarienne: Bilan et perspectives de recherche*, ed. Jacques Cotnam, Yves Frenette, and Agnès Whitfield, 17–51. Ottawa: Nordir 1995.

Boulay, Gérard. *Du privé au public: Les écoles secondaires franco-ontariennes à la fin des années soixante*. Sudbury: Université de Sudbury 1987.

Bourasssa, Henri. "The French Language and the Future of Our Race." In *French-Canadian Nationalism: An Anthology*, ed. Ramsay Cook, 132–46. Toronto: Macmillan 1969.

Bourhis, Richard, ed. *Conflict and Language Planning in Quebec*. Clevedon: Multilingual Matters 1984.

Breton, Raymond, and Pierre Savard, eds. *The Quebec and Acadian Diaspora in North America*. Toronto: Multicultural History Society of Ontario 1982.

Brodie, Ian. "Interest Group Litigation and the Embedded State: Canada's Court Challenges Program." *Canadian Journal of Political Science* 34(2) (June 2001): 357–76.

Brown, Robert Craig, and Ramsay Cook. *Canada 1896–1921: A Nation Transformed*. Toronto: McClelland and Stewart 1974.

Bureau, Brigitte. *Mêlez-vous de vos affaires: 20 ans de luttes franco-ontariennes*. Ottawa: L'Association canadienne française de l'Ontario 1989.

Cairns, Alan. "The Embedded State: State-Society Relations in Canada." In *State and Society: Canada in Comparative Perspective*, ed. Keith Banting, 53–86. Toronto: University of Toronto Press 1986.

– "From Interstate to Intrastate Federalism in Canada?" *Bulletin of Canadian Studies* 2 (1979): 13–34.

– "The Past and Future of the Canadian Administrative State." In *Reconfigurations: Canadian Citizenship and Constitutional Change*, ed. Douglas E. Williams, 62–97. Toronto: McClelland and Stewart 1995.

Cairns, Alan, and Cynthia Williams, eds. *The Politics of Gender, Ethnicity, and Language in Canada*. Toronto: University of Toronto Press 1986.

Cameron, David. "The Structures of Intergovernmental Relations." *International Social Science Journal* 167 (March 2001): 121–7.

Cameron, David, and Richard Simeon. "Intergovernmental Relations in Canada: The Emergence of Collaborative Federalism." *Publius: The Journal of Federalism* 32 (2) (spring 2002): 49–71.

Cardinal, Linda. *Chroniques d'un vie politique mouvementée*. Ottawa: Éditions Nordir 2001.

Carrière, Fernan. "La métamorphose de la communauté franco-ontarienne, 1960–1985." In *Les Franco-Ontariens*, ed. Cornelius Jaenen, 305–40. Ottawa: Les Presses de l'Université d'Ottawa 1993.

Cartwright, Donald G. "Linguistic Territorialization: Is Canada Approaching the Belgian Model?" *Journal of Cultural Geography* 8 (1988): 115–34.
- *Official Language Populations in Canada: Patterns and Contacts*. Montreal: Institute for Research on Public Policy 1980.
Castonguay, Charles. *Aperçu démolinguistique de la francophonie ontarienne.* 1977.
- *L'assimilation linguistique: Mesure et évolution, 1971–1986*. Ste-Foy: Conseil de la langue française 1994.
- *L'avenir du français au Canada et au Québec*. Québec: Mouvement national des Québécois 1975.
- "The Decline of French as a Home Language in the Quebec and Acadian Diaspora of Canada and the United States." In *The Quebec and Acadian Diaspora in North America*, ed. Raymond Breton and Pierre Savard, 91–100. Toronto: Multicultural History Society of Ontario 1982.
Choquette, Robert. *Language and Religion: A history of English-French Conflict in Ontario*. Ottawa: University of Ottawa Press 1975.
Clarkson, Stephen, and Christina McCall. *Trudeau and Our Times*. Vol. I, *The Magnificent Obsession*. Toronto: McClelland and Stewart 1990.
Coleman, William. "From Bill 22 to Bill 101: The Politics of Language under the Parti Québécois." *Canadian Journal of Political Science* 14(3) (September 1981): 459–85.
Comeault, Gilberte-L. "L'Affaire Forest: Franco-Manitobans in Search of Cultural and Linguistic Duality." In *The Quebec and Acadian Diaspora in North America*, ed. Raymond Breton and Pierre Savard, 101–21. Toronto: Muticultural History Society of Ontario 1982.
Conlan, Timothy. *From New Federalism to Devolution: Twenty-five Years of Intergovernmental Reform*. Washington, DC: Brookings Institution Press 1998.
Cormier, Michel, and Achille Michaud. *Richard Hatfield: Power and Disobedience*. Fredericton: Goose Lane Publications 1992.
Cotnam, Jacques, Yves Frenette, and Agnès Whitfield, eds. *La francophonie ontarienne: Bilan et perspectives de recherche*. Ottawa: Nordir 1995.
Cousineau, Marc. "Langue et justice: L'experience de la minorité francophone de l'Ontario." In *Towards a Language Agenda: Futurist Outlook on the United Nations*, ed. Sylvie Léger, 207–22. Ottawa: Canadian Centre for Linguistic Rights 1995.
Crunican, Paul. *Priests and Politicians: Manitoba Schools and the Election of 1896*. Toronto: University of Toronto Press 1974.
Daigle, Jean, ed. *Acadia of the Maritimes*. Moncton: Chaire d'études acadiennes 1995.
- *The Acadians of the Maritimes*. Moncton: Centre des études acadiennes 1982.

D'Anglejan, Alison. "Language Planning in Quebec: An Historical Overview and Future Trends." In *Conflict and Language Planning in Quebec*, ed. Richard Bourhis, 29–52. Clevedon: Multilingual Matters 1984.

de Vries, John. *Towards a Sociology of Languages in Canada*. Quebec: International Centre for Research on Bilingualism 1986.

Dion, Léon. *Le duel constitutionnel Québec-Canada*. Montreal: Boréal 1995.

– *Pour une véritable politique linguistique*. Québec: Ministère des Communications 1981.

Dufour, Andrée. *Histoire de l'éducation au Québec*. Montreal: Boréal 1997.

Dye, Thomas. *American Federalism: Competition among Governments*. Lexington: Lexington Books 1990.

Eastman, Carole. *Language Planning: An Introduction*. San Francisco: Chandler and Sharp 1983.

Edwards, Viviane. "French Immersion in New Brunswick: The Early Years, 1969–85." MEd diss., University of New Brunswick 1986.

– "The Social and Political Implications of French Immersion in New Brunswick." *Language and Society* (31 August 1983).

Esman, Milton J. "The Politics of Official Bilingualism in Canada." *Political Science Quarterly* 97 (summer 1982): 233–53.

Fishman, Joshua, ed. *Advances in Language Planning*. The Hague: Mouton 1974.

Fortier, D'Iberville. "Official Languages Policies in Canada: A Quiet Revolution." *International Journal of the Sociology of Language* 105–106 (1994): 69–97.

Fraser, Graham. *PQ: René Lévesque and the Parti Québécois in Power*. Toronto: MacMillan 1984.

Gaffield, Chad. *Language, Schooling and Cultural Conflict: The Origins of the French-Language Controversy in Ontario*. Montreal: McGill-Queen's University Press 1987.

Gagnon, Alain. *Quebec: Beyond the Quiet Revolution*. Scarborough, ON: Nelson 1990.

Galligan, Brian, ed. *Australian Federalism*. Melbourne: Longman Cheshire 1989.

Gérin, Odile. *D'un obstacle à l'autre: Vers le Conseil scolaire de langue française*. Ottawa: Éditions L'Interligne 1998.

Gervais, Gaétan. *Des gens de résolution: Le passage du Canada français à l'Ontario français*. Ottawa: Éditions Prise de parole 2003.

Gilbert, Anne. "Les espaces de la francophonie ontarienne." In *Francophonies minoritaires au Canada: L'état des lieux*, ed. Joseph Yvon Thériault, 55–75. Moncton: Éditions d'Acadie 1999.

Gill, Robert. "Bilingualism in New Brunswick and the Future of l'Acadie." *American Review of Canadian Studies* 10 (1980): 56–74.

- "Federal and Provincial Language Policy in Ontario and the Future of the Franco-Ontarians." *American Review of Canadian Studies* 13 (1983): 13–43.
- "Language Policy in Saskatchewan, Alberta, and British Columbia and the Future of French in the West." *American Review of Canadian Studies* 15(1) (1985): 16–37.
- Hargraves, Susan. "Federal Intervention in Canadian Education." In *Federal-Provincial Relations: Education Canada*, ed. J.W. George Ivany and Michael E. Manley-Casimir, 23–33. Toronto: Ontario Institute for Studies in Education 1981.
- Harvey, Louis-Georges. "The French Canadian and Acadian Diaspora." *Acadiensis*, 15(1) (1985): 174–186.
- Hayday, Matthew. "Confusing and Conflicting Agendas: Federalism, Official Languages, and the Development of the Bilingualism in Education Program." *Journal of Canadian Studies* 36(1) (spring 2001): 50–79.
- "Pas de problème: The Development of French Language Health Services in Ontario, 1968–86." *Ontario History* 94(2) (fall 2002): 183–200.
- Hébert, Raymond. "Francophone Perspectives on Multiculturalism." In *20 Years of Multiculturalism: Successes and Failures*, ed. Stella Hryniuk, 59–72. Winnipeg: St John's College Press 1992.
- "Historique de la législation scolaire au Manitoba." *Revue de l'Association canadienne d'éducation de langue française*, 6(2) (1976): 11–12.
- "The Manitoba French-Language Crisis, 1983–84: Origins and Early Legislative Debates." PHD diss., University of Manitoba 1991.
- "Historique de l'enseignement en français au Nouveau-Brunswick." *Revue de l'Association canadienne d'éducation de langue française*, 6(3) (1976): 7–11.
- Hoy, Claire. *Bill Davis*. Toronto: Methuen 1985.
- Hryniuk, Stella, ed. *20 Years of Multiculturalism: Successes and Failures*. Winnipeg: St John's College Press 1992.
- Jaenen, Cornelius, ed. *Les Franco-Ontariens*. Ottawa: Les Presses de l'Université d'Ottawa 1993.
- Jakes, Harold, and Hanne Mawhinney. *An Historical Overview of Franco-Ontarian Educational Governance*. Ottawa: University of Ottawa 1990.
- Johnson, Marc, and Isabelle McKee-Allain. "La société et l'identité de l'Acadie contemporaine." In *Francophones minoritaires au Canada: État des lieux*, ed. J. Yvon Thériault, 209–38. Moncton: Éditions d'Acadie 1999.
- Jones, Richard. "Politics and the Reinforcement of the French Language in the Province of Quebec, 1960–1986." In *Quebec since 1945: Selected Readings*, ed. Michael Behiels, 223–40. Toronto: Copp Clark Pitman 1987.
- Joy, Richard. *Canada's Official Languages: The Progress of Bilingualism*. Toronto: University of Toronto Press 1992.
- Julien, Richard. "Chéticamp: An Acadian Community in Conflict." *Historical Studies in Education* 2(2) (1990): 265–85.

Juteau-Lee, Danielle, "The Franco-Ontarian Collectivity: Material and Symbolic Dimensions of its Minority Status." In *The Quebec and Acadian Diaspora in North America*, ed. Raymond Breton and Pierre Savard, 167–82. Toronto: Multicultural History Society of Ontario, 1982.
Juteau-Lee, Danielle, and Jean Lapointe. "From French-Canadians to Franco-Ontarians and Ontarois – New Boundaries, New Identities." In *Two Nations, Many Cultures: Ethnic Groups in Canada*, ed. Jean Leonard Elliott, 173–86. Scarborough, ON: Prentice-Hall 1983.
Kingsley, Marie-France. "Le rôle de l'ACFO dans la production et l'institutionnalisation légale et politique de l'identité franco-ontarienne." PHD diss., Université Laval 1999.
Klassen, Thomas R., and Steffen Schneider. "Similar Challenges, Different Solutions: Reforming Labour Market Policies in Germany and Canada during the 1990s." *Canadian Public Policy* 28(1) (2002): 51–69.
Labrie, Normand. "Complémentarité et concurrence des politiques linguistiques au Canada: Le choix du médium d'instruction au Québec et en Ontario." *Bulletin suisse de linguistique appliqué* 62 (1995): 9–33.
Laferrière, Michel. "Languages, Ideologies and Multicultural Education in Canada: Some Historical and Sociological Perspectives." In *Multiculturalism in Canada: Social and Educational Perspectives*, ed. Ronald Samuda, John Berry, and Michel Laferrière, 171–82. Toronto: Allyn & Bacon 1984.
Laforest, Guy. *Trudeau and the End of a Canadian Dream*. Montreal: McGill-Queen's University Press 1995.
Lamarre, Jean. *Le devenir de la nation québécoise selon Maurice Séguin, Guy Frégault, et Michel Brunet*. Sillery: Septentrion 1993.
Landry, Rodrigue, and Réal Allard, "Choix de la langue d'enseignement: Une analyse chez des parents francophones en milieu bilingue soustractif." *La revue canadienne des langues vivantes/The Canadian Modern Language Review* 44 (1985): 480–500.
– "Contact des langues et développement bilingue: Un modèle macroscopique." *La revue canadienne des langues vivantes/The Canadian Modern Language Review* 46 (1990): 527–53.
Lapierre, André, Patricia Smart, and Pierre Savard, ed. *Language, Culture and Values in Canada at the Dawn of the Twenty-first Century*. Ottawa: Carleton University Press 1996.
Laponce, Jean. *Languages and Their Territories*. Toronto: University of Toronto Press 1987.
– "Protecting the French Language in Canada: From Neurophysiology to Geography to Politics, the Regional Imperative." *Journal of Commonwealth and Comparative Politics* 23 (1985): 157–70.
Laporte, Pierre E. "Language Planning and the Status of French in Quebec." In *Two Nations, Many Cultures: Ethnic Groups in Canada*, ed. Jean Leonard Elliott, 91–110. Scarborough, ON: Prentice-Hall 1983.

LaSelva, Samuel. *The Moral Foundations of Canadian Federalism: Paradoxes, Achievements, and Tragedies of Nationhood*. Montreal: McGill-Queen's University Press 1996.
Laxer, Robert M., ed. *Bilingual Tensions in Canada*. Toronto: Ontario Institute for Studies in Education 1979.
LeBlanc, Gilberte Couturier, Alcide Godin, and Aldéo Renaud. "French Education in the Maritimes, 1604–1992." In *Acadia of the Maritimes*, ed. Jean Daigle, 523–62. Moncton: Chaire d'études acadiennes 1995.
Leblanc, Paul-Emile. "L'enseignement français au Manitoba, 1916–1968." MA diss., University of Ottawa, 1969.
Levasseur-Ouimet, France, et al. "L'éducation dans l'Ouest canadien." In *Francophonies minoritaires au Canada: L'état des lieux*, ed. Joseph Yvon Thériault, 475–93. Moncton: Éditions d'Acadie 1999.
Levine, Marc V. *The Reconquest of Montreal: Language Policy and Social Change in a Bilingual City*. Philadelphia: Temple University Press 1990.
Linteau, Paul-André, René Durocher, and Jean-Claude Robert. *Quebec: A History, 1967–1929*. Toronto: Lorimer 1983.
Little, Jack. "Watching the Frontier Disappear: English-Speaking Reaction to French-Canadian Colonisation in the Eastern Townships, 1844–1890." In *Quebec since 1800*, ed. Michael Behiels, 369–95. Toronto: Irwin 2002.
Macdonald, Robert J. "In Search of a Language Policy: Francophone Reactions to Bill 85 and 63." In *Quebec's Language Policies: Background and Response*, ed. John Mallea, 219–42. Québec: Les Presses de l'Université Laval 1977.
Mackey, William F. "Language Policy and Language Planning." *Journal of Communication* 29 (1979): 48–53.
MacMillan, C. Michael. *The Practice of Language Rights in Canada*. Toronto: University of Toronto Press 1998.
Magnet, Joseph Eliot. *Official Languages of Canada*. Montreal: Les Éditions Yvon Blais 1995.
Makropoulous, Josée. "Sociopolitical Analysis of French Immersion Developments in Canada." MA diss., OISE/University of Toronto, 1998.
Mallea, John, ed. *Quebec's Language Policies: Background and Response*. Québec: Les Presses de l'Université Laval 1977.
Mansfield, Joan Clarke. *History of the Canadian Home and School Federation, 1964- 1996*. Ottawa: CHSF 1999.
Marshall, David F., ed. *Language Planning: Focusschrift in Honour of Joshua A. Fishman on the Occasion of His Sixty-fifth Birthday*. Vol. 3. Amsterdam: John Benjamins Publishing 1991.
Martel, Angéline. *Official Language Minority Education Rights in Canada: From Instruction to Management*. Ottawa: Commissioner for Official Languages 1991.
– *Rights, Schools, and Communities in Minority Contexts: 1986–2002*. Ottawa: Commissioner of Official Languages 2001.

Martel, Marcel. *Le deuil d'un pays imaginé: Rêves, luttes et déroute du Canada français*. Ottawa: Les Presses de l'Université d'Ottawa 1997.
McAllister, James A. *The Government of Edward Schreyer: Democratic Socialism in Manitoba*. Montreal: McGill-Queen's University Press 1984.
McDougall, Allan Kerr. *John P. Robarts: His Life and Government*. Toronto: University of Toronto Press 1986.
McRae, Kenneth. "Official Bilingualism: From the 1960s to the 1990s." In *Language in Canada*, ed. John Edwards, 61–83. Cambridge: Cambridge University Press 1998.
– "The Principle of Territoriality and the Principle of Personality in Multilingual States." *International Journal of the Sociology of Language* 4 (1975): 33–54.
McRoberts, Kenneth. "Making Canada Bilingual: Illusions and Delusions of Federal Language Policy." In *Federalism and Political Community: Essays in Honour of Donald Smiley*, ed. David P. Shugarman and Reg Whitaker, 141–71. Peterborough, ON: Broadview Press 1989.
– *Misconceiving Canada: The Struggle for National Unity*. Toronto: Oxford University Press 1997.
– *Quebec: Social Change and Political Crisis*. Toronto: McClelland and Stewart 1993.
– "Unilateralism, Bilateralism and Multilateralism: Approaches to Canadian Federalism." In *Intergovernmental Relations*, ed. Richard Simeon, 71–129. Toronto: University of Toronto Press 1985.
McWhinney, Edward. *Canada and the Constitution 1979–1982: Patriation and the Charter of Rights*. Toronto: University of Toronto Press 1982.
Mezey, Susan Gluck. "The U.S. Supreme Court's Federalism Jurisprudence: *Alden v. Maine* and the Enhancement of State Sovereignty." *Publius: The Journal of Federalism* 30 (1-2) (winter/spring 2000): 21–38.
Monière, Denis. *Le développement des idéologies au Québec: Des origines à nos jours*. Montreal: Éditions Québec-Amérique 1977.
Mosimann-Barbier, Marie-Claude. *Immersion et bilinguisme en Ontario*. Rouen: Publications de l'Université de Rouen 1992.
Nice, David. *Federalism: The Politics of Intergovernmental Relations*. New York: St Martin's Press 1987.
Nordlinger, Eric. *On the Autonomy of the Democratic State*. Cambridge: Harvard University Press 1981.
Oliver, Michael. "The Impact of the Royal Commission on Bilingualism and Biculturalism on Constitutional Thought and Practice in Canada." *International Journal of Canadian Studies* 7–8 (1993): 315–22.
Ouellet, Fernand. "L'évolution de la présence francophone en Ontario: Une perspective économique et sociale." In *Les Franco-Ontariens*, ed. Cornelius Jaenen, 127–99. Ottawa: Les Presses de l'Université d'Ottawa 1993.
– "L'historiographie francophone traditionelle au Canada." In *Francophonies minoritaires au Canada: L'état des lieux*, ed. Joseph Yvon Thériault, 99–130. Moncton: Éditions d'Acadie 1999.

Owram, Doug. *Born at the Right Time: A History of the Baby Boom Generation.* Toronto: University of Toronto Press 1996.

Pal, Leslie. *Interests of State: The Politics of Language, Multiculturalism, and Feminism in Canada.* Montreal: McGill-Queen's University Press 1993.

Pelletier, Gérard. *L'aventure du pouvoir, 1968–1975.* Québec: Les éditions internationales Alain Stanké 1992.

Pelletier, Réjean. "La francophonie canadienne: Un déclin irréversible?" Lecture delivered at Freie Universität Berlin, 9 December 2002.

Pichette, Robert. "Culture and Official Languages." In *The Robichaud Era, 1960–1970 – Colloquium Proceedings,* 67–86. Canadian Institute for Regional Development 2001.

Piret, Nadine. "Le bilinguisme fonctionnel du gouvernement ontarien ou les origines et la réception des services en français, 1976–1986." MA diss., University of Ottawa 1997.

Poyen, Janet McCrae. "Canadian Parents for French: A National Pressure Group in Canadian Education." MA diss., University of Calgary 1989.

Rainville, Maurice, and Simone LeBlanc Rainville. *Le Rassembleur – Léger Comeau.* Moncton: Les Éditions d'Acadie 2000.

Redonnet, Jean-Claude. "La francophonie canadienne." *Mondes et Cultures* 49 (1989): 145–50.

Richard, Sacha. "Prelude to a Second Acadian Renaissance: The Acadian Bicentennial Celebrations of 1955." Presented at the Canadian Historical Association Annual Meeting, May 2002.

Richards, John, François Vaillancourt, and William G. Watson, eds. *Survival: Official Language Rights in Canada.* Toronto: C.D. Howe Institute 1992.

Ross, Sally. *Les écoles acadiennes en Nouvelle-Écosse, 1758–2000.* Moncton: Centre d'études acadiennes 2001.

Ross, Sally, and Alphonse Deveau. *The Acadians of Nova Scotia Past and Present.* Halifax: Nimbus Publishing 1992.

Roy, Muriel. "Demography and Demolinguistics in Acadia, 1871–1991." In *Acadia of the Maritimes,* ed. Jean Daigle, 135–200. Moncton: Chaire d'études acadiennes 1995.

– "Settlement and Population Growth in Acadia." In *The Acadians of the Maritimes,* ed. Jean Daigle, 125–96. Moncton: Centre des études acadiennes 1982.

Rudin, Ronald. *The Forgotten Quebeckers: A History of English-Speaking Quebec, 1759–1980.* Québec: Institut québécois de recherche sur la culture 1985.

Russell, Peter H. *Constitutional Odyssey: Can Canadians Become a Sovereign People?* Toronto: University of Toronto Press 1993.

Safty, Adel. "Effectiveness and French Immersion: A Socio-Political Analysis." *Canadian Journal of Education* 17 (winter 1992): 23–32.

Savas, Daniel. "L'impact des politiques d'aide du Secrétariat d'État sur l'évolution financière de la Fédération des Franco-Colombiens." In *Les outils de la francophonie: Les actes du sixième colloque du centre d'études franco-canadiennes de l'ouest tenu à Richmond, Colombie-Britannique les 10 et 11 octobre, 1986*, ed. Monique Bournot-Trites, 11–54. Saint Boniface: Centre d'études franco-canadiennes de l'Ouest 1988.

Savoie, Alexandre-J. "Education in Acadia: 1604–1970." In *The Acadians of the Maritimes*, ed. Jean Daigle, 383–428. Moncton: Centre des études acadiennes 1982.

Savoie, Donald. *The Politics of Language*. Kingston: Institute for Intergovernmental Relations 1991.

Sawatsky, John. *Mulroney: The Politics of Ambition*. Toronto: McClelland and Stewart 1991.

Shapson, Stan, and Vincent D'Oyley, eds. *Bilingual and Multicultural Education: Canadian Perspectives*. Clevedon, UK: Multilingual Matters 1984.

Sharman, Campbell, ed. *Parties and Federalism in Australia and Canada*. Canberra: Australian National University 1994.

Silver, Arthur. *The French-Canadian Idea of Confederation*, 2d ed. Toronto: University of Toronto Press 1997.

Simeon, Richard, and Ian Robinson. *State, Society, and the Development of Canadian Federalism*. Toronto: University of Toronto Press 1990.

Skogstad, Grace. "Federalism and Agricultural Policy." In *Federalism and the Role of the State*, ed. Herman Bakvis and William Chandler, 187–215. Toronto: University of Toronto Press 1987.

Smiley, Donald, and Ronald Watts, eds. *Intrastate Federalism in Canada*. Toronto: University of Toronto Press 1985.

Smith, C.D.C. "Invasion, Succession and Conflict: The Case of St Leonard, Quebec." PHD diss., Pennsylvania State University 1974.

Smith, Miriam. *Lesbian and Gay Rights in Canada: Social Movements and Equality-Seeking, 1971–1995*. Toronto: University of Toronto Press 1997.

Sniderman, Paul M., Joseph F. Fletcher, Peter H. Russell, and Philip E. Tetlock. "Political Culture and the Problem of Double Standards: Mass and Elite Attitudes toward Language Rights in the Canadian Charter of Rights and Freedoms." *Canadian Journal of Political Science* 22 (June 1989): 259–84.

Stanley, Della. *Louis Robichaud: A Decade of Power*. Halifax: Nimbus Publishing 1984.

Stevenson, Garth. *Community Besieged: The Anglophone Minority and the Politics of Quebec*. Montreal: McGill-Queen's University Press 1999.

– *Unfulfilled Union: Canadian Federalism and National Unity*, 3d ed. Toronto: Gage Publishing 1989.

Stevenson, Hugh. "The Federal Presence in Canadian Education, 1939–1980." In *Federal-Provincial Relations: Education Canada*, ed. J.W. George Ivany and Michael E. Manley-Casimir, 3–22. Toronto: Ontario Institute for Studies in Education 1981.

Sylvestre, Paul-François. *Penetang: L'école de la résistance*. Sudbury: Éditions Prise de Parole 1980.

Taddeo, Donat J., and Raymond C. Taras. *Le débat linguistique au Québec: La communauté italienne et la langue d'enseignement*. Montreal: Les Presses de l'Université de Montréal 1987.
Thériault, Joseph Yvon. "L'Acadie politique et la politique en Acadie." In *L'identité à l'épreuve de la modernité*, ed. Joseph Yvon Thériault, 30–50. Moncton: Les Éditions de l'Acadie 1995.
– *Francophonies minoritaires au Canada: L'état des lieux*. Moncton: Éditions d'Acadie 1999.
Thériault, Léon. "Acadia 1763–1978: An Historical Synthesis." In *The Acadians of the Maritimes*, ed. Jean Daigle, 47–86. Moncton: Centre des études acadiennes 1982.
Thomson, Dale. *Jean Lesage and the Quiet Revolution*. Toronto: MacMillan 1984.
Trofimenkoff, Susan Mann. *The Dream of Nation: A Social and Intellectual History of Quebec*. Toronto: Gage Publishing 1983.
Viaud, Gilles. "La géographie du peuplement francophone de l'Ouest." In *Francophones minoritaires au Canada*, ed. J. Yvon Thériault, 75–96. Moncton: Éditions Acadie 1999.
Vigod, Bernard L. *Quebec before Duplessis: The Political Career of Louis-Alexandre Taschereau*. Montreal: McGill-Queen's University Press 1986.
Waddell, Eric. "State, Language, and Society: The Vicissitudes of French in Quebec and Canada." In *The Politics of Gender, Ethnicity, and Language in Canada*, ed. Alan Cairns and Cynthia Williams, 67–110. Toronto: University of Toronto Press 1986.
Wardhaugh, Ronald. *Language and Nationhood: The Canadian Experience*. Vancouver: New Star Books 1983.
Watts, Ronald. *Comparing Federal Systems*. Montreal: McGill-Queen's University Press 1999.
Welch, David. "The Social Construction of Franco-Ontarian Interests towards French-Language Schooling – Nineteenth Century to 1980s." PHD diss., University of Toronto 1988.
Williams, Douglas E., ed. *Reconfigurations: Canadian Citizenship and Constitutional Change*. Toronto: McClelland and Stewart 1995.
Woehrling, José. "L'évolution des rapports minorité-majorité au Canada et au Québec de 1867 à nos jours." *Zeitschrift für Kanada-Studien* 12 (1992): 93–112.
Yalden, Max. "La réforme linguistique au Canada en 1981." *Vie Française* 35 (1981): 24–30.
Young, Robert. "The Program of Equal Opportunity." In *The Robichaud Era, 1960–1970 – Colloquium Proceedings*, 22–35. Canadian Institute for Regional Development 2001.

Index

Acadians: in New Brunswick, 19, 49, 82–4; in Nova Scotia, 20, 28, 85, 124. *See also* Fédération acadienne de la Nouvelle-Écosse; Fédération francophone de la Nouvelle-Écosse; Société des Acadiens du Nouveau-Brunswick; Société nationale des Acadiens
Act Respecting Public Schools (Manitoba), 21
Act Respecting the Department of Education (Manitoba), 21
Alberta, 22, 27, 52–4, 56, 69–72, 115–18, 126, 129–30, 145–7, 149, 153, 156–9, 161; elementary education, 70, 130; English-language requirements, 21, 53; French immersion, 70–1, 116–17, 161, 163; implementation of OLEP, 69–70, 97, 117, 129; minority-language education, 22, 27, 52, 69–72, 117, 163–4; multilingualism, 39, 53, 71–2, 116; postsecondary education, 54, 72; response to B & B Commission recommendations, 52–3; secondary education, 70, 130; second-language instruction, 52, 69–70, 130, 174
Alberta Cultural Heritage Association, 130
Alberta Teachers' Association, 130
Alliance for the Preservation of English in Canada (APEC), 2, 121, 132
Allmand, Warren, 134

André, Harvie, 92–3
Andrew, Jock, 3–4
anglicization. *See* assimilation
assimilation, 20, 28, 30–1, 40, 70, 124, 179–80, 185. *See also* bilingualism, demographics, exogamy
Association acadienne d'éducation en Nouvelle-Écosse, 7
Association canadienne d'éducation de langue française (ACELF), 72, 87, 127, 144, 147
Association canadienne-française d'éducation de l'Ontario (ACFEO), 18–19, 26, 36–7, 50. *See also* Association canadienne-française de l'Ontario
Association canadienne-française de l'Alberta (ACFA), 22, 36–7, 53–4, 70–2, 116–18, 130, 138–9, 141, 182–3; collaboration with CPF, 116, 130; fiftieth anniversary of, 72
Association canadienne-française de l'Ontario (ACFO), 26, 51, 78, 121, 183. *See also* Association canadienne-française d'éducation de l'Ontario
Association des éducateurs canadiens-français du Manitoba (AECFM), 21, 27, 36–7. *See also* Société franco-manitobaine
Association des enseignants francophones de l'Ontario (AEFO), 121, 132, 183

Association des enseignants francophones du Nouveau-Brunswick (AEFNB), 122
Association des surintendants francophones de l'Ontario (ASFO), 121
autonomy bills (Alberta and Saskatchewan), 21

B & B Commission. *See* Royal Commission on Bilingualism and Biculturalism
Bain, Bruce, 117
Beauregard, Claude, 93
Bériault report, 26
Bertrand, Jean-Jacques, 24, 46–7
biculturalism, 36, 43, 53, 64; double-compact theory of, 43. *See also* Bourassa, Henri; Laurendeau, André; multiculturalism; Royal Commission on Bilingualism and Biculturalism; Trudeau, Pierre
Bilingual Today, French Tomorrow, 3–4
bilingualism, 3–10, 32, 48, 179–81, 183–4; bilingual belt, 12; bilingual districts, 54; in civil service, 42, 43, 67, 69, 100, 107–10, 117; youth option, 100, 107–10, 181. *See also* French immersion, language policy, language rights, minority-language education, Official Languages in Education Program, Royal Commission on Bilingualism and Biculturalism, second-language instruction
Bilingualism in Education Program (BEP). *See* Official Languages in Education Program
Bill 22 (Manitoba), 119
Bill 22 (Quebec), 91, 94
Bill 59 (Manitoba), 27
Bill 63 (Quebec), 46, 89–90; regulation 6, 47
Bill 65 (Nova Scotia), 137
Bill 71 (Manitoba), 75
Bill 88, An Act Recognizing the Equality of the Two Linguistic Communities (New Brunswick), 135
Bill 101 (Quebec), 102, 104, 106, 114–15, 134, 149; section 86 reciprocal agreements, 102–6, 124
Bill 113 (Manitoba), 52, 73–5, 119; as model for Alberta, 53–4, 72
Bill 140 (Ontario), 26, 78
Bill 141 (Ontario), 26, 78
Blakeney, Allan, 104
Bloc Québécois, 170

Bourassa, Henri, 43
Bourassa, Robert, 69, 88–90, 92, 169
British Columbia, 158
British North America Act, 1867, 7, 17; provisions for official languages, 17, 19
Buchanan, John, 125
Bureau de l'éducation française (BEF), 76–7, 118–20, 131, 162; created, 75; équipes d'interlocuteurs, 76–7, 118; model for Alberta, 117
Byrne Commission on Municipal Taxation, 25

Campbell, Gordon, 21
Canadian Association of Second Language Teachers, 174
Canadian Charter of Rights and Freedoms, 101, 128, 131, 134, 139, 170, 180, 184; section 23, 134, 137, 140–2, 148, 170–1, 173, 179, 180. *See also* Constitution Act, 1982; language rights; *Mahé* decision
Canadian Council of Christians and Jews, 130
Canadian Home and School and Parent-Teacher Federation (CHSPTF), 153
Canadian Parents for French (CPF), 101, 111, 116, 119, 127, 130–1, 136, 140–1, 144, 146–9, 153–4, 166, 182–3
Canadian School Trustees Association (CSTA), 148
Canadian Teachers Federation (CTF), 147
Carleton Catholic School Board, 79, 121, 132
Carrière, Laurier, 79
Castonguay, Charles, 30–1. *See also* assimilation, exogamy
Catholic Church, 5, 21–2, 31–2. *See also* identity
Charlottetown Accord, 170
Charter of the French Language (Quebec). *See* Bill 101
Chrétien, Jean, 107, 168, 170
Churchill, Stacy, 76, 121, 171
civil service: bilingualism in, 28, 42–4, 50
Clark, Joe, 93, 126, 133, 137, 144, 170; on Canadian federalism, 137
Cohen, Maxwell, 49
Collège St-Jean, 54, 71–2
Collège universitaire Saint-Boniface, 75, 162

Commission of Inquiry on the Position of the French Language Rights in Quebec. *See* Gendron Commission
Commissioner of Official Languages, 38, 44, 82, 89, 150. *See also* Canadian Parents for French; Spicer, Keith; Yalden, Maxwell
Common Schools Act (New Brunswick), 19
Confederation of Tomorrow Conference, 27, 29, 33, 50, 54
Conseil de la vie française (CVF), 5, 31
Conservative Party, 45, 69, 174
Constitution Act, 1982, 133, 135–6, 139, 141, 159. *See also* Canadian Charter of Rights and Freedoms
Constitutional Conference of 1968–71, 44, 49, 55, 57; continuing committee of ministers on the constitution, 44; ministerial committee on official languages, 45, 55–7; subcommittee of officials on official languages, 52, 64
constitutional reform, 33, 44, 49–50, 60–1, 106, 127–8, 133. *See also* Canadian Charter of Rights and Freedoms; Charlottetown Accord; Confederation of Tomorrow Conference; Constitution Act, 1982; Constitutional Conference of 1968–71; language rights; Meech Lake Accord; Victoria Charter
Copps, Sheila, 168
Council of Ministers of Education, Canada (CMEC), 28–9, 46, 61, 65–6, 104–5, 111–13, 122, 133, 142, 144, 146, 154–6, 158, 160, 163–4, 166, 171, 177; Quebec's participation in, 105, 113, 133, 142, 156, 159–60; Report on the state of the minority language, 104–5, 112
Council of Quebec Minorities, 115
Council on French-Language Schools, 78–9
Crosbie, John, 144
Cummins, James, 117

Davis, William, 51, 78, 103, 121, 133, 140, 182
demographics, 6, 30, 32, 66. *See also* assimilation, bilingualism, exogamy
Desjardins, Larry, 51
Dion, Léon, 4
Dion, Stéphane, 3, 172, 175

Dobell, Jane, 68
Donahoe, Terence, 125–6, 138, 182
Doucet, Gérard, 54
Duhamel, Ronald, 131
Dunton, Davidson, 28, 40–1
Duplessis, Maurice, 5, 24
Durham Report, 16–17. *See also* Les Héritiers du Lord Durham

Edmonton Catholic School Board, 70
Edmonton Public School Board, 116
education. *See* Alberta, elementary education, French immersion, homogeneous schools, Manitoba, minority-language education, New Brunswick, Nova Scotia, Official Languages in Education Program, Ontario, postsecondary education, Quebec, secondary education, second-language instruction
elementary education, 32, 65–6, 171; in Alberta, 70, 130
embedded state, 7, 64, 98, 101, 120, 131–2, 165, 176, 181–3; and civil servants, 12, 96–7; defined, 11
Equal Opportunities Program, 25–6, 48, 81
Évangéline, 82–4, 87
exogamy, 12, 31

Faulkner, Hugh, 67, 95
federalism, 9–12, 36, 50, 60–1, 96, 109, 165, 177–9, 185; co-operative, 9–10, 61; decentralized, 6; executive, 9–10, 61; interstate, 9–10, 12, 29–30, 46, 61, 93, 96, 100, 102, 112, 127, 156–7, 159, 164–5, 170, 176–9; intrastate, 9–10, 12, 41, 48–9, 55, 61, 90, 96, 101, 104, 112, 123–4, 127, 142, 146, 157, 164–5, 170, 175–9
Fédération acadienne de la Nouvelle-Écosse (FANE), 28, 87, 94, 124–5, 136–7, 182–3. *See also* Fédération francophone de la Nouvelle-Écosse
Fédération canadienne-française de l'Ouest (FCFO), 67
Féderation des communautés francophones et acadiennes du Canada (FCFAC). *See* Fédération des francophones hors-Québec
Fédération des francophones hors-Québec (FFHQ), 95, 104, 108, 112, 131, 144, 147, 165–6, 183; "De l'action, s.v.p.,"

112, "Les gouvernements jouent," 112; "Les Héritiers du Lord Durham," 95; "Premiers concernés," 112
Fédération francophone de la Nouvelle-Écosse (FFNE), 28, 85–6. *See also* Fédération acadienne de la Nouvelle-Écosse
Fédération des parents acadiens de la Nouvelle-Écosse (FPANE), 137
Fédération provinciale des comités de parents (FPCP), 77
Finn-Elliott Commission, 135
Firth, Royce, 40
Forest, Georges, 119, 130
Fox, Marcel, 134
Franco-Albertans, 53, 70, 117; hesitations about French-language schools, 70. *See also* Association canadienne-française de l'Alberta
Franco-Manitobans, 21, 27, 51–2, 73–4, 77, 119. *See also* Association des éducateurs canadiens-français du Manitoba, Société franco-manitobaine
Franco-Ontarians, 80, 121–2, 132–3, 146. *See also* Association canadienne-française d'éducation de l'Ontario; Association canadienne-française de l'Ontario
Frawley, J.J., 52
French immersion, 59, 66, 99, 142, 147–8, 164, 166, 172, 174–5, 180–1, 185; in Alberta, 70–1, 116–17, 161, 163; in Manitoba, 76, 119, 131; in New Brunswick, 83–4, 122, 135; in Nova Scotia, 85, 88, 125; in Ontario, 80, 120; in Quebec, 24, 89, 92. *See also* Canadian Parents for French
Front de Libération du Québec (FLQ), 89

Gallagher, Charles, 141, 150, 159
Gauthier, Hubert, 95
Gauthier, Jean-Robert, 67
Gendron Commission, 46, 90–1
Graham Commission, 86–8
Grand Falls: French immersion controversy in, 135
Greenway-Laurier Compromise, 21

Hanuschak, Ben, 75
Hatfield, Richard, 49, 81, 84, 103, 123, 136, 140

Hébert, Raymond, 77, 182
homogeneous schools, 40, 68, 70, 137. *See also* Canadian Charter of Rights and Freedoms; New Brunswick, bilingual schools and districts; Ontario, bilingual schools
House of Commons, 45, 90, 134; as forum for regional interests, 10

identity: Canadian, 7, 167, 177, 181, 185; French Canadian, 7, 32; Québécois, 5–6, 24–5, 32. *See also* national unity
interstate federalism. *See* federalism
intrastate federalism. *See* federalism

Johnson, Daniel, 24
Johnston, Dick, 139
Joy, Richard, 12, 32. *See also* bilingual belt
Joyal, Serge: as member of Parliament, 95; as secretary of state, 144, 160–1

King, David, 129, 159–60
Koziak, Julian, 72, 116

Lacoste, Paul, 40–1
Laforest, Guy, 4
Laing, Gertrude, 39–40
language policy, 3–13, 36–45, 64–9; in Belgium, 4, 37; federal role in, 36–7, 39, 55, 149–51, 165, 169–70, 176–7; in Finland, 38; personality principle, 37; in South Africa, 37; in Switzerland, 4, 37; territoriality principle, 4, 37. *See also* biculturalism, bilingualism, Bill 22, Bill 59, Bill 63, Bill 65, Bill 71, Bill 88, Bill 101, Bill 113, Bill 140, Bill 141, Canadian Charter of Rights and Freedoms, language rights, multilingualism, New Brunswick Official Languages Act, Official Languages Act, Official Languages in Education Program, Royal Commission on Bilingualism and Biculturalism
language rights, 37–8, 40, 49–50, 56, 72, 87, 101, 103, 106, 110, 115, 117, 127, 130, 133, 140–2, 178. *See also* Canadian Charter of Rights and Freedoms, language policy, New Brunswick Official Languages Act, Official Languages Act

Laurendeau, André, 28–9, 35, 40, 47; philosophy of bilingualism, 4, 42–3
Laurier, Wilfrid, 21–2
Laurin, Camille, 102, 160
Lavergne law, 24
Le Petit Courrier, 28
Leblanc, Roméo, 67
Léger, Jules, 45
Lemieux, Raymond, 25
Lesage, Jean, 5, 24
Lévesque, René, 102, 113, 126, 134, 140
Liberal Party, 45
Ligue pour l'intégration scolaire, 25
lobby groups, 98; strategy of, 53–4, 70–2, 112–13, 165–6, 176, 182–3. See also Alliance for the Preservation of English in Canada, Association canadienne d'éducation de langue française, Association canadienne-française de l'Alberta, Association canadienne-française d'éducation de l'Ontario, Association canadienne-française de l'Ontario, Association des éducateurs canadiens-français du Manitoba, Association des enseignants francophones de l'Ontario, Canadian Parents for French, embedded state, Fédération acadienne de la Nouvelle-Écosse, Fédération des francophones hors-Québec, Fédération francophone de la Nouvelle-Écosse, Protestant School Board of Greater Montreal, Quebec Federation of Home and School Associations, Société des Acadiens du Nouveau-Brunswick, Société franco-manitobaine, Société nationale des Acadiens
Lougheed, Peter, 115
Loyalist Associations, 2, 50
Lyon, Sterling, 118–20, 130–1, 139–40

Macdonald, David, 137, 143–4
MacFarlane Commission, 21
MacKenzie Commission, 20
Mahé decision, 170–1
Malmberg, Harvey, 123
Manitoba, 20–1, 27, 51–2, 73–7, 110, 116, 118–20, 126, 130–2, 145–6, 152, 154–8, 161–3; Catholic schools, 20–1; French immersion, 76, 119, 131; implementation of OLEP, 73–4, 76, 97, 118–20; minority-language education, 21,
27, 51–2, 73–7, 119, 131, 162–4; second-language instruction, 131, 174; transportation costs, 119
Manitoba Act, 1870, 20, 119
Manitoba Official Language Act, 21, 119, 130
Manning, Ernest, 53
marriage. See exogamy
Matte, René, 69
McLeod-Pinet Commission, 82–4; "Education of Tomorrow," 83–4
McRoberts, Kenneth, 4, 183–4
Meech Lake Accord, 169–70
Merchant report, 18
Ministerial Commission on French-language Secondary Education. See Symons Commission
minority-language communities, 4–6, 42, 179–80, 184–5. See also Acadians; Canadian Charter of Rights and Freedoms; Franco-Albertans; Franco-Manitobans; Franco-Ontarians; minority-language education; Quebec, anglophones; Royal Commission on Bilingualism and Biculturalism
minority-language education, 37, 39–41, 65–6, 97–8, 112, 141–2, 147–8, 163–4, 166, 173–4, 180, 184, 188; in Alberta, 22, 27, 52, 69–72, 117, 163–4; in Manitoba, 21, 27, 51–2, 73–7, 119, 131, 162–4; in New Brunswick, 19, 25–6, 49, 81–4, 149; in Nova Scotia, 20, 85–7, 125, 161, 163–4; in Ontario, 18–19, 26, 50–1, 78–80, 120, 132; in Quebec, 23, 25, 46–8, 102
Mitchell, George, 124
Montreal declaration on minority language education, 105, 127, 179
Moreau, Joseph, 70
Morin, Claude, 105–6
Morin, Jacques-Yvan, 140–5, 122
Mulroney, Brian, 168–9
multiculturalism, 36, 38–9, 43, 53, 183–4; directorate, 64; French Canadian reaction to, 64. See also biculturalism; multilingualism; Royal Commission on Bilingualism and Biculturalism; Rudnyckyj, Jaroslav
multilingualism, 21, 39, 53, 71–2, 116; German, 21, 39, 116; Ukrainian, 21, 39, 116. See also Alberta; bilingualism;

Edmonton Public School Board; Manitoba; multiculturalism; Royal Commission on Bilingualism and Biculturalism; Rudnyckyj, Jaroslav

"National Understanding, A," 107
national unity, 5–6, 10, 41, 48, 51, 55, 57, 61, 87, 107, 117, 149, 150, 165, 179, 181, 185. *See also* Constitutional reform; Quebec
Neatby, Blair, 40–1
neo-institutionalism: as policy formulation model, 10–11
New Brunswick Official Languages Act, 48
New Brunswick Teachers' Association (NBTA), 123
New Brunswick, 19–20, 25–6, 38, 44, 48–50, 56, 81–5, 110, 122–4, 126, 134–6, 145–6, 151–2, 157–9, 161, 163; anglophone protest against bilingualism, 123; bilingual schools and districts, 19, 82–4, 123, 135; confessional schools, 19; English minority-language education, 149; French immersion, 83–4, 122, 135; French minority-language education, 19, 25–6, 49, 81–4, 149; implementation of OLEP, 81–2, 97; response to B & B Commission recommendations, 48; second-language instruction, 49, 83–4, 122–3, 135, 174
New Democratic Party, 45, 69
Newfoundland, 136, 158
newspapers, 53, 59–60, 68
"Next Act, The," 4
Nogue, Alain, 117
Northwest Territories, 67
Northwest Territories Act, 1875, 22
Nova Scotia, 20, 27–8, 44, 54–5, 85–8, 124–6, 136–7, 143, 155, 161–2; Acadian schools, 27–8, 124–5, 136–7; Argyle County, 20, 124; Chéticamp, 88, 137; Clare County, 20, 85; French immersion, 85, 88, 125; Halifax, 85; implementation of OLEP, 85–6, 88, 97, 124–5, 136; Inverness County, 20, 88; Kings County, 20, 88; minority-language education, 20, 85–7, 125, 161, 163–4; reaction to B & B Commission recommendations, 54; regional disparity payments, 54; Richmond County, 20, 88; secondary education, 137; second-language instruction, 28, 87–8, 124, 161

October Crisis, 89
Official Language Act (Quebec). *See* Bill 22
Official Language Minority Groups Program (OLMG), 64, 94, 98, 169, 175, 180
Official Language Monitors Program, 65, 110, 165
Official Languages Act, 1969, 3, 45, 47, 55, 169; created, 43; proposed by B & B Commission, 38; renewed in 1988, 169–70, 181
Official Languages in Education Program (OLEP), 7–8, 60–1, 64–9, 161; accountability, 59, 67, 71, 93, 96, 108, 111, 114–15, 125, 133–4, 137, 152–3, 158, 166, 176; additional costs concept, 39–41, 57–8, 93, 95–6, 108, 114, 151–2; administration of agreements, 93, 155–6; in Alberta, 69–70, 97, 117, 129; annex programs, 58–9, 64–5, 68; announced, 57; Basic Program Option, 157, 159, 161, 178; cultural enrichment, 41, 108, 148–9, 185; development of new programs, 45, 47, 49, 54, 58–9, 95, 110, 114, 118, 151, 172; discussed by B & B Commission, 39–42; duration of agreements, 57–9, 109, 148; evaluation, 45–6, 59, 65, 93, 95, 110, 115, 154–5, 167–8, 171–2, 184; federal-provincial bilateral agreements, 161–4; formula payments, 40–1, 45, 51, 53, 56, 58, 66, 80, 108–9, 115–16, 120–1, 128, 145–8; full-time equivalents, 58; funding levels, 33, 40–2, 44–5, 49–51, 56, 58, 65, 96, 108–9, 116, 123, 126, 128, 143–8, 159, 171–2, 187–92; initial development of, 44–5, 55–9; jurisdiction, 41, 53, 59, 61, 114, 149–51; maintenance of ongoing programs, 45, 95, 100, 110, 122, 151; in Manitoba, 73–4, 76, 97, 118–20; Negotiation Option, 57–8, 159, 161, 165, 178; new agreement of 1983, 139–67; in New Brunswick, 81–2, 97; nonformula payments, 109; in Nova Scotia, 85–6, 88, 97, 124–5, 136; objectives, 7, 47, 51, 59, 67–8, 91, 114, 148–51; in Ontario, 79–

81, 97, 120, 147; principle of parental choice, 39, 45, 51, 59, 68, 91; protocol agreement, 142–61, 171, 175; in Quebec, 89–93, 97, 113–14; renamed from BEP, 128; renewals, 67–9, 126, 128, 144, 161, 168, 171, 172; special projects, 58, 65–6, 76, 80, 93, 95–6, 125, 161–3, 190; structure of agreement, 57, 61, 108, 153, 156–8, 177; transportation costs, 54, 56, 66, 129; visibility of federal contributions, 67, 125, 153–4
Ontario, 18–19, 26–7, 44, 49, 50–1, 56, 77–81, 110, 116, 120–2, 126, 132–3, 146–7, 151–3, 155, 157–8, 161, 177; bilingual schools, 18–19, 78–9, 121, 132; Catholic schools, 17, 26; Essex county school crisis, 81; French immersion, 80, 120; implementation of OLEP, 79–81, 97, 120, 147; minority-language education, 18–19, 26, 50–1, 78–80, 120, 132; Penetanguishene school crisis, 132; postsecondary education, 50; response to B & B Commission recommendations, 38, 50–1; school management, 121; secondary education, 19, 26, 50, 78–9; second-language instruction, 50–1, 79–80, 116, 120–2, 174; Sturgeon Falls school crisis, 78, 81
Ontario Institute for Studies in Education (OISE), 121
Orange Order, 2, 18, 50
Ordre de Jacques Cartier (OJC), 5, 28, 31
Orlikow, Lionel, 75–6; fired under Sterling Lyon, 119

Parent Commission, 24
Parizeau, Jacques, 170
Parti Acadien, 123
Parti Québécois, 94, 101, 113, 126–7, 142, 170
patriation of the Constitution. *See* Constitution Act, 1982
Pawley, Howard, 131
Pearson, Lester, 27, 29, 44, 48
Pelletier, Gerard, 7, 44–5, 51, 56
Pepin-Roberts Task Force on Canadian Unity, 106
postsecondary education: in Alberta, 54, 72; in Ontario, 50; university admission requirements, 33, 79
Potter, Winifred, 92

Pour un réseau d'écoles françaises au Manitoba, 77
press coverage, 53, 59–60, 68
Prince Edward Island, 155, 158, 174
Promotion of Official Languages Program, 175. *See also* Official Language Minority Groups Program
Protestant School Board of Greater Montreal (PSBGM), 89, 92, 106, 114–15, 134, 140–1, 162, 166

Quebec Association of Protestant School Boards, 92, 134
Quebec Federation of Home and School Associations (QFHSA), 89–94, 115, 140, 149, 162, 166
Quebec, 5, 22–5, 32, 36, 43, 46–8, 56, 69, 88–94, 99, 100, 113–15, 126, 133–4, 141–2, 145–6, 151, 153, 156–8, 160, 162, 171, 177; 1980 referendum, 126–7, 133, 138–9, 165; 1995 referendum, 170; allophone communities, 25, 91; anglophone communities, 13, 23–4, 69, 91, 108, 114–15; bilingual classes, 25, 46; Catholic schools, 23, 114; confessional schools, 46; French immersion, 24, 89, 92; implementation of OLEP, 89–93, 97, 113–14; Jewish students, 23; minority-language education, 23, 25, 46–8, 102; nationalism, separatism, and sovereignty-association, 6, 10, 32, 89, 101, 115, 133, 170, 179, 183–4; participation in the CMEC, 105, 113, 133, 142, 156, 159–60; Protestant schools, 17, 23, 114; response to B & B Commission recommendations, 46–7; second-language instruction, 46–7, 89, 91–3, 134, 162
Quiet Revolution, 5–6, 10, 16, 24, 35

Rapport Frechette, 74
referendum. *See* Quebec
Regan, Gerald: as premier of Nova Scotia, 88, 103, 124; as secretary of state, 160
regulation 17, 18–19
Reid, Scott, 174
Robarts, John, 26–7, 29, 50
Roberts, John, 108
Robichaud, Louis, 25, 48–9, 61, 89
Roblin, Duff, 27, 51
Roy, Albert, 121

Royal Commission on Bilingualism and Biculturalism, 4, 7, 28–9, 35–42, 51; federal response to recommendations, 42–5
Royal Commission on Education, Public Services and Provincial-Municipal Relations. *See* Graham Commission
Rudnyckyj, Jaroslav, 38–9, 41. *See also* multilingualism, multiculturalism
Ryerson, Egerton, 18

Saintonge, Armand, 123
Saskatchewan, 104, 153, 158, 161
school governance, 170. *See also* Canadian Charter of Rights and Freedoms
schools. *See* Alberta, elementary education, French immersion, homogeneous schools, Manitoba, minority-language education, New Brunswick, Nova Scotia, Official Languages in Education Program, Ontario, postsecondary education, Quebec, secondary education, second-language instruction
Schreyer, Edward, 51, 61, 73
Scott, Frank, 39–41
Second Language Bursary Program, 65, 110
secondary education, 32, 65–6, 171, 180; in Alberta, 70, 130; in Nova Scotia, 137; in Ontario, 19, 26, 50, 78–9; second-language instruction, 41–2, 44–5, 56, 65–6, 97–9, 111, 142, 148, 171, 174, 180, 184–5, 189; in Alberta, 52, 69–70, 130, 174; in Manitoba, 131, 174; in New Brunswick, 49, 83–4, 122–3, 135, 174; in Nova Scotia, 28, 87–8, 124, 161; in Ontario, 50–1, 79–80, 116, 120–2, 174; in Quebec, 46–7, 89, 91–3, 134, 162
Senate, 10
Sifton, Clifford, 22
Smith, George, 54–5
Social Credit Party, 69
Société des Acadiens du Nouveau-Brunswick (SANB), 82, 84, 94, 122, 138, 183; and French immersion, 135. *See also* Société nationale des Acadiens

Société franco-manitobaine (SFM), 27, 73, 131, 138, 182–3. *See also* Association des éducateurs canadiens-français du Manitoba
Société nationale des Acadiens (SNA), 26, 36–7, 67, 82, 183; complaint to commissioner of official languages, 82; reorganization, 94. *See also* Société des Acadiens du Nouveau-Brunswick
Société St-Jean Baptiste (SSJB), 23
spending power, 7, 48–9, 57, 169. *See also* constitutional reform, federalism, Official Languages in Education Program
Spicer, Keith, 107, 111
St Andrews Conference, 103–5, 155; declaration on minority-language education rights, 104, 106, 114, 124, 127, 178–9. *See also* Canadian Charter of Rights and Freedoms, Montreal declaration on minority-language education rights
St Léonard School Crisis, 24, 46
Stanfield, Robert, 45
Stephenson, Bette, 122
Stevens, H., 54
Stevens, Sinclair, 144
Strom, Harold, 53
Symons, Thomas, 78
Symons Commission, 78, 80

Tremblay, Olivier, 74–7; report, 74–5
Trudeau, Pierre Elliott, 3–8, 48–9, 91, 103, 106–7, 126–7, 133, 139, 168; on bilingualism, 42–3; on individual rights, 43–5, 106
Turnbull, Ian, 118
Turner, John, 168

Victoria Charter, 57

Watson, Ian, 92
Wells, Thomas, 79–80, 120, 133
World War I, 18–19
Worth Commission on Educational Planning, 71

Yalden, Maxwell, 45, 111
Yukon Territory, 67